THE ULTIMATE GUIDE TO TRADITIONAL ARCHERY

RICK SAPP

Skyhorse Publishing

Skyhorse Publishing books may be purchased in bulk at special discounts for sales promotion, corporate gifts, fund-raising, or educational purposes. Special editions can also be created to specifications.

For details, contact the Special Sales Department, Skyhorse Publishing, 307 West 36th Street, 11th Floor, New York, NY 10018 or info@skyhorsepublishing.com.

Skyhorse® and Skyhorse Publishing® are registered trademarks of Skyhorse Publishing, Inc.®, a Delaware corporation.

www.skyhorsepublishing.com

10 9 8 7 6 5 4 3 2

Library of Congress Cataloging-in-Publication Data is available on file.

ISBN: 978-1-62087-575-9

Printed in China

TABLE OF CONTENTS

INTRODUCTION

WHAT IS IT ABOUT ARCHERY?

It's all about you.

With just two sticks and one string, you can become rich and famous beyond your wildest dreams. Okay, not rich in the financial sense, or famous like a celebrity, but who knows? We live, after all, in a world of unlimited possibilities . . .

Whoever coined the expression about *life being short, so play hard* was probably trying to sell you something. Something expensive and electronic, something fragile, breakable, something that will go out of style or out of service or need "up-grading" next year. It will be something you don't need, but the advertising won't say that, choosing instead to stimulate your desire to be cool.

But those sticks and a string? They could hook you forever, make you a devotee, an addict, in a sense. Without trying. An addict in a good way.

If you believe it is high time you found the spot of gold at your center, these two sticks—a bow, an arrow—and a bowstring can take you there.

It's archery, of course. Archery in its purest form. Stripped of modern time—and energy—and thought-saving conveniences. Stripped of artificial. Stripped of the futility of searching endlessly for meaning and community. Many people—thousands, hundreds of thousands—think of it as "traditional archery."

They think of it this way . . .

The long, arcing flight of an arrow cast from a bow is a useful metaphor for our lives. We experience a specific instant of conception and then birth; we also experience a final conscious instant that we call death. What happens on the great curve between those points—what we do, how we think, exchange, initiate, and respond in the world—ultimately defines us because we have little or no power over the beginning or the ending. Launch and impact are beyond our control.

Archery represents the mindful life, the pure sweeping arc from beginning to end, the arrow buffeted by elements climactic and historic and personal, ultimately hitting or missing its thoughtful goal, but always coming to rest in a target. And it allows you to take charge.

In *The Ultimate Guide to Traditional Archery*, we are going to dissect the process of living a full and complete life through archery in its most elemental form. We will do so from the initiation of your arrow's flight to its final resting moment.

Family Life. We tend to suppose that life before the invention of writing, before the invention of "history," was somehow primitive, but the men and women of 50,000 years ago surely wanted the same things from life that you want: a little love, a little laughter, a full belly, and a good night's sleep. Although we do not know when the bow was "invented," it surely made providing food, clothing, and tools easier for families whose very existence depended on forces far beyond their control. (©Libor Balak, Antropak, Czech Republic)

We will cover dozens of topics from gear to 3D shooting, but archery isn't about a dozen things. It's about one thing. It is all about you.

BENDING SPOONS WITH YOUR MIND

We only think we understand the universe. We feel what we cannot see. A woman walks into the room; she falls in love with you. You feel the love, but you cannot practically define it. And occasionally we see what we cannot feel. We imagine connections and consequences or their absence.

Archery is both deceptively simple and difficult to define. You can with no trouble wrap your mind around shooting the bow, pulling an arrow out of a target. And yet, archery is a multifaceted Zen puzzle of infinite variation and levels of complexity, even amusement. It is all that it appears and more. It is the sound of one hand clapping.

Look up a definition of archery and you will read that it is the art of shooting the bow and arrow. Yet that only lists an action with ingredients, artifacts. As if a cake were the act of baking flour mixed with and eggs and sugar. You may also read that archery is the art, practice, or skill of shooting the bow and arrow. Still the emphasis on the obvious, the non-explanation. As if by calling archery an "art," one accepts the mystery at the center as the answer instead of the opportunity to explore. The sightless sight.

Here's what archery is and what sets it apart in the universe: Archery is an act of imaginative creation. It is the practice of exercising one's power over inanimate objects, causing them to fly through the air and arrive at a goal using little more than the effort of your will. Archery is magic. Archery is levitation and bending spoons.

We imagine an arrow and it appears. We imagine a bow and it rests in our hand, light and tense and filled with potential. But these objects, these sticks with a string, are no more than stones in a river bed until we imagine them into action.

Eugen Herrigel studied *kyudo*, the art of the Japanese bow, under Zen master Awa Kenzo in the 1920s. Awa convinced Herrigel that through complete inner stillness and concentration, as well as through continuing dedication to the art form, he could walk blindfolded into a dark room, pick up the bow and arrow, and extinguish a distant burning candle with his shot. Herrigel's book *Zen in the Art of Archery* was published in 1948. If he could imagine such a shot, could you not also move mountains with your mind?

Think about it like this: Let your hand lie flat on a desk or table. Relax and tell your index finger to move. What happens? Nothing. No matter how many times you order it to move, what tone of voice you use, whether you shout or whisper, the finger is little more than a stone in the river. Order the lily in the planter to flower and it remains as still as your finger. How do you make a finger move? Certainly, it does not move of its own volition. The stone in the river bed requires force: gravity or rushing water or the scratch of a bear. The plant beside you flutters if you blow its leaves or if the vacuum rocks the pot. So where is the force, the energy and willpower that moves your hand, that picks up the rock, that animates the plant, that shoots the arrow?

When we imagine shooting the bow, it quivers with anticipation, with hidden reserves of energy waiting to be unleashed and applied by simply placing an arrow onto the string, pulling back, and setting it free. When we do that, we empower these inanimate objects—the sticks and string, the rocks of the river-bed, even our fingertips—and bring them into conscious, willful existence. We transform the elemental structure of the universe from lifeless points of matter to vibrating strings with our mind. Nothing exists unless we first create it with our imagination.

If life is energy, concentrated into discrete, non-random packages—and modern String Theory argues that it is—the definition of archery is this: Archery is an act of creating life with inanimate objects. The bow and arrow, the feathers on the arrow, the plastic nock, the leather glove—these things are only tools, trinkets. Yet they possess potential, like a fingertip or the riverbed rock, for coming to life and altering the course of human history and thereby attaining the ebb and flow of life on earth as surely as the beat of a butterfly's wing, the grumble of a lion, or the sudden flash of a meteor on a dark night.

Archery is the life bringer. Archery is the act of endowing inanimate objects with power, and traditional archery is its purest, most elemental form.

The Life Sport. *Archery has a deeper and more meaningful side than just the enjoyment of shooting arrows, although that would be sufficient reason for trying the "stick and string." Archery is a lifetime sport, like riding a bicycle, with—paradoxi-cally—more to teach and more to offer than one could possibly absorb in one lifetime. Archery opens a world-wide community of interest and fellowship.*

IS IT ALL RELATIVE, REALLY?

Traditional archery is stripped down, shucked off, and shorn of the technical advances of the twentieth and twenty-first centuries, or most of them. Yet, reasonable people disagree, and so we have to take a quick trip in time, facing backward.

It is almost certainly in the very nature of men and women to seek to improve their lives, to fix things that break, to puzzle over the tools of existence, to worry about their children. That desire may be rolled into the DNA of man, the inquisitive tinkerer, the accumulator. And so the concept of "traditional archery" might be evasive.

Let's face it. What we call "traditional" is usually nothing more than what makes us comfortable.

"Traditional" customarily indicates the manner something was accomplished or the way something looked or felt when we were young. We customarily rented a beach house for the summer; it became a family tradition. The ball players refused to wash their socks when they were winning; a team tradition. We opened presents together. We are Jew or Christian or Muslim not because of some rational personal choice among competing sets of benefits and requirements, but because we were born that way.

Yet it is the nature of an arrow's flight that, just as everyone was once a child, everyone is eventually released from the bow to fly away, to dispense with tradition, to make a new tradition. And yet we take the notions of home and hearth, of custom and family with us wherever we go, however far we travel. Home, where we were born and raised, and tradition give us identity and community. They relieve us of the responsibility of making some difficult choices, of selecting our targets. People who grow up without such grounding often have difficulty forming close, identifying associations and wander through life searching for targets.

So tradition is both a winging flight to freedom and an anchor holding us securely to "the way we were." Tradition can be liberating, allowing us "to be," without questioning every action or second cousin. Tradition can also be smothering.

Traditional for an armored knight on horseback just a thousand years ago meant a world without powerful bows. No less a personage than the Roman Catholic Pope condemned and banned the crossbow. Tradition meant the "good old days" before iron bodkin arrow points. It meant those days before massed archers shooting heavy longbows could destroy mounted formations of cavalry (the archers being more or less average citizens; the cavalry, members of the aristocratic families).

Traditional for Oetzi the Ice Man, discovered in the Alps in 1991, meant something altogether different. Oetzi was about forty-five years old and a hunter or perhaps a high-altitude shepherd when he was killed and entombed in ice 5,000 years ago. Oetzi collapsed from an arrow wound to his shoulder and probably died from a blow to his skull. He carried a copper axe, a flint-[br] bladed knife, an unfinished yew longbow, and a quiver holding fourteen arrows with viburnum and dogwood shafts. Traditional for Oetzi in a pre-literate, pre-industrial society was exactly his personal tool kit, yet he carried that valuable copper axe, and that certainly was not traditional for common hunters or shepherds.

In American football, the traditional ball was a pig skin. Literally. Or perhaps a pig's bladder tied into a deer skin cover (Scotland, 1540).

A traditional marriage is that between a man and a woman.

In a traditional economy, one has a choice of farming and hunting—or hunting and farming.

Traditional depends on your point of view. It depends on where you stand, which direction you look, when you make the call.

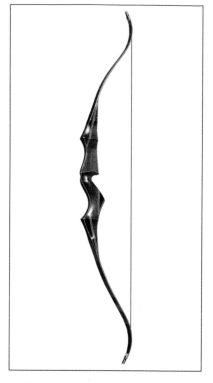

Traditional. The sixty-four-inch Nomad one-piece recurve from PSE exhibits classic traditional styling with multiple inlays and is available in draw weights from thirty-five to fifty pounds. It is sold with a synthetic Fast Flight string and multiple layers of fiberglass and exotic woods: beech, cassia, siamea, ebony, and maple.

NAKED, CLONED, AND STUCK IN THE MIDDLE

To appreciate traditional archery, one only needs to look at the modern archer and understand, then peel away, the technological advantages. He or she—mostly he, by a significant margin, though perhaps that is only because of historic and demographic customs—wears glasses that are not glass and clothing that varies by the season. Neither the flowing mantle of Shiva the Destroyer nor the loincloth of the Biblical Nimrod, neither of whom carried a cell phone into the field. In winter, this clothing is stuffed with a scientifically formulated material such as Thinsulate—essentially oil, and then a mixture of Polyethylene tere-phthalate and polypropylene spun into tiny fibers—designed to trap body heat but allow perspiration to wick away and evaporate. And of course the warm, battery-powered mittens and socks. Summer fabrics might be Gore-Tex, waterproof but breathable.

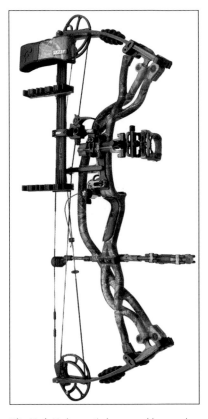

The most jaw dropping aspect of the modern archer, however, is the archery tackle, the equipment itself. To refer to modern gear as "stick and string" is sweetly poetic, but either overestimates the potential of the stick or underestimates human imagination, like referring to the family automobile as a "horseless carriage."

The modern bow is designed to win the lottery, to reduce the archery learning curve, to give the archer power without effort. A compound bow equipped with limb-tip cams and connecting bowstring and cables is built around a machined aluminum handle (also called a riser), which is carved out of a solid aluminum bar on a high-speed computerized lathe, a CNC machine. Unless there is some hidden flaw in the aluminum, a hundred or a thousand handles can be produced precisely to the data programmed into the computer. Unlike Oetzi the Ice Man's bow or the yew bows of the storied English longbowmen or even the crossbows of Swiss hero William

UltraMod. Modern vertical compound bows such as this Carbon Matrix G3 with hollow carbon riser design from Hoyt are marvels of modern engineering. They shoot a very fast arrow and, loaded with accessories, weigh approximately the same as a hunting rifle.

Tell's era, all of which were produced one at a time, by hand, by craftsmen, each of today's modern bows will be exactly, perfectly, precisely identical. They are clones.

The limbs of the modern compound bow are frequently called "carbon" and sometimes called "glass," but they are in reality a fiberglass-based composite. Basically, a slurry or matrix is poured into a tray that contains stretched fiberglass strands. Then, under extreme heat and pressure, a limb is molded within certain tensile boundaries—which we non-scientists eventually understand as a bow's draw weight. It is then matched to a correspondingly strong limb and clamped into the riser.

So the modern compound is a marvel of engineering. It is a space-age miracle, but it is certainly not "traditional," unless one views this era from perhaps a century or two in the future. Unfortunately the asymmetry or arrow of time is unidirectional in the known universe and we're stuck here, in the middle, forced to plod forward without sight and look backward without movement.

GET OUT OF JAIL FREE?

The bow is only the ingenious beginning of the modern archer's opportunity to escape from "traditional." Numerous accessory items, as well as the arrows themselves, are attached to the compound bow besides its cams and cables. Often, especially for hunting archers, the arrow rest is linked by a cord to the down-cable of a compound. Thus, after an archer releases the string, the rest supports about a third of the length of the moving arrow before dropping away; because it drops or falls away it does not interfere with the arrow's fletching. Sometimes, the prongs holding the arrow are a complicated mechanical system of brushes or Teflon-coated fingers, Teflon being, according to its inventors at DuPont, "the slickest material known to man."

Today's arrow rest is a far cry from that of Ishi, the "last wild Indian (or last free man) in North America." According to Saxton Pope's classic *Hunting with the Bow and Arrow* (1923), the Yana hunter, who stumbled out of the wilderness, starving, near Oroville, California in 1911, laid an arrow "across the bow on its right side where it lay between the extended fingers of his left hand." Such was a truly traditional arrow rest.

The sight on a modern bow is usually structured to hold delicate fiber optic cables. It may also include a rheostat-controlled, battery-powered light (usually with a red or blue lens) to provide illumination to the glowing fiber tips in early morning or late evening hours, when ambient light is dim but when deer are most frequently encountered. Fiber optics, of course, are tiny scientific miracles. They have the ability to channel light through colored plastic or glass cables, until they exit through the head of the cable, which is affixed in the sight bracket. The cable end or pin head appears to glow. Fibers are coated or "clad" with a material that encapsulates the light—regardless of whether light is a particle or a beam—and in effect channels it toward the archer's eye.

Ishi, of course, shot by sheer instinct. Rock-and-roll bowhunter Ted Nugent, the Motor City Madman, claims that his first bow sight was a match stick taped to the back of his recurve bow. Just fifty years ago, a sight attached to a bow was rare, usually a single pin, which might be fixed in position or else could slide up and down a scale that was screwed into the bow handle, bow handles in those days being made of wood.

The arrow shot from a modern compound is no longer a stick, of course, arrows having evolved technologically in an astonishing manner. Two decades ago the most common arrow was a lightweight aluminum tube that had been drawn over a mandrel and shaped precisely to within a few thousandths of an inch.

Although the manufacturing has taken a quarter century to perfect, aluminum has by and large been replaced by carbon. Not only does that material sound cutting edge and space age, but lightweight, durable products can be made from it. Bend an aluminum tube by holding both ends and it will break or, if one stops bending it before it breaks, it will take a permanent, precision-debilitating bend that is almost impossible to repair. Bend a carbon composite arrow, also a hollow tube although the walls are inevitably thicker, and its material "memory" snaps it back to near perfect shape (unless it is bent radically or held in an extreme "U" position for a lengthy period).

There is no question that carbon allows the manufacture of superior, sophisticated arrows. And yet, Princess Merida of Scotland in the animated 2012 Disney movie *Brave* used stout wooden shafts . . . as did Robin Hood in Sherwood Forest and even the "Skraelings" who drove the Vikings from North America a thousand years ago. Very traditional.

Modern arrows are tipped with modern components. The butt end that attaches to the bowstring is set with a plastic nock that both holds the arrow in place and allows for clean separation from the string upon release. And while the fletching on today's arrows provides the same steering and stabilizing function that it has for hundreds of generations, it is inevitably plastic and cut short, but in the shape of the traditionally trimmed or burned turkey feathers. Plastic vanes are moisture resistant. They are quieter in flight and are very durable.

Feather fletching has a reputation for being more "forgiving," though forgiveness, whether physical or spiritual, has always been difficult to quantify. Achilles,

Diana. Women handle the bow and arrow as effectively as men. The mystique of shooting traditional equipment is not lost on Jenia Gladziejewski of Australia, who easily handles a thirty-three-pound White Wolf longbow. Jenia follows in the footsteps of female warriors of myth and legend, goddesses like Diana and Artemis and warriors such as the Amazons of ancient history. (Photo courtesy of Denise, The Nise Works, Perth, AU)

the Greek hero of Homer's *Iliad* and arguably the greatest warrior the world ever produced, died—according to legend—from an arrow wound inflicted by the Trojan prince Paris and guided to Achilles' vulnerable heel by the god Apollo. Ouch!

On the forward end of the arrow shaft, the modern archer typically fastens a lightweight metal insert that allows various types of heads to be screwed in and removed: sleek field and target points for competition or sharp broadheads for hunting or oddly shaped wire heads for short-range or bird shooting.

Today's hunting broadheads can be one of two general varieties. Both use factory-sharpened removable blades; when a blade becomes dull, one simply removes it, trashes it, and replaces it with a sharp blade. Such heads are either fixed or mechanical, the difference being not that the fixed head is such a rock-solid cutting platform, but that it does not open upon contact with the target. The first decade of the twenty-first century saw a flowering of intricately moveable mechanical heads—which had an early reputation for performing less than desirably, but they may now surpass fixed heads in total sales volume.

The flaked obsidian arrow points that Ishi fashioned would fare poorly on a modern compound bow . . . and would not be preferred by the modern archer shooting traditional equipment, either. Though very sharp, Ishi's hand-shaped points would be too heavy, too poorly centered in construction even for today's longbows and recurves, and so traditional archers today use a style of fixed, steel heads that are able to be resharpened.

It's not unusual to see the occasional laser-aiming device on a modern bow, although many states—Pennsylvania, for example, with 350,000 or so bowhunters—do not allow the use of electronic devices for hunting. A hand-held laser range finder is a marvelous device, and when the batteries are fresh and one is ranging to a reflective or "hard" target that is not moving, they are extremely reliable and efficient beyond a thousand yards, far beyond the effective range of even the most powerful commercial bow.

Speaking of range, American archer Harry Drake, a specialist in long-distance (called "flight") shooting, lay on his back to fire a wooden "foot bow"—a very short, one-of-a-kind, hand-made recurve, often good for only a single great shot before shattering—more than a mile on more than one occasion. Of course, even flight archery pales when compared to the Iranian legend of Arash the Archer, whose shot traveled either a) a thousand leagues or b) from dawn to dusk or c) a forty-day walk, depending upon which source is consulted.

The popular device that truly and irrevocably separates modern from traditional, however, is the release aid. Not long ago, engineer and expert archery analyst Norbert Mullaney of Wisconsin defined archery as a "hand drawn, hand held, hand released" sport based on fingers (protected in a glove or soft pad) drawing and holding the bowstring . . . but in those days the hand-held release was in its infancy. The variety and sophistication of twenty-first-century release aids is astonishing.

The theory of a release, whether the object holding the string is another string or a metal bar or even opposing ball bearings, is that the less mass holding the string the easier and swifter, the crisper, will be its release. Three fingers on a bowstring in the classic Mediterranean draw, one finger above the arrow and two below, place several inches of soft, yielding tissue around the string. A string or metal attachment might measure an eighth to a quarter inch wide. When it is time to let the string go, the best educated fingers hardly move, with precision, whereas a metal bar or a looped string will snap off the bowstring instantaneously.

Using a modern release aid undoubtedly gives a better bowstring release on a compound bow. And a better release means, all other things being equal, that less torque will be imparted to the string and hence to the arrow speeding away. Release aid plus modern compound bow equals very accurate shooting, shooting that requires little practice and archery that requires little understanding.

* * *

So it is this complex of gadgetry—and much more, besides—that separates modern from traditional archery. Traditional is archery stripped of lasers and fiber optics, of cams and batteries, of magically opening broadheads and space-age release aids. Traditional is not space age.

Do these improvements—the improvements of the twentieth and twenty-first centuries—make one a better archer? The answer to that question depends on how one defines "better."

Speed

A modern archer shoots a faster arrow than a traditional archer, sometimes twice as fast: typically 175 fps (119 mph) for a traditional set-up versus 300, 350, even 400 fps (273 mph) for a modern set-up. Shot from a cam bow, today's carbon arrow carries more kinetic energy over a flatter trajectory than a wood arrow. (Wood arrows are *not* recommended for compound bows.) Thus, precise distance estimation is not so critical for the modern archer.

Accuracy and Distance

A modern archer shoots a more accurate arrow more consistently at almost any distance although it will take him longer to break over the cam, decide on a pin, aim, and release. Use of a release aid with precision manufactured and balanced components is simply far more effective, as determined by long-range accuracy, than using soft fingers encased in a leather glove or protected by a tab. (Use of a release aid with a longbow or recurve *invites disaster* as traditional bows are meant for the dynamic of fingers!)

The Learning Curve

A modern archer learns to manage his gear much faster than a traditional archer. Holding and aiming a seventy-pound compound bow, for instance, requires pulling the bowstring through a stiff arc of resistance. Then just before one comes to full draw, the cams roll over and compensate for the power in the bow. This is called "let-off" and it can be as much as 80 percent, so that at full draw the modern archer is actually holding about fourteen pounds, and one can hold that practically all day.

It would take a real beast to draw and hold a seventy-pound recurve or longbow at full draw for more than a few seconds, because to draw a seventy-pound bow is to hold a full seventy pounds. Thus, with a modern compound, an archer has time to think through his shot, relax, aim, and execute. Once a traditional archer pulls to full draw, though, he is committed to making a rapid shot or else letting down (not shooting) quickly.

If one is keeping score and measures like these—speed, accuracy at distance, length of the learning cycle—are the determinants, the modern bow is unquestionably "better." But are these the correct indicators of which tool kit is best? Perhaps there are other considerations.

ALL KIDDING ASIDE . . .

What sets traditional archery aside from "modern archery" is attitude. It's a desire to, at least in one small and optional phase of life, refuse to do things the easiest way. You probably did not choose to become a U.S. Navy SEAL or an Army Ranger or run marathon races, but chances are you drive a car to work rather than walking or riding a bicycle. You enjoy air conditioning and buy at a grocery store rather than growing your own vegetables or raising and slaughtering chickens.

Life requires accommodation, compromise. Yet in this one wee area—a recreational endeavor that you could arguably live without, but choose not to—you refuse to compromise or, in truth, you compromise less.

Every culture throughout man's brief history has relied on a tool kit for survival advantages. We are not the fastest animals on the planet or the most ferocious. We don't have great fangs and claws. But we are adaptable and, at some point millions of years ago, became tired of getting our butts kicked around the playground by every fierce species, lions to bears to baboons, and began to assemble a tool kit.

It surely was not a conscious decision, using that first club. In a sense it just "happened," and then happened again. We learned and our tool kit has since continued to evolve over millions of years from a rock and a stick to a couple sticks and a string to computers and submarines and spaceships.

So choosing to shoot the bow and arrow in the traditional manner means returning to some former stage of our tool kit's evolution. And right there you pick up the bow and loose an arrow.

Today's traditional archers are an amalgam. The instruments are the bows and arrows of roughly a century ago, but a century ago many of the components would surely be considered state-of-the-art, even high tech and non-traditional—real advances in the art of bow making. But a century ago, archery was in a state of decline in America and around much of the world, just as firearms—repeating rifles and handguns shooting smokeless, factory-loaded cartridges—were gaining an ascendency for use in hunting, recreational shooting . . . and war. And of course much of our traditional archery tool kit is built using modern equipment like a belt sander instead of a soapstone rock for sanding limbs.

And so "traditional" is a matter of perspective.

What Is "Traditional"? A question we will wrestle with throughout the book is how to define "traditional archery" . . . and how to define ourselves as traditional archers. What distinguishes traditional from modern? A recurve bow is typically considered traditional, but in searching for new designs and materials, free market manufacturers often defy cherished concepts and present intriguing puzzles. The limb-riser system of Hoyt's Formula HPX is designed for NAA/FITA (Olympic) style shooting. Can we properly consider this recurve "traditional"?

CHAPTER ONE

ARCHERY FOR THE AGES

MAYBE WE'RE SPECIAL . . . MAYBE WE'RE NOT

A Story in Paint. *Before agriculture tied people to the land, the hunting bands roaming what is now Spain used ravines and rock shelters for temporary camps. Artists among them decorated cavern walls with paintings of hunting scenes, legitimate forerunners to the illustrated books and magazines that would come 25,000 years later. This painting is preserved in the Lascaux caves in France.*

When did the bow and arrow first appear? Nobody knows. Several writers have suggested that beings escaping a dying planet, maybe Mars or Krypton, brought advanced technology to Earth. Probably not.

The archery tool complex—bow, string, arrow, fletching, and arrowhead—probably evolved in several areas, independently, over a long period of time. Certainly men used bows and arrows 20,000 years ago.

Some researchers claim the archaeological record provides a longer timeline—as much as 65,000 years. But even 20,000 years is 800 human generations. Imagine. Me to Dad to Grandpa—three generations. Unless he was rich or famous, few people remember their great grandfather, and that would only be four generations . . .

Whatever the timeframe, ancient archery artifacts—mostly stone points—have been found in caves and graves on every continent except Australia and Antarctica. Migrating over the Bering land bridge, people carried archery technology from Asia to the Americas. Oddly, bows and arrows did not appear in Australia, where the native aborigines used the spear thrower and the bizarrely effective boomerang. Surviving art and religious fragments—cave paintings, carvings on tusks, and bones—dating thousands of years before today's major religions crept onto the scene, offer teasing images of archery's ancestry.

What is surely true is that people were just as inventive, just as intellectually bold in those distant eras as they are today. Individuals were just as keen then as now to solve the existential problems of living, or sometimes were keen to say, "To hell with it," pick up their bow, and go to war. When people lived closer to the earth, when beefsteak and shoe leather, breakfast and dinner came not in little boxes or in sanitized containers, but raw in tooth and fang, one daily problem was eating. Another problem was to keep from being eaten.

Human feet and teeth, and our marvelously dexterous and inquisitive hands, were essential to survival in a world where food was hand-to-mouth. So grabbing and gobbling sufficed for our *Australopithecine* ancestors. Those dining habits also suffice for baboons and chimpanzees today, both of which species are stronger, faster, and more ferocious than humans are and arguably just as clever. Surviving in a world where one is born naked and hairless and helpless, and where the infant-to-adult cycle lasted for years, has always been a challenge. Thus, for millions of years, men and women led short, hard lives.

By the time of our *Neanderthal* and *Cro-Magnon* relatives, however, the human brain had doubled in size and was beginning to figure things out. Perhaps, as some scientists speculate, there was strong but subtle feedback between the brain and the hands.

The more those early humans played with or experimented with the sticks and stones and bones in their environment, the more they imagined things such as an inflated animal bladder being used as a flotation device; the more their brains were stimulated to increasing creativity; the more their tool complex groped toward the bow and arrow.

CUTTING OUT HEARTS, SMASHING HEADS

Atlatl. Prehistoric aboriginal rock art of kangaroo hunting with the atlatl—called a woomera in Australia—and a long dart, from the Anbangbang Rock Shelter, Kakadu National Park, Australia. (Photo courtesy of Thomas Schoch)

The atlatl, or spear thrower (called a "woomera" in Australia), came first, perhaps a quarter million years ago! The atlatl is an extension of the arm, a throwing aid, a longer lever that allows an extended dart to travel a greater distance at greater speed and hit with significantly greater force than is possible with the unaided arm. Atlatl allowed hunters to distance themselves from dangerous game animals or stampeding herds or enemy warriors and throw a light but deadly missile at the speed of a major league fastball, as much as 100 miles per hour.

23

The word "atlatl" is derived from the Nahuatl language, from the Aztecs, although for thousands and thousands of years the tool must have been known by many terms. Records of the conquest of Mexico tell of native warriors skilled with the atlatl. Armed with matchlocks, fine steel cutting weapons, and war horses, and confident in their racial and religious superiority, the Spanish Conquistadores confronted the Aztecs wearing leather padded with cotton for protection. Defending their homeland from invasion, their families from impoverishment and slavery, but otherwise the scourge of Central America, the Aztecs threw long darts with barbed stone tips that drove through the padded leather and into the men or horses behind that soft armor. The barbed heads could not be pulled out without causing excruciating pain. (Despite earlier accounts, the stone heads would not penetrate a Spanish knight's steel plate armor, but few of the Conquistadores belonged to this social class and so plate armor was rare.)

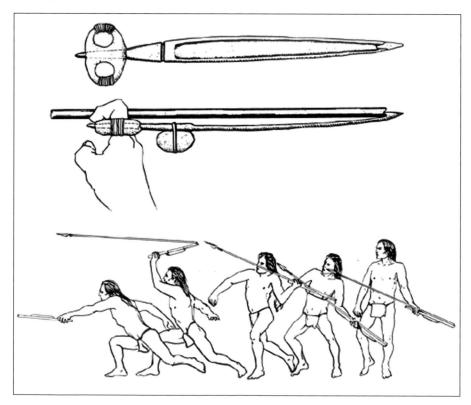

Fast and Lethal. In the 1500s, Spanish Conquistadores invading Mexico feared that thrown atlatl darts would penetrate light armor. The balancing and throwing movement was simple and extended the reach and power of a hand-held spear by several times. (Photo courtesy of Mexicolore)

So what, exactly, is an atlatl?

The atlatl is a wooden handle about two feet long. It is generally grooved along the centerline. On one end is a grip, which is held in the throwing hand; at the other is a hook or a point designed to hold the butt end of the dart in place. A warrior or hunter—in the heyday of the atlatl they were one and the same—fitted his dart, which could be six feet long, into the hook at the end. He then laid the dart in the groove and grasped the dart with the thumb and first finger of the throwing hand in preparation for the cast.

The dart differed from the traditional spear (which is, in any case, a thrusting weapon) or even the javelin (which one throws by hand) in that it typically had a flexible rather than rigid shaft. A thinner, lighter, more flexible shaft was easier to throw and was able to travel a greater distance. Its supple nature—flexing as it was thrown, before stabilizing—also gave it better flight characteristics. The warriors who fought the Conquistadores were capable of hitting a target at 100 yards with tremendous power (thus the heavy Spanish reliance on native troops). The dart's back end was slightly concave so that it would fit over the pin at the base of the atlatl, and feathers were attached to the rear of the shaft for steering. In totality, it was a dart that looked like an oversized arrow.

To throw a dart with an atlatl, a warrior swung his arm back and then swept it forward, releasing the dart from his thumb-forefinger grip along the way. Midway through the cast, centrifugal force lifted the dart off the pin holding it in place—similar

Father of the Arrow. The ***Codex Borgia*** *is a Mesoamerican ritual and divinatory manuscript probably written before the Spanish conquest of Mexico. Made of animal skins, this panel shows Venus, as an owl, striking Tezcatlipoca, as god of the north. Venus is holding an atlatl and dart. Most scholars and archaeologists believe the atlatl preceded the bow and arrow, and its fully fletched dart served as a model for the flight of an arrow. (Photo courtesy of Codex Borgia)*

to an arrow separating from a bowstring and lifting off the arrow shelf midway through a shot—and it flew into the air and away toward its target.

In ages past, the tips of the original weapons might simply have been sharpened, dried, and fire-hardened, but soon they were tipped with sharp flint or obsidian heads, and ultimately even with bronze and iron. In recent decades, people have again become interested in the atlatl, although now it is a toy, albeit a traditional toy.

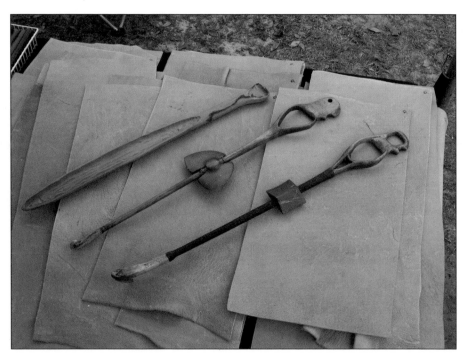

The Modern Atlatl. *We take up an old craft because it should remain alive, a part of the living tool kit of humanity. These modern atlatls will deliver a powerful feathered dart on target at dozens, perhaps scores, of yards. Bob Berg of Thunderbird AtlAtl builds them in a variety of hardwoods chosen for grain, texture, and strength. Blanks are rough sawn and stored in a dry atmosphere "until stresses in the wood are released." Finished atlatls are hand-crafted from seasoned blanks and then hand-rubbed with a tung oil finish. A tine is tied to the head with simulated sinew. The spurs are expertly carved and polished from several different materials including but not limited to bone, antler, or horn.*

* * *

The men of pre-history also developed the sling. Working on the same principle as the atlatl, the sling had an effective distance of hundreds of yards and it proved to be a smashing success.

Other than a bare rock thrown by hand, the sling may have been mankind's first, true projectile weapon. It didn't amount to much really, and yet required an imaginative leap of consciousness and in skilled hands became a deadly tool. The concept was similar to that of the atlatl, the length of the sling providing greater mechanical advantage than the thrower's unaided arms.

Basically, a sling consisted of two cords and a connecting pouch. The cords were held in one hand, one end looped around a finger, the other end knotted for a secure hold, while a projectile—usually stone, but for certain Roman infantry a specifically manufactured lead weight—was placed in the pouch. The thrower whirled the pouch to gain momentum, loosed the knotted cord end and the stone whirled away.

Many historical sources describe the sling's extraordinary performance. In some instances the sling was preferred to the bow and arrow, because a sling could deliver tremendous impact at a long range and stones were certainly simpler projectiles than balanced, fletched arrows. In practice, stones can be thrown a quarter of a mile at speeds exceeding 200 mph! Still, the arcing throw of the sling was merely an extension of the user's body. Its power and accuracy were the result of the slinger's skill, and it could be deadly accurate in experienced hands.

The biblical story of David meeting the Philistine champion Goliath in single combat illustrates the effect of a single stone cast by a sling. From the New International Version, 1 Samuel 17, 48-51:

> As the Philistine moved closer to attack him, David ran quickly toward the battle line to meet him. Reaching into his bag and taking out a stone, he slung it and struck the Philistine on the forehead. The stone sank into his forehead, and he fell face down on the ground.
>
> So David triumphed over the Philistine with a sling and a stone; without a sword in his hand he struck down the Philistine and killed him.
>
> David ran and stood over him. He took hold of the Philistine's sword and drew it from the sheath. After he killed him, he cut off his head with the sword. When the Philistines saw that their hero was dead, they turned and ran.

The sling was also a weapon of terror. Slinging hollow, clay-fired pots filled with burning pitch over the walls of a besieged town where most houses were wood and thatch, or at a highly combustible wooden ship, would have caused panic and enormous devastation. Once lighted, the pitch was hard to extinguish and water only spread it. (George R. R. Martin described this antique device, which was used with deadly effect to defend the city of King's Landing in his novel *Game of Thrones: A Clash of Kings*.)

Use of the sling diminished after the fall of the Roman Empire. (Rome was destroyed in 476 CE.) Nevertheless, the weapon's supremacy as the premier personal long-range weapon (not to be confused with giant ballista or siege engines) was not supplanted

Rome ballista of 1/2 talent caliber

WMD. *Two thousand years ago, the ballista was a fearsome weapon of mass destruction. It could be built in practically any size, and although it was slow to fire, its bolts delivered shattering trauma to lines of troops and even to horses, oxen, and lightly constructed walls. (Photo courtesy of Retro Brit)*

until the fifteenth century. After all, it was cheap, effective, easy to manufacture, and its weights picked up on the battlefield could instantly be reused. Ultimately, changes in society, technology, and military tactics rendered the sling ineffective in large-scale, organized warfare. Transporting thousands of stones may simply have become impractical, with effective stones for warfare weighing perhaps half-a-pound. Nevertheless, the sling continues to be used in less formalized conflicts—young Palestinians use them, for instance, against the Israeli Defense Force—and by hobbyists.

* * *

How man made the leap to the bow is a mystery. The first bow might have been a musical instrument played around the hearth of a skin hut, or a child's toy or even a utilitarian gadget like a fire drill. Still, someone recognized its possibilities, and the primitive bow and arrow spread to every inhabited continent except Australia. Where a man could carry three or four darts and an atlatl, an archer could carry a bow and several dozen arrows in a back quiver, leaving his hands free for other tasks. Plus, he could shoot at distance with greater accuracy and with less overall body movement than when hurling a javelin or an atlatl dart or a stone from a sling.

HARNESSING THE POWER OF THE GODS

The bow and arrow not only used a man's strength but harnessed the power of nature. That brought the gods into the game. Almost every ancient culture celebrated the capabilities of the bow and arrow and associated it with their mythical beings.

In literary contexts, Apollo represents harmony, order, and reason, but the god had a dark side. During the Trojan War Apollo shot arrows infected with the plague into the Greek encampment.

Warrior goddess Satet protected the Pharaoh and the southern borders of ancient Egypt. In her dual role as goddess of fertility, she flooded the Nile River valley every year and purified the deceased with water from the underworld.

The Old Testament in the Hebrew tradition is filled with direct references to archery. Genesis 27, 3–4: "Now then, please take your gear, your quiver and your bow, and go out to the field and hunt game for me; and prepare a savory dish for me such as I love, and bring it to me that I may eat . . ."

In Hindu lore, Rama, the seventh avatar of Vishnu, shot an undying arrow across all of time and the universe. Supposedly, the day the arrow falls to earth will bring the end of the world or perhaps the end of evil, thus upholding dharma and righteousness.

On the Great Plains of North America, a Blackfoot Indian myth tells how Old Man (Napi) walked north, creating as he went. He created bighorn sheep and buffalo. He molded people from clay and realized they were poor and naked; they did

The Gods. *The ancients endowed their gods with bows and arrows. These tools, along with the spear, were the means by which men managed their existence in a world without weather satellites or internal combustion engines. Today, artists continue to reinterpret these legends hoping to sift truth and beauty from the ashes of history. This statue of the Roman goddess Diana was created in bronze by Augustus Saint-Gaudens, 1892–93. It is now on display in the Metropolitan Museum of Art in New York City. (Photo courtesy of Postdlf, 2006)*

not know how to care for themselves. So Old Man taught them how to make bows and arrows and how to hunt animals for food.

Whatever the origin or relation to the supernatural, men slowly discovered the best raw materials and techniques for shaping bows and straightening arrows. Some woods, for example, were more suited to the stress of simultaneous stretching on one side and compression on the opposite side than others. If not locally available, the best wood was traded, sometimes over long distances. Fifty thousand years ago men knew, from experience with spears and atlatl darts, that sharp, hardened arrowheads could penetrate the skin of animals. They learned to shape extraordinarily sharp heads from rocks and fasten them to arrows—downsizing them from the larger, heavier spear heads—using the dried and greased intestinal strings of animals or even a glue made from boiled fish skin and bones. They discovered that bird feathers fixed to the rear of an arrow shaft stabilized its flight and gave it greater accuracy. They embarked on an inventive, adaptive process that to this very day has not ended.

IT WASN'T ALL FUN AND GAMES

The bow and arrow have been immensely effective as weapons. Long before men refined gunpowder to fire lethal projectiles, bows and arrows were incorporated into armies and used by assassins.

Prior to the modern era, warlords in the classical civilizations—Mongols, Parthians, Assyrians, Persians, Koreans, Japanese—fielded battalions of archers. Mounted warriors raced over the fields, their iron-tipped arrows deadly at hundreds of yards and especially destructive to masses of lightly-armored infantry.

Wherever elephants lived, archers rode them into battle. The immense, armored beasts maddened by the pricks of spears and arrows, the screams of the wounded and dying, and carrying partially protected archers—protected from short-range melee weapons—swords and spears—but otherwise excellent targets for other archers or slingers—could be as effective against infantry as are modern battle tanks. Alexander faced them in person in Asia Minor and Hannibal marched them over the Alps and into Italy. J. R. R. Tolkien imagined them as "oliphaunts" in *The Lord of the Rings* saga.

The ingenuity of bow makers (traditionally called bowyers) developed continually over thousands of years. A pinnacle of the art combined mounted warriors with recurved composite bows. These short, powerful bows were wielded with devastating effectiveness by the Great Khan's Mongol cavalry. Horsemen could shower death

Tank Power! Elephants were used in warfare for thousands of years. Against poorly trained troops, they were terrifying, and the archers on their backs were inevitably decisive; but against seasoned veterans, they could be hit-and-miss as instruments of terror and destruction. Foes quickly learned to mass their archery firepower against the men on their backs or to shoot for the elephant's eyes, which would madden it. Then it might do as much harm to one's own forces as to the enemy. In such a case, the mahout (in a sense, the driver) held a stake ready to drive into the elephant's brain, killing it instantly.

on opponents from a quarter mile away and were credited with defeating the massed war elephants of Burma.

These archery kits were no simple stick-and-string. Beginning with a core of wood, Mongol bowyers laminated this stave with a thin layer of horn on the belly (the string side). They then applied a layer of sinew to the back (side opposite the string), thus allowing for tremendous rigidity: stretching on the sinew side and compression on the horn side. This composition was bound together with glue made from boiled animal skins, and Temujin's warriors rode it across the vast steppes of Mongolia and Russia into central Europe.

The bow and arrow were also effective in the hands of ninjas and assassins. Nearly 5,300 years ago a tattooed, forty-five-year-old man climbed into the Alps along what is today the Austrian-Italian border. He wore warm fur garments and carried a bow and fourteen arrows in various states of development, a sharp flint knife, and a valuable copper axe. At some point, he was shot in the back with a flint-tipped arrow and then his skull was bashed in with a rock. We refer to him as "Oetzi—the Iceman."

The incident most infamously demonstrating the effect of a single arrow dates to the Battle of Hastings, October 14, 1066. That afternoon Harold Godwinson, the putative King of England, led his Anglo-Saxon army against a Norman invasion directed by Duke William. Struck in the eye by an arrow, Harold collapsed in agony.

Tool of History. The famous 230-foot Bayeux Tapestry depicts Harold Godwinson, the putative King of England, as he is shot in the eye with an arrow, effectively turning the tide of British history, collapsing the English resistance, and allowing William, Duke of Normandy, to gain the title William the Conqueror.

With their leader dead or dying, the English resistance also collapsed and William—suddenly William "the Conqueror"—swept on to total victory.

The great age of the bow and arrow was ultimately doomed, of course, as chemists around the globe experimented with the dynamic force of explosive powders: sulfur, charcoal, and potassium nitrate. Still, the bow continued to make news, even if the dates and actual events cannot always be verified.

Under the Roman Catholic Pope Innocent II, the Second Lateran Council in 1139 ruled on matters of the faith. Canon 10, for instance, excommunicated laity who failed to pay tithes due to bishops. It also banned the use of crossbows . . . but only against other Christians.

In Switzerland, a local patriot and crossbow sharpshooter named William Tell and his son were marked for execution because they challenged the authority of Austrian overlord Albrecht Gessler. According to legend, Tell was forced to shoot an apple off his son's head (1307). Soon thereafter he killed Gessler. His defiance stoked the Swiss fever for an independent confederation.

Legendary. *According to legend, William Tell was a strong man and an expert shot with the crossbow. In 1307, he refused to bow before the hat of Gessler, the Austrian overlord, and was forced to shoot an apple off his son's head. Tell later assassinated the cruel Austrian and sparked the rebellion that led to Swiss independence. The bronze statue of Tell shows the Swiss national hero with his crossbow and accompanied by his son, Walter. Erected in 1895, the monument stands in Altdorf, Switzerland. (Photo courtesy of Library of Congress Prints and Photographs Division)*

In competition before the Sheriff of Nottingham, Robin Hood shot arrows so accurately that they split other arrow shafts down the center in the very heart of the targets (1260s). Today, to split one arrow by shooting another is called "a Robin Hood."

In France, at the battles of Crecy (1346) and Poitiers (1356), a small army, principally of English longbowmen, obliterated the massed power of French knighthood. The English archers shot bows with—by today's standards—astonishingly heavy draw weights, to 200 pounds and even beyond. The archers' hands and shoulders could be permanently disfigured from the extreme effort and the legally mandated weekly practice sessions. It is no wonder that conventional lightweight armor was little defense against the iron tipped arrows.

The Middle Ages was a time of mounted knights and minstrels, of nobility and serfs, of the Black Plague and the growth of a commercial class, of the coalescence of nation-states . . . and it literally ended with a bang.

YOU'VE BEEN SERVED . . .

Men worked with gunpowder a thousand years ago, although the powders were generally suitable only for fireworks and magic tricks. In the Middle Ages, these formulations filtered out of China along the spice routes to Europe and North Africa. In all of these regions, men experimented with saltpeter, finding that it was eminently suitable to propel iron balls with terrifying, body-splintering results. Indeed, primitive firearms may have been present at the Battle of Crecy (1346), arguably the pinnacle of archery supremacy. If that is so, at that moment the bow and arrow were served notice that their favored position in hunting and the military were doomed.

As firearms grew in sophistication over the course of half a millennium, archery declined. With it went the lance and pike, the axe and mace, the sword and spear and dagger, all replaced by hand cannons and flintlocks. And yet, little ever completely disappears from the earth. Myths take on new meaning. Micro-biologists sequence dinosaur DNA. Politicians reinvent themselves. Tools are put to new uses.

As late as the middle of the Second Millennium, the reloading process of those early guns was so tedious that a skilled archer could accurately shoot a dozen arrows in the space of one musket shot. And because early firearms required a great deal of care and support, the bow and arrow never entirely disappeared. North American Indians famously hunted buffalo with the bow and arrow, both on foot and from horseback into the late nineteenth century. In a famous scene from the 1990 Kevin Costner movie *Dances with Wolves*, the flatulent white teamster Timmons (Robert Pastorelli) is shot full of arrows. American archer and manufacturer Fred Bear purchased a diminutive bow from a Central African pygmy hunter in the 1960s. And as late as 2008, tribesmen in the Amazon jungles were filmed attempting to bring down an airplane belonging to Brazil's National Indian Foundation with bows and arrows.

Eventually, however, faced with the development of repeating firearms, smokeless powders, and self-contained cartridges, the bow and arrow almost disappeared from civilized society. Firearms were simply more effective for warfare and hunting. Firearms were easier.

And yet, the archery tradition persisted. In Japan, when the emperor outlawed the samurai class, archery merged into a meditative corner of Zen Buddhism. On the steppes of Asia and as far west as Hungary, descendants of Mongol cavalry continued to enjoy mounted shooting. Today, public archery is often a festival-driven competition such as the Mongolian *Naadam*, or "three games of men" (with wrestling and horse racing). Archery persists because it is fun.

In Europe, a more formal archery was incorporated into the modern Olympic Games in Paris in 1900. Eight years later at the London games, women were allowed to participate. But some national sports teams emphasized shooting from horseback; others preferred the crossbow; others excluded women. (In 1904 Lida Howell Scott became America's first female gold medalist in archery. Though women were allowed to compete in swimming events at the 1912 Olympic games, the United States refused to take part because of a national rule that prohibited female athletes from participating in events unless they wore long skirts.)

The sport strayed as far as the variously spelled "popinjay," which tied birds (originally live parrots or pigeons; later only tufts of feathers) to tall poles for target practice. The lack of uniform international rules caused archery to be dropped from the Olympic program after 1920. It was not included again until the ill-fated 1972 games in Munich.

Archery remained a sports step-child until 1931 when the International Archery Federation, or Federation International de Tir a l'Arc (FITA), was founded. Today, FITA is composed of nearly 150 member associations representing the world's nation-states. Its purpose remains Olympic-focused, conducting archery events that conform to the highly stylized and—does anyone dare say boring?—static Olympic rules.

The 1972 Olympic Games in Munich—the venue interrupted by the terrorist murders of Israeli athletes—were the proving ground for FITA's new rules. Competitors shot thirty-six arrows for a single competition and seventy-two arrows for a double. Men shot from ninety, seventy, fifty, and thirty meters; women shot from seventy, sixty, fifty, and thirty meters. Team competition was added in the 1988 Games in Seoul, Korea.

Archery reinvented itself in the twentieth century. While isolated pockets of subsistence hunters remain in several backwaters of the world, archery basically takes two forms today: Olympic-style competition and hunting with the bow and arrow. Other contests, often nationalistic, sometimes historically themed, persist though: from horseback, popinjay, archery golf, kyudo, and, in the United States, 3D shooting.

A MAN CALLED ISHI AND THE RISE OF MODERN BOWHUNTING

Millions of archers hunt recreationally with the bow, primarily in economically prosperous countries, the United States, Canada, and, to a lesser extent, Continental Europe. Thousands of them travel to hunt the exotic game still found in less prosperous countries such as Namibia or Uzbekistan or Mozambique.

The rise of modern archery hunting or bowhunting began in the nineteenth century, principally in the United States with men like the brothers Maurice and Will Thompson. Paradoxically, widespread admiration of the Native American way of life coexisted with a lust to exterminate the Indian tribes and seize their land and its resources; a love of freedom and wilderness coexisted with a fear of the wild and an urge to huddle together around the fireplace.

And so in 1911, the sole surviving member of the Yahi tribe, a middle-aged man called "Ishi" (it was not his true given name, which he never spoke and no one ever recorded), fled starving from the isolation of the northern California forest. He was eventually given refuge by anthropologists at the University of California–Berkeley, where he lived for five years as both a specimen and a research assistant. Prior to his death from tuberculosis, Ishi became a popular character at the museum and taught many people to enjoy native crafts, among them building and shooting the bow and arrow. One of the people he befriended and eventually hunted with was his doctor, Saxton Pope.

Because there is a thread of continuity that runs through human affairs, Pope befriended Art Young. Young had learned about the bow and arrow from Will Compton, who learned from Sioux Indians. Young, Pope, and Compton built bows and arrows and hunted together. Eventually Pope and Young hunted grizzly bears and African lions, even traveling together to Greenland and Alaska. Young also

Photo source: Online Archive of California

Photo source: Online Archive of California

Last Wild Indian. *A forty-nine-year-old man named Ishi stumbled out of the California wilderness in 1911. Alone and starving, his Yana people had been hunted to extinction, and he was the last surviving member. Ishi lived the final years of his life in the Museum of the University of California–Berkeley, where he passed along such skills as fire-making, sewing with native tools, and both building and hunting with the bow and arrow. He became friends with his doctor, Saxton Pope, and taught him to shoot "Indian style."*

lectured to popularize archery, and one of the young men he energized in Michigan was Fred Bear, who founded Bear Archery.

Today there are three million licensed bowhunters in North America, all of whom participate in their hobby in direct descent from Ishi. Furthermore, state wildlife departments recognize the bow and arrow as being sufficient for taking any big-game animal, whitetail deer to musk ox, and thousands of American and International archers travel the world to bowhunt: Florida for alligator, Mozambique for lion, Australia for water buffalo, Alaska for moose, Russia for brown bears.

The basic instrument of archers around the world is still the traditionally styled longbow or recurve, the particular design of which varies region to region. In North America and perhaps in Europe though, the modern compound bow has a greater number of adherents, but the infrastructure to support this complex tool kit—repair,

Master Teaches Master. *This is a 1929 photo taken at the Detroit Archery Club range. Each man is shooting a longbow: (left to right) Leonard Osberg, Art Young, Carl Strang, Fred Bear, and Ray Stannard. Ishi taught Pope and Will Compton taught Young. Eventually the four men hunted together in California, until Ishi's death from tuberculosis. These men are credited with introducing thousands to the thrill of big-game hunting with their bow by lecturing and presenting slide shows across the United States. (Photo courtesy of Bear Archery)*

accessories, pro shops, organization, and leisure time—is not available everywhere in the world or is simply too expensive.

Thus, in most areas, from the deep forests of Tanzania to the arid plains of Mongolia, a form of traditional archery still prevails. And so one who learns to shoot the longbow or recurve will find a welcoming community of archers in every country. Indeed, learning the traditions of a host country—most archery communities practice archery in different games than those in the United States and Canada, the bows, grip, and targets being different—is an exciting international opportunity for those who take up the stick and string.

That being said, man is an inquisitive and inventive tool-making animal. So he maintains traditions such as archery, even though they are not practical or necessary, day to day. He continues to think up innovative solutions to problems, experiment with new materials, and even add new instruments to his repertoire. But archery has always been a craft that rewarded innovation, even after its original benefits as a survival tool complex became antiquated. Now, startling new instruments are finding their way into hunting camps and competition venues across the world, overwhelming the old styles and inventing new ones.

HUNGRY GAMES

Archery continually reinvents itself, except at the fossilized level of international competition where it seems to continually hyperventilate for lack of oxygen. At the private level, however, archery is both a communally shared myth and a privately held desire.

It is for this reason that almost all ancient arts and their tool kits persist through time. Hand quilting, embroidery, and needlework are passed down the generations in the face of giant computerized machines that can stitch more perfectly than the most skilled seamstress. The machines can select color variations even more complementary and pleasing to the eye than a Hong Kong tailor. People continue to learn the art of canning, preserving vegetables and meats, although most of them would admit that the practice is out of date, no longer necessary and perhaps even more expensive than purchasing from the local grocery.

The myth-desire division is obvious in the current industry-driven mania for the black gun, the MSR. An MSR is a modern sporting rifle, a semi-automatic AR15, and it costs between $1,000 and $1,500. It is being promoted as the "New Hunting Rifle." MSR manufacturers and their mouthpieces at the National Rifle Association and National Shooting Sports Foundation are working very hard to convince gun hunters that their "daddy's rifle" is old fashioned. The old rifle style was a classic single-shot, bolt action wooden stock hunter, and it was tremendously effective in a variety of old-fashioned calibers . . . and yet people continue to learn the arts of axe throwing and atlatl building and black powder shooting.

The crux of the matter is that shooting a zeroed .223 caliber AR15 loaded with Wal-Mart 69-grain HPBT cartridges can give a more precise pattern down-range, and a shot will cover a greater distance—as much as a half-mile—in less time than a blast from your black powder rifle. On the other hand, the half-ounce lead ball you produced with a mold and fired from a muzzleloader, perhaps built and personalized from a kit that drops a whitetail deer at eighty yards, leaves you feeling far more satisfied. Used within their specifications, the muzzleloader and the MSR are effective, but there is a *je ne sais quoi* difference that all of us feel, even if we struggle to explain it.

It's similar to what factory bosses are learning. An employee who stamps and inspects door bolts all day, every day, eventually becomes a discipline problem, and his work begins to suffer because he is bored. Bolts are rejected, doors fail. Contrarily, an employee who may have a single primary responsibility but has the opportunity to follow work through to the end product—the finished, painted, ready-to-hang door, for example—is happier, more attentive to his work, and the work itself measures up to a higher standard because has made a personal connection with the process.

Never-Ending Story. Once men generally learn a skill such as lithic reduction, some few will always be loathe to give it up. Hence, with men orbiting Earth in a space station, when scientifically formulated, pre-fabricated rifle cartridges are cheap and easily available, some men and women pick up rocks and a set of simple tools and learn to fashion arrowheads in the same manner their forefathers used 100 or 20,000 years ago. It is a messy art; just right for old men and little boys!

In the public imagination, we continue to tell stories about archery that reinvent and reinforce the art. The Robin Hood legend has been told and re-told a half-dozen times in films, and more are undoubtedly on the horizon, because each generation experiences life and thus reinterprets the ancient legends and archery arts differently. Here are a few interpretations that have appeared recently:

Rambo: First Blood: Based on the 1972 book by David Morrell, this 1982 film featured Sylvester Stallone as the principal character. Stallone portrayed a tormented and misunderstood veteran of the Vietnam War. Four movies and a video game have been made from the Rambo franchise. In the earliest movie, Stallone carried a modern compound bow into combat, shooting conventionally and exploding heads. Bow manufacturer Hoyt USA built the bows for the movies, advertised them widely, and produced a black Rambo bow. The action adventure film was credited with interesting thousands of people in archery . . . and in exploding heads.

The Lord of the Rings: This film trilogy in 2001, 2002, and 2003 followed the fantasy books of J. R. R. Tolkien closely in imaginative detail. Orlando Bloom played the elf Legolas, a prince of the Woodland Realm and one of nine members of the Fellowship of the Ring. Legolas used numerous bows, but his Mirkwood bow was a dark but elegant sixty-inch recurve, possibly hickory, and decorated with gilded ivy leaves and tendrils around the handgrip and tips. In Tolkien's imagination, the bow drew an astonishing 150 pounds, but as a stage prop it would have been closer to fifteen pounds to avoid arm fatigue. These films became the highest grossing motion picture trilogy of all time, with a worldwide total of $2.91 billion.

Brave: In this 2012 animated film, Princess Merida (voiced by Kelly Macdonald) uses her skills as an archer in a time when women weren't traditionally trained in the arts of war. When her archery gets her into trouble, she must use her wits and her instincts to break the curse she has caused and return everything back to normal. This is a charming tale with traditional archery at its center.

The Hunger Games: Set in a future where the Capitol selects a boy and girl from each of the twelve districts to fight to the death on live television, young Katniss Everdeen—played by Jennifer Lawrence—volunteers to take her younger sister's place. In the story, the heroine hunts for food for her family with the bow and arrow and must subsequently use these practical skills to kill rivals in the "games." The 2012 movie was based on a 2008 young adult novel by Suzanne Collins. Perhaps because of the success of the film, thousands of young people have been drawn to Easton Archery Centers and the National Archery in the Schools Program to learn the art of archery. (According to sources in the film industry, three sequel films based on the two sequel books have been announced.)

All things, even straight lines, followed to their conclusion are eventually circular. With television shows (*Arrow*, *Game of Thrones*, etc.) and more movies featuring archery in the programming and production stages, there is sure to be a continuing boomlet in interest. Shooting venues will be crowded and archery instructors will be in demand . . . for a while. But it is in the nature of things that the boom eventually collapses on itself, the sound and fury dissipate, the fog clears. What's left is archery, pure and simple, traditional and eternal, and you can be a part of this timeless passion.

Archery and Friendship. *Archery brings people together, whether it is for hunting, competition, or simply the enjoyment of like-minded companionship. This photo was taken twenty-five years ago at Grousehaven, Fred Bear's hunting camp near Rose City, Michigan. A great deal has changed in that quarter century, and several of the individuals in this photo have since passed away, including the Great Bear himself (seated third from the left). The author is standing, second from the right. Rock and roll bowhunter Ted Nugent, with an Irish setter named Pinecone, is seated at the far left.*

CHAPTER TWO

BOWS OF THE WORLD

Several distinct types of bows—some traditional and some not so traditional—are shot around the world. The names applied to these bows are usually taken from the shape, especially when viewed from the side: straight, recurve, crossbow, or compound.

The most primitive of all bows, the stick bow, has a brilliant heritage, dating back thousands of years before the complex recurve bows shot by mounted Mongol warriors or even the heavy longbows wielded by English yeomen. Early crossbows, essentially a short, stiff horizontal bow mounted on a wooden stock, appeared in Asia maybe a thousand years BCE. The compound or wheel bow— old-time traditional shooters sneer at its complex system of cables and cams as "training wheels"—was effectively invented in the middle of the twentieth century.

Pyramid Bow. *A "pyramid" bow is a style of primitive bow that is rarely seen on shooting venues except among the most dedicated archery historians. A pyramid bow's limbs taper evenly from the center. (Photo courtesy of Richard Keatinge)*

Because archery is a living exercise, its tools or artifacts continue to evolve. We no longer need to shoot arrows dipped in poison to slow down a mastodon so that we can kill and butcher it by hand. We no longer *need* to hunt (or grow a garden or learn swordsmanship or learn how to cure animal skins), though millions of people choose to keep these antique skills alive. We are no longer called to take up a bow to defend our nation from invasion. We no longer need to build everything we need to survive. On the other hand, who knows what the future may bring?

Today we take up archery because it gives so much back. Imagine yourself handling the archery tools of prehistory. Imagine the feel of roughly tanned skin clothing, the taste of meat and vegetables grilled over an open fire, and the tight intensity of a small, self-reliant group of family. The people of 10,000 BCE or 100,000 BCE were much like us. They had many of the same interests and dreams: love, children, a good life, to live without fear, and to "be somebody" in their community. They prospered within their extended family unit. They hunted and fished and ate seasonal fruits. They sewed their clothes from the skins of animals, walked everywhere, and were subject to unpredictable acts of nature. They depended on a personal tool kit made by hand from the stones, sticks, and bones they found in or wrenched from their environment. This chapter looks at several stages in the evolution of those tools, stages we now refer to as "traditional."

ARCHERY FOREPLAY

It can be a little scary to learn about traditional or "old style" concepts. After all, they require a certain grasp of technologies and ways of learning with which few of us are any longer familiar. Under the personal instruction of your father or a master bowyer, you pick up the draw knife and wood rasp instead of the car keys, cultivate your sharp eye and steady hand instead of typing with your thumbs on a smartphone. It's no different than golf or painting. You can buy your paints from an art store or learn to crush and mix pigments to meet your own ideas of a great color palate. You can purchase bows from bowyers and accessories from commercial outlets, or you can learn to build everything yourself, even the tools. But you can go as deep into this art as you wish, and you can stop at any time without prejudice.

Perhaps the best way to begin is to focus on enjoying a satisfying moment—an arrow well-fletched, a single shot perfectly executed. Then, if your curiosity drives you deeper into the traditional community, you will discover that the hobby is truly international and intellectually stimulating.

A useful way to look at the art of traditional archery is in contrast, the airplane, for example. For a decade, a well-funded research and engineering team under the auspices of the National Geographic Society attempted to re-build the airplane flown by the Wright brothers in 1901. Unfortunately, only old photos exist because the Wrights left no blueprints behind; indeed, they did not work from blueprints.

The Wright Flyer is a good analogy to traditional bows and arrows. So many questions remain about the development and manufacture, the uses and capabilities of archery gear. How deep you want to fly away in this mystery and how long you want to stay involved is up to you, but understanding archery can become a lifetime passion.

And the Wright brothers airplane reconstruction? They still can't get it to fly.

Bob Popularizes Archery. *For more than half a century, California trick-shot artist Bob Markworth has traveled the world popularizing archery with his entertaining archery and night club show. In 1954, he recruited three beautiful women to pose for a press photo and wrote, "Just starting into show business at the age of 16, I posed with three of my assistants [left to right]: Dolores Andrews, Marjean Faulkner, and Caleta Bakus." (Photo courtesy of Bob Markworth)*

LONGBOWS—MEET THE SELF BOW: "STRAIGHT," BUT NOT SIMPLE

The longbow looks so simple, so clean, as if it is the easiest tool in the world to understand, build, and shoot. Just chop a stick and tie a string to both ends.

Looks are deceiving.

Longbows probably began as a single straight piece of wood, straight in side-view profile when they are not strung. The earliest versions are often referred to as straight bows, despite some minor curves of the natural wood grain or any "set" or curvature the wood takes during use or any slight curvature built into the tips. Today, we refer to that most basic longbow as a self bow (or perhaps a flat bow). As we will see however, basic doesn't mean simple, even if the self bow was the very first purposefully constructed bow.

Self Bow. *A self bow made of straight but knotty and poor-quality yew wood. The contour of the wood will add character to the finished product even if it does not promote excellent shooting.*

The self bow is still in use around the world, although in Europe and North America only a handful of skilled archery aficionados continue to build and shoot them. Still, a self bow can be an effective hunting weapon, although it is a tool that requires practice, as well as physical and mental discipline and concentration, to shoot well. And when it is backed with snake skin or when other woods and rawhide strips are applied around the grip, this basic tool can become a thing of immense beauty.

In cross-sectional shape, the working or flexing parts of a flat bow resemble a rectangle, and many different types of woods can be used in its construction. A skilled bowyer can make a workable self bow in less than a day, but much longer is truly needed to coax peak performance from a shaped stick. Self bows have to be long from tip to tip to perform efficiently. The overall length of the bending wood must be about 2.3 times the archer's draw length, which will give the bow a tip-to-tip length of sixty-two to seventy inches. The longer the bow and the longer the draw, the faster and more efficient the arrow will be . . . and every inch of that long shape needs special attention.

The self bow is at once durable and fragile. Dried, scraped, greased, and sanded, then notched to hold a string (linen or hemp, vegetable fibers, sinew, or silk in the old days, stronger-than-steel synthetic materials today), it performs well with wooden arrows tipped with either a tiny knapped flint or bone arrowhead (or with modern equivalents, though we will consider those in later chapters). It also performs very adequately with more modern arrows, properly spined aluminum and carbon and broadheads.

Cutting or grooving notches, even shallow notches, into the bow's tips for the string can weaken the bow by giving the wood low-pressure lines along which it can easily develop a split. So bowyers long ago learned to glue horn or bone laminates on the ends to strengthen those delicate tips. Traditionally, bowyers also beefed up the handles or spliced additional, sometimes decorative, woods into the "non-working" grip area to reinforce what might otherwise be the self bow's central weakness.

Of all the types of bows that are practical for building in a home workshop, the self bow is the best because it is at once the simplest and the easiest to learn with, yet the result can be an effective and attractive bow. (Of course, if one becomes hooked on building primitive weapons, simple can soon become complicated, elaborate, and truly modern works of singular craftsmanship.)

To begin building a bow, bowyers usually prefer a stave with a straight grain. Interesting and workable bows can be made from wood with complex curves and grain structures, though.

The cellulose wood fibers on the back of a self bow (the side away from the shooter) should be fairly continuous, however, and there are two ways to ensure this. The hard way is to use the outer, under-bark surface of the tree as the back of the bow, by the painstaking process of removing outer growth rings. This is often the manner of shaping yew and Osage orange staves. The easier way is by making or following a cut or split surface that happens to have continuous grain (customary if starting with commercially sawn wood).

As they are bent, denser heavier woods typically store energy better than less dense woods. They can also be made into narrower, more efficient bows with less woodworking effort. Yew has, perhaps for thousands of years, been prized for bow-making, and it was much sought after for the traditional European version of the longbow. Good yew staves are more difficult to find these days. (At the time of this writing, a commercial Osage orange stave was about $100 and a yew stave was about twice that amount, plus shipping.) The Eastern Woodland Indians of North America used hickory. Tribes in parts of the southwestern United States began the tradition of using Osage, which can make wonderful bows but has a reputation for being a difficult subject, twisty and wormy. Tribes of the Brazilian rainforest used palm wood, among others. Woods that are more common, such as maple, ash, elm, and even oak, will make fine self or flat bows and are easier to obtain.

With less dense timber, the self-design sometimes results in the bow taking excessive set (also called string follow) or even breaking. Hence the practice of reinforcing soft wood bows at or near their center.

Approximately the same mass of wood is required, whatever the density of the particular timber. The overall length of bending wood, the working sections in the upper and lower limb, as opposed to the static handle and tip sections, must be (as mentioned earlier) about 2.3 times the draw length. Thus, a bow with a twenty-eight-inch draw will have sixty-plus inches of working limb, thirty inches or so in top and bottom. Narrow longbows actually bend slightly in the handle section. The widest bows (these are known as "flat bows," but the distinctions can be minute) must be narrow in the handle if they are to be practical, but the handle must be made thicker so as not to bend, and the complete bow will therefore tend to be longer.

Let's Build a Bow!

Just for fun.

Here are the steps to follow when building your own self bow. First, begin with the end in mind. Decide things in advance that will determine how you handle some of the steps, how the bow should fit, and how you want it to perform. For instance, how long will you make it, what draw length and weight are you aiming for, and do you intend to back it with sinew and perhaps snake skin? Have a plan—not inflexible, but a guideline—then get busy.

This section is not meant as a precise "how-to" but will give you an idea of the steps, the tools, and the general objectives to show that even traditional or "primitive" construction is a sophisticated and intellectual process, a true craft. Now, imagine performing all these steps without modern conveniences, such as electricity that operates drills and saws and sanders. Imagine that before the sun rises, you get up in the gray dawn to begin work, and when the sun sets, you set your tools aside and gather by the firelight, kissing the children and petting the dog, the day's chores completed . . .

Building a bow is more difficult than learning to drive a car with a stick shift. If you're not satisfied with your first few attempts . . . excellent! You are on the right path. Becoming a bowyer does not resemble the agonizing learning curve for the Bride ninja in the *Kill Bill* movie series. So take your time; enjoy the process; learn from your mistakes.

1. First, select a suitable wood for your bow. Many woods will do: oak, hickory, yew, Osage orange, Ipe (Brazilian walnut), and even some types of bamboo (which is actually a grass). A dense wood with plenty of width and a long, consistent grain will ensure that yours becomes a stout bow. Otherwise it may break if pulled too far. And of course, the more the stave (in archery, a "stave" is a full-length piece of wood used to make a bow) is shaped and thinned, the faster it dries. Left to its own devices, it might take a year for the stave to fully dry, and unless you are operating an assembly line, that's too long to wait to sustain interest in your first bow.

2. Now, cut a six-foot length with the grain. Carefully peel or strip off the bark. It's important to do so without damaging the outer layer of wood, which will become the back of the new bow.

3. Next, draw the bow's rough profile on the bare wood of the stave.

    a. The longer the bow, the more energy it will store; but ounce-for-ounce, the less efficient it will be. The total length depends on the draw length of the archer who will shoot it. Something between sixty and seventy inches is generally preferred, but it can be any manageable size.

    b. Begin with a bow width of two-plus inches as this helps narrow the stave, makes it more manageable, promotes drying, and allows gentle narrowing to the handle and at the tips. Imagine that the handle area will be between four and five inches long and the fades, the sections that angle or transition into the working limbs, will be another couple inches on either side of the grip. The thickness of the handle—1½ to 2¼ inches or so—is a matter of personal taste (what fits your hand). A thicker handle is generally more stable, but a little harder to manage.

    c. Determining the specific gravity of the wood (its weight divided by the weight of an equal volume of water) helps estimate the final draw weight. Each wood has its own specific gravity. Ash has a specific gravity of .64 and, at the lengths we are considering, will give a final draw weight of about sixty-four pounds; southern cypress .51; hickory .77; black maple .75. For a lighter draw weight, trim the width.

4. With the final profile in mind, begin to cut and shape the wood. This is the "roughing out" step. You must pay attention to the grain and not cut across it. The self bow does not have to be "straight," just internally consistent, meaning a bow cut along the line of the grain. Trim the stave to width first and then worry about thickness. Bring it relatively close to final dimensions, making sure the limbs are as parallel as possible given any curvature of the grain. As you work the stave in the direction of a bow, you'll want to monitor its thickness. What you must avoid are thin or low spots, areas where you have cut a bit too deep, because the bow will break there. An even taper in all sections is desirable.

5. Final drying of the roughed-out stave comes next. Drying is very important and must be thoughtfully approached, but it is not a science. Bowyers who are really "into" building bows, who perhaps build them commercially, will have an assembly area with a number of staves moving along and drying at their own pace.

   a. Most people don't have that much available space (or time), however, and so a simple "dry box" is easy to build. It's a simple container that holds the stave, is lined on the inside with foil, and is heated with several continuously burning sixty-Watt bulbs. The secret is to not become impatient. If you don't have a dry box and don't want to hammer one together—it doesn't need to be fancy, just functional—finding a dry, flat spot on a shelf of the house or in the sun while turning the stave regularly will accomplish the same purpose, but will take a lot longer (especially if it's outside and you allow it to get wet from rain or dew).

   b. You can check your stave either with a commercial moisture meter ($50 to $500) or by becoming sensitive to the wood—which is perhaps as easy as becoming sensitive to your spouse or girl/boyfriend—but within a week to ten days in the box it will lose its "wet weight." You can detect this by weighing it. If you have a relatively lightweight stave, try giving it a good bend by hand.

If it doesn't remain in the bent position, but quickly moves back to straight, you're getting close. A month or so in the drying box and your stave will be ready to progress to further cutting and shaping.

6. Now it's time to finish shaping and tempering the bow, beginning with scraping the limbs to their final dimensions. Remember that you are, in a sense, a partner with the wood in this process. Some of the final shape will be determined by your attention and craftsmanship; some will be inherent in the grain and quality of the wood. Begin in the middle of each limb and begin to taper from about two inches wide at six to eight inches from the fades, down to about ½ or ⅜ inches at the tip.

    a.   Numerous types of bend can be built in to your bow. Several procedures, all compatible with a simple home workshop, are practical. You can hold it over a fire or, more practically, steam it or use a heat gun (a heavy-duty hair dryer). Remember to bend the bow slightly past your design point and then clamp it down and let it sit for several days. The same simple technique—and like anything else, the more you practice, the better you'll get— works for steaming. Cover the spot in which you want to induce a bend with foil and hold it over boiling water for an hour, then induce the bend and clamp it in place for several days.

    b.   The essential tool for tempering your stave is the heat gun. The idea of tempering is to harden the belly of the bow, the side toward the archer. Give each limb an hour or so of heat until the limb turns dark. You don't want to set them on fire, but a wee wisp of smoke indicating the tempering process is complete is not an altogether bad sign. (If you're really into "primitive," suspend the bow over a bed of hardwood coals, a practice that might require experimentation!)

    c.   Now gently begin to file the bow so the edges of the back and belly are smooth and rounded. This is a good time to remove any tool marks and begin smoothing the handle or perhaps building it up by adding a section of wood. Filing to shape is the essential step before final sanding.

d. Trim each limb tip for bowstring nocks. Go lightly at this point, as the string needs very little shoulder to hold it in place.

7. Tiller and bend the limbs to shape.

a. "Tiller" is the difference between the distance of the upper limb and the lower limb, measured on the perpendicular, from the bowstring to the belly at the fadeouts. Traditionally, bows are tillered to produce a stiffer lower limb. This only means the distance from the bowstring to the belly is less on the lower limb than on the upper limb. In bow building, one adjusts the tiller by sanding or filing wood from a bow limb, or in some cases, both limbs.

b. Tiller can be affected by the manner in which the bow is shot. A bow tillered for a three-finger under-grip on the string may have an even tiller, meaning the distance from the upper and lower limbs to the string is about the same. For a split-finger shooter, one finger above and two below, the upper limb is usually $1/8$ to $1/4$ inch longer than the similar distance on the lower limb. This is called a positive measurement.

The Mediterranean Grip. *The classic Mediterranean grip is customarily, though is by no means exclusively, used in the United States. It requires three fingers to draw the bowstring, one finger above the arrow and two beneath. This gives the archer control without pinching the arrow off the string. Optionally, some archers shoot with all three fingers beneath the arrow.*

c. The concept of tillering is sometimes more difficult than the practice. The purpose is to produce a smooth, even pull. To change tiller, bowyers sometimes narrow or round the edges of the strong limb or sand it after fiberglass is applied. This is a painstaking process. Removing material is easy, but building it up is usually impossible. If the bow loses weight during the tillering process, it may need additional drying time. (You will hear a lot about tiller in the traditional community. It's important, or not, but it's nice to understand.)

d. Depending on its design, a bow will vary in the amount of tillering needed. The trick is to get it close and then apply a nock-set to the string (with nock-set pliers) before shooting a handful of arrows. The nock-set can be adjusted up or down the string to reduce, though it will never entirely eliminate, wallowing or porpoising of the arrow (the horizontal or vertical oscillations of archer's paradox that can sometimes be observed after a shot).

e. Some bowyers begin with "floor tillering," a crude process of bending the bow tips against the floor to feel how heavy the limbs are and to watch for stiff or weak spots. The more practice one has in bow building, the easier—and more understandable—this becomes.

8. Build in the finishing touches. During the tillering process you will have strung and shot the bow a few times. It might shoot as smooth as butter, but chances are it will have one or two characteristic problems that you need to address.

a. If your self bow's limb tips are too heavy, you will, curiously, feel it in excessive hand shock (not unusual in shooting longbows of any variety, however). This requires a smidgen of trimming. What nock size is best depends on the draw weight of the bow and your shooting preferences. In fact, the limbs might need to be shaved or filed slightly. This is sometimes called an "Eiffel Tower" taper and it can run all the way to the limb tips, though here individual preference dictates how thin to make the limb.

b. Adjusting the thickness of the handle, the "arrow pass," is another consideration prior to applying the finishing touches. A narrow handle does not allow much choice since there is so little to work with, but a wider handle allows a little variation on a self bow. This is a moment when arrow shaft selection is critical and will help make any decision, because you will at first want to shoot the bow with a bare shaft (no fletching) to find out what flies best.

c.   Another consideration is adjusting the draw weight. If it is too light, you may want to shorten the bow by a couple of inches from each limb or, if you have time and patience, give it reflex tips if you have not already done so (check step 6a). This will boost the weight substantially. Of course, shortening it and then backing it with sinew will also cause the bow to develop a heavier weight, as much as twenty to twenty-five pounds. If you desire to use snake skins, those are best applied before the finish; the same with sinew. Sinew bows are especially susceptible to moisture, so snake or even fish skin covers are usually best for protection.

9. Finally, this bow has taken a chunk of your life. Why not make it a personal statement. There are as many ways to decorate a bow as there are possibilities. Several coatings of the right wood stain can help bring out the grain, and there is a wide range of color options. Polyurethanes make a good finish, though as you become more experienced you may want to experiment with shellac and other alternatives. Some bowyers have used paraffin (canning wax) successfully on bare bows, melting the wax into the bow with a heat gun. The purpose of sealing the bow is to prevent the wood from soaking up moisture. An uneven coating of the finish, leaving an uncoated spot, can cause a split and ruined bow. When you have finished, fight your impulse to take it to the range and shoot it: allow the bow to dry. Let it lie braced on a flat surface for half a day. Next, unstring it, let it sit for an hour, and then check its draw weight. If you have done a good job and there is not a lot of "string follow" (the bow has not taken an unusual set, a permanent bend, in the direction of the string), what you measure now for weight and length should be final and it is time to use the handle grip, limb wraps, strike plates, backings such as snake skin, and decorations that appeal to you. The shelf can be covered with leather or even a contrasting splice of wood, such as rosewood.

A "D" for Effort

A step up from the self bow in power and resilience is the true longbow, whose cross section is built in a "D" shape rather than a rectangle. The classic longbow has long, narrow limbs, often less than two inches wide. Bow lengths of approximately a shooter's height or a little less give the archer a long but manageable draw and maximize the bow's stored energy as well.

The traditional longbow could be called a "D-bow." Robin Hood and the English longbow archers shot it, as did many Native Americans. The longbow bends almost throughout its length, often without a significantly thicker or narrowed handle. These are heavyweight bows, capable of drawing well over a hundred pounds, because they are narrow but stiff. Strung and ready to shoot, they are under a great deal of stress.

This style bow exhibits the characteristic stick bow profile: narrow at the tips (even if the tips are bent into a reflex shape, in other words, bending away from the archer in such a way that the tips are essentially non-functional), slightly wider in the center or action section of the limbs, and narrowing slightly into the riser.

Longbows like self bows may be built from various woods—Osage orange and mulberry, even bamboo, lemonwood, pine, or hickory—but the qualities of yew attracted early bowyers. Sectioning a yew tree to make classic longbows requires careful attention to the layering of the bole, because the heartwood has excellent compressive characteristics while the outer sapwood is good in tension.

Longbow Strengths and Weaknesses

The strength of the traditional longbow was that a skilled bowyer could finish several per day. Unfortunately, it had three weaknesses.

1. It was especially vulnerable to splitting at the narrow tip, which had to be notched to hold the string on the bow's centerline. This was eventually remedied by gluing overlays or notched horn or even bone to the tip and placing the string in the notch of the overlays.

2. The longbow was, as its name implies, "long." Thus, while it was entirely adequate for foot soldiers or even for hunting, it could not be shot effectively from horseback. And its five-foot length made it a bit cumbersome, even though the traditional longbow weighed less than a pound.

3. The longbow required extensive training before one became proficient at shooting it and continuing practice was necessary. According to legend, French soldiers cut a finger or two off the right hand of any English archer they captured. Better than beheading, but effectively ending one's pleasure in archery and hence this urban legend:

   a. Agincourt, France—October 1415: The heavily favored French versus the English: The French propose to cut off the middle finger of captured English longbowmen. Lacking a middle finger, they could not draw their heavy bows, typically made from the native English Yew tree. The act of drawing the longbow was known as "plucking the yew" (or maybe only "pluck yew").

   b. Astonishing the French—perhaps even to this day—the English are victorious. They mock the defeated Frenchmen by holding up their middle fingers thus demonstrating that they can still "Pluck yew!"

   c. Over time, this became a symbolic gesture, much admired (although not by parents or defeated adversaries) and copied around the world with a concomitant change in consonants as the symbols swirled through the world's linguistic maze.

   d. It has since been suggested that because pheasant feathers stabilized the English arrows, the symbolic gesture has been retranslated into the more intimate "flipping the bird."

   e. Alas, such an endearing story has little or no basis in historic fact and so the longbow must stand or fall on merits all its own. Traditionalists may take no pride in nor, conversely, may they feel shame for the development of such an internationally recognized sign.

Today, the longbow has returned to fashion among a growing crowd of traditional enthusiasts. This group has by and large resisted the archery speed craze that has driven arrow speeds upwards of 300 and even 400 fps. The typical arrow launched from a well-constructed longbow is in the neighborhood of 170–180 fps. Nevertheless, its sub-group popularity could be a reaction to the pervasive commercial culture . . . or perhaps because of it. To meet this need, bowyers skilled in longbow (and recurve) production have proliferated to the point that excellent trees and hence fine-grained wood staves—the raw, un-worked wooden staffs from which the bow is constructed—are increasingly rare, and that means more expensive. It is said that good yew for English longbows was already becoming rare in the sixteenth century!

Bowyers building longbows, especially in America and England, are crafting beautiful and eminently functional bows today. Modern longbows are often laminated with dyed wood and fiberglass or are even built in a take-down model with a metal hinge in the center of the riser or with special hinges and take-down limbs. A take-down version allows the bow to be shipped and stored more easily. Here are a few current examples chosen at random from America's many fine bowyers:

- Allegheny Mountain Bows (Jeff Strauss, New Jersey): "Some woods available: zebra, bocote, maple, red elm, ash, bamboo, birdseye maple, bubinga, cocobolo, walnut, and many others."

- Acadian Woods (Tim Mullins, Louisiana): The Three-Piece Tree Stick take-down longbow has a sixteen-inch riser with a ridged, grooved shelf and is cut $3/16$ inch past center. It is $1\frac{7}{16}$ inches at its widest point and comes with a Fast Flight string and bow stringer. The take-down comes standard with a bamboo core, "riser wood of your choice and domestic veneer options."

- Pacific Yew (Jay St. Charles, Washington): Pacific Yew classic and take-down laminated longbows are available in one-piece and take-down versions. Crafted from multiple laminations of select, naturally seasoned Pacific yew, they are backed and faced with clear fiberglass and so have the look and feel of an all-wood bow. All Pacific Yew classic longbows have steer horn–tip overlays and a secure buckskin grip. Pacific Yew classic longbows are fully hand-tillered. Price includes fleece bow sock and two hand-laid Flemish splice bowstrings.

- Thunderhorn (Duane Jessop, Montana): "The Three-Piece Takedown is currently available in the HeartStopper model" with rustic maple veneer limbs and myrtlewood/macassar ebony riser.

The modern recurve stickbow is a "take-down." This means the limbs are built separately from the handle and are often different materials entirely. They fasten to the handle in metal clips or more often with bolts. This obviously trims the size of a shipping or storage container by half from about 60 to 30 inches. Single-piece and take-down models are commercially offered and aluminum or impact-resistant plastic shipping containers are available for both.

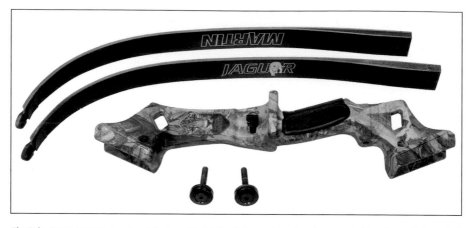

The Take-Down Recurve. A modern take-down, like this Martin Jaguar, is much easier to travel with and store. Limbs are built separately from the handle and are often different materials entirely. They fasten to the handle in metal clips or brackets or, more often, with bolts. This obviously trims the size of a shipping or storage container by half from about sixty to thirty inches. Single-piece and take-down models are commercially offered and aluminum or impact-resistant plastic shipping containers are available for both.

When selecting a traveling case, you have a choice of anodized aluminum or impact-resistant plastic. (You will see the term "HDPE," which stands for high-density polyethylene.) Look for a bow case that lets you carry arrows and the taken-apart bow in protective foam, perhaps a case that has cut-outs for an extra set of limbs as well. Weight is important, but so is the quality of the locks and latches and the ability to seal out moisture. A double case, one that holds two take-down bows and a dozen or more arrows, costs more to transport by commercial air, but considering the rare adventure that awaits and the opportunity to hunt or shoot in some exotic shooting locale, the extra expense is insurance that you will arrive with intact gear. For traveling to an adjoining state with the bow packed in the back of the truck, a padded, water-resistant nylon case may be plenty.

The point of a bow case is to protect your investment. Spend more rather than less. A fine take-down and accessories may only cost a thousand dollars, but a trip to shoot in a tournament in France or to hunt in Africa should never be ruined because your case was not able to resist the quality of care we have grown to expect from commercial baggage wrestlers.

Your Bowstring

In the "old days," a Flemish twist string was standard for European longbows. "Flemish" refers to Flanders, the region of Europe bordering the North Sea, which has often been disputed between France, Belgium, the Netherlands, and other powers. It has been fought over from ancient to recent times, and inspired John McCrae's heart-breaking World War I poem "In Flanders Fields."

A particular style of bowstring came out of the Flanders area in the Middle Ages, long before strings were made from Dacron or Fast Flight synthetic materials. Flemish strings were carefully constructed from thin strands of natural materials, such as shredded linen and hemp, perhaps even silk. Strands were rolled together and woven into bundles, usually two or three deep, in such a way that the loops were plaited from material without a serving. In most hand-making processes, wax was used to lubricate the strings and keep the bundles together. Today, bundles (called "lays") are often different colors.

The lays of a Flemish twist string allow for various design differences. Two-lay designs, normally in two accenting colors, are made using ten, twelve, fourteen, sixteen, or eighteen strands. The three-lay string is made with nine, twelve, fifteen, or eighteen strands in two or three colors. What's best? Practically speaking, there is little difference in performance, though the point will be argued endlessly by old time traditional shooters who tend to prefer the three-lay string.

You can typically purchase a Flemish twist string built to your bow's dimensions for less than $20. It will be pre-stretched, center-served, waxed, and ready to tie on the bow and shoot.

When you have time, you may want to find a mentor to teach you the art of string building. After all, your increasing archery skills beg a slight investment in this finishing touch. Building your own strings is easy after the first one or two, and quite fast. A hand-built string will complete your set-up . . . at least until you begin to build your own arrows, quivers, arrowheads . . .

Another type of string is called the "endless loop." The performance difference in terms of speed between it and a Flemish twist string is miniscule and may depend on the calibration of the chronograph or the string release or other factors. Endless loop strings are durable, with loop ends served for protection from rubbing and scraping; because they are the contact points with the bow, the loops are the points of greatest string stress. Built to precise specifications, identical endless loop strings can be constructed. For 100 percent efficiency, the endless loop has the slightest margin advantage in speed, but it also produces a slightly greater noise than the Flemish string.

Today's new traditional bows come with fitted strings. The sixty-two-inch Quarbon Nano GrizzlyStick from Alaska Bowhunting Supply, for example, is a reflexed take-down longbow with a carbon riser and carbon/foam limbs: 47.5 pounds at twenty-eight inches draw. The center sight window is cut to ⁷⁄₁₆-inch past center. No wood here . . .

The Quarbon Nano comes with a handmade fifteen-strand Flemish bowstring, constructed from high-performance Astro Flight. A note attaches to the string: Always keep a Flemish string twisted. Removing too many twists will cause the string to unravel.

So is this what "traditional" has come to? Should we call the book high-tech traditional? No. Plenty of bowyers still produce superb wood longbows, but they are all sold with a string made from modern synthetic material.

Kota's wooden Prairie Fire longbow, for instance, comes with tips of antler or horn and use handmade Flemish strings in Brownell Fast Flight or Dyna Flight. (The recurves, incidentally, are sold with Dyna Flight or Dacron.)

Longbow strings may still be built in the traditional Flemish twist manner, but the materials now are most likely a petro-chemical-based synthetic, such as DynaFlight 97 or B50 Dacron. Here are a few of the non-traditional materials suitable for and now used for stick bows:

- Astro Flight: Called "next generation" bowstring material by Brownell Archery, it promises no "creep" (the modular lengthening of a string when it is subjected to heat, continuing stress from remaining string for long periods, or being shot repeatedly). In addition, the company says it is "20 percent stronger, offers fast arrow speed, is durable and stable, offering a soft shot, and performs like a combination material." It is 100 percent HMPE (high-modulus polyethylene).

- B500 Dacron: Just a generation ago, Dacron bowstrings were standard and bows were built to accept the string's known peculiarities: stretch and creep. With a relatively low tensile strength, Dacron allowed a bow's brace height to change over time. Still, it is safe, inexpensive, and makes an acceptable string. Not high performance and not as durable, it needs to be replaced at least every year. If you have an older bow, one that is not Fast Flight compatible, choose Dacron. B500 from BCY Fibers are sold in 1¼-pound spools. Waxed, it tests to a tensile strength of 4,300 ft/lb. (BCY says its 100 percent polyester B55 is similar to Dacron but with better durability and very low stretch, also 4,300 ft/lb.)

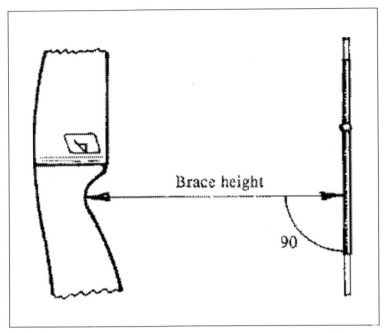

Brace Height. *The traditional term was "fistmele," which refers to the equivalent length of a closed fist with the thumb extended, indicating the proper traditional distance used between the deepest part of the grip and the string.*

- 450+: If your bow is Fast Flight compatible, this material, a blend of HMPE and Vectran, is excellent. Vectran is "stable," which means it does not creep or stretch in traditional bows. A little thicker and heavier than DynaFlight 97, it is a touch slower, but it will nail the brace height of your bow unless temperatures in the bow case exceed 100 degrees Fahrenheit or you leave your bow strung at seventy pounds over the summer. 450+ from BCY Fibers are sold in 1¼-pound spools. Waxed, it tests to a tensile strength of 4,500 ft/lb.
- DynaFlight 97: An exceptional string material and creep-free, it is 100 percent HMPE (high-modulus polyethylene). Other names are Spectra or Dyneema—high strength, low stretch and creep, and, at around 125 pounds per strand, very fast. Thus, a small, lightweight, twelve-strand DynaFlight 97 string nets approximately 1,500 pounds tensile strength, and that will handle any traditional bow you can pull to full draw. Dynaflight 97 from BCY Fibers are sold in 1¼-pound spools. Waxed, it tests to a tensile strength of 6,700 ft/lb

Bowstring. *If you become invested in the beauty, lore, science, and enjoyment of traditional archery, you may progress to building your own bows. One day, that will lead to building your own bowstrings, and at that point, when your hobby has taken over the basement or the garage, you may consider yourself fully "hooked." B500 Dacron from BCY is an excellent all-around traditional string material.*

A note about Halo center serving: Great for finger shooters and traditional bows because it feels slick to the fingers, it is sold as a premium serving material, more expensive than braided Dacron or monofilament. It is extremely abrasion resistant, grips the string tightly, and does not wear quickly. Thus, serving separation is not a problem.

Three Harmonious Notes about Bowstrings

A quick note about string terminology or "creep versus stretch."

Creep is non-recoverable elongation, unlike stretch, which is basically elasticity or recoverable elongation. Bubble gum creeps when you hold a chewed piece between your fingers on a hot day, and then must be wadded back into a ball to be chewed. A rubber band stretches when you pull at either end, but when you relax the tension—assuming you have not pulled it so far it breaks—it returns to its original position. Some elasticity is necessary in a bowstring, but creep is a problem. It can cause a traditional bow to lose its customary tiller, a compound bow to go out of time, and a peep sight to rotate. Ultimately, creep may cause the draw weight and the draw length to increase or decrease.

To wax or not to wax. Applied to a hairy leg, hot wax goes on soothingly and comes off like an angry hornet. Your bowstring will appreciate a bit of rubbed-in wax, however. It is said that wax lubricates the fibers and prevents "fiber-to-fiber" abrasion, helps keep the strands together in a stable bundle, prevents water absorption, and extends the life of the string.

Bowstring material manufacturers normally apply a generous amount of synthetic wax in liquid form. This insures that from its origin the bowstring material is well-lubricated inside the lay and outside. This protects the material from abrasion and keeps the bundles of strands together.

Generally the type of wax you should use would be a good quality standard "tacky" wax, but do not use a wax with silicone until after a string is built. A "maintenance" wax that contains some silicone is a good idea because the silicone promotes penetration into the string material and keeps the tightly twisted fibers on the inside as well as the outside slick. Wax can be applied with fingers, with a cloth, or with chamois leather. It should be applied frequently and rubbed vigorously into the string, omitting the serving, except perhaps on areas that show wear.

About breaking the string, it has been calculated that on a high poundage bow, seventy-five to eighty pounds, it is possible to generate as much as 200 pounds total tension or more while drawing. Compare this to the breaking strength of a string using eighteen strands of BCY's 8125 material, which has a ninety-pound breaking strength. There is more than 1,000 pounds margin for error, a five to one safety factor.

Breaking strength is rarely, if ever, the cause of a string failure, notes BCY Fibers. The most likely causes for traditional shooters are: over-twisting when trying to manipulate brace height, lack of string care and maintenance (lubrication), abrasion on rocks or from a tree stand, a nock-point locator crimped so tightly on the string that it cuts a strand, and compressive failure due to an extremely tight serving.

THE RECURVE BOW—TRADITIONAL TO MODERN

The recurve bow is easy to spot in a crowd. Like the friend that always wears the porkpie hat or the mom in the play group who has twins. It stands out because of its beautiful shape. Rather than being straight or only slightly curved, its limb tips curve dramatically, first toward and then away from the archer. It's sleek, sinuous, and deadly.

The Required Historical Note

No one is quite certain where or when or even why the recurve evolved. Politically correct thinking says it probably evolved from the longbow, but this may not be the case. It may well have been an independent innovation.

What is known is that complex recurve bows have been around for thousands of years. They were preferred by horse cultures on the arid steppes of Euro-Asia for hunting, for warfare, and for competition. This style of bow could very well have its origins in China from whence it spread westward to Central Asia and the Mediterranean world. Certainly the Greeks and Egyptians and even the Romans used it. Perhaps it fell out of style in Europe simply because, inch-for-inch, its design and the complexity of its manufacture were more difficult than the longbow. Perhaps it reminded the Europeans of the Mongols who nearly drove them into the sea, or perhaps the extra effort and technical expertise required to build and care for a recurve was just unnecessary for the advantages it offered.

Ready to Hunt. *Except for the additions of options such as string silencers and brush buttons, this recurve is ready to hunt.*

Energy

The recurve design is a master of energy storage. With limb tips that curve away from the shooter when the bow is strung, the bowstring is not only hooked through the notches in the limb tips, but it actually rests against the top and bottom limbs.

Engineers refer to the recurve as "pre-stressed," which means it takes advantage of its gently curving limbs. When tension in a stressed element rounds a corner, energy is either lost or gained. By building limbs that are pre-curved at rest (hence, "pre-stressed"), system energy is gained. This allows a very compact bow to deliver a great deal of energy, whereas a straight bow of equal length and strength would experience a short draw before breaking (or before the string slid off the limbs). All things being equal, recurve bows give greater arrow speed than longbows of equally rated strength.

Recurves store more energy than longbows, of whatever style, because they have more working limb, a greater storage capacity for energy. This is significant in a world where arrow speed is important and deer are thought to "duck the arrow."

Using a recurve bow, archers could achieve the same results as a longbow with a shorter instrument. A recurve stores and delivers energy more efficiently and this is tremendously important when, for example, shooting from horseback.

We Have Contact

If you want to pick every last weevil out of the cotton, you can call the modern recurve a "contact recurve." The string lies against or stays in contact with the limbs. It is at the point in the draw that the string lifts off the limb, the belly surface, that the effective force of the bow increases, and that distinguishes it dramatically from straight bows. If it lifts too early, it does not maximize the potential of the design. If it lifts later, it harnesses more energy.

In a mechanical sense, the recurve bow itself becomes a pulley or cam as it is drawn. Because of its tightly curved shape—an unstrung, composite Mongol bow's limbs circled back on themselves in the shape of a backward "C," almost to a complete "B"—a bow with recurved limb tips provides even more leverage for the string throughout the draw.

As the string is drawn off the belly, the recurve in a sense grows longer, and the longer the draw, the greater the wallop and whack of energy delivery.

There are "working recurves" and there are "static recurves." Suffice it to say the distinction is real but immaterial to most of us. A working limb bends and does work during the draw. A static recurve has limb tips that do not bend, tips that stay tightly curved during the draw, and hence the string stays in contact with a portion of the limb even at full draw. Perhaps the advantage of a static recurve is that it increases string angle at full draw and this allows the shorter bow to effectively shoot as if it were longer. Static recurves typically launch a faster arrow and possess a smoother draw. The disadvantage is they are more difficult to build and also can be harder to string without applying torque to the delicate recurve limbs.

And . . . Today, Materials

Archers of 5,000 years ago would recognize today's recurve bows because the shape is timeless. The one notable difference between those ancient bows and twenty-first century bows is that today's highest-quality manufactured recurves are take-downs or take-aparts. This means the limbs can be quickly removed when the bow is unstrung, a superb feature for travel, storage, or limb interchangeability. In fact, all Olympic champions since 1972, when archery was reinstituted as an Olympic sport after a fifty-two-year hiatus, have shot take-downs rather than one-piece recurves.

There are other exotic differences between today's commercial recurves and those made in the skin tent workshops of Mongolian nomads preparing to invade Europe in the thirteenth century. The limbs of a modern recurve are manufactured from multiple layers of fiberglass and carbon sheeting, sometimes with hard rock maple or a carbon foam core, though wood is going out of style as consistent performance becomes more critical on international shooting venues.

The riser or handle of a high end recurve is usually, though not always, aluminum. (A technical note about "riser:" in a one-piece bow such as a longbow, the built-up center section rises from the limbs in a gentle taper and thereby spreads the stress.) Some risers in perfectly functional bows are now made principally of carbon with metal fittings.

Most significant commercial archery manufacturers produce aluminum riser recurves for hunting and competition. Precision Shooting Equipment (PSE) and Hoyt USA compete on the international stage with the Korean manufacturer Win & Win.

Several of the commercial manufacturers also have strong divisions producing traditional wooden bows. Bear Archery offers a series of adult and youth recurves, one of them a take-down, the adult bows having a crowned, cut-past center arrow shelf with Bear Hair Rest and leather side plate and grip, sold with a Dynaflight 97 Flemish String. Bear also offers several full-length longbows.

Martin Archery says it builds more custom bows than anyone and has more combined staff experience than any other traditional bow manufacturer. Building on the tradition of Gale Martin, one of the founders of the bowhunting record-keeping Pope and Young Club, Martin Archery offers a strong line-up of recurves, several of them built for hunting with take-down composition, and a couple of longbows as well as a strong line-up of entry-level accessories for traditional shooting.

Bamboo Viper. The riser is bubinga and the limbs are made of a bamboo core that is carbon fiber backed with clear glass on the belly to show the bamboo. The sixty-four-inch Bamboo Viper comes in draw weights of forty to sixty-five pounds and brace heights from seven to 7 ¾ inches, and it weighs one pound, seven ounces.

Martin also operates the Damon Howatt custom bow line. "Because we hand-craft our bows one at a time, we can offer many custom options on the model of your choice. We can provide custom draw weights, measured at your personal draw length: 52#, 27", for example. Add a message or name to be applied beneath your bows finish, such as 'Custom Made for John Archer.' Describe your preferred grip style and we'll do our very best to shape your grip accordingly. We even offer custom installation of sight, quiver, and bowfishing mounts."

Between the mass producers and the tiny, custom manufacturers are a few companies like Black Widow Bows. Black Widow has been in business fifty-six years and has a reputation for producing superior recurve bows with many designs and types of woods available. Bows are stocked and also may be custom ordered. Black Widow says that bows in stock take two to four weeks to finish, but they can be tillered for split finger or three fingers under. We can also put the laser overlays or snake skins on the bows as well as your name. In most cases, the bows may be able to be reduced in weight one to five pounds, depending upon the length and poundage of the bow." If it isn't custom, it's close.

Other custom shops are well-known and respected names in archery: Bill Stewart Custom Bows, Bob Lee Bows, Bill Forman's Great Plains Traditional Bows, Dale Karch's Tomahawk Bows, White Wolf, Palmer, and many others. The smallest but most hands-on manufacturers are Americas thousands of custom bowyers. Smaller than Martin or even Black Widow, these men produce bows that are functional and beautiful, hand crafted one at a time. Chances are there is one near you.

Custom Bows. Archery is like any sport or hobby. Once you become enamored with it, you want to spend more money and time learning about it and practicing. One aspect of that interest is the purchase of a fine custom bow and, fortunately, there are dozens of superior custom longbow and recurve manufacturers in the United States . . . hundreds around the world.

About "Systemic Misdirection"

Is the recurve bow easier to shoot—and learn to shoot well—than the longbow? Without question, yes. This makes it an excellent choice for archery newbies.

A couple of basic features are responsible for the shorter learning curve. First, the arrow shelf design. The shelf is cut to or beyond the center point of the riser and this puts the arrow close to the direction of string travel. (Here, for instance, is [edited] how Black Widow Bows describes its PTF X Exotic recurve: "The one-piece PTF has a radiused shelf, which makes it great for the instinctive shooter who prefers shooting off the shelf.") Forces applied to the arrow are thus more unidirectional in a manner called "columnar loading," and so there is less "systemic misdirection" for which the archer must compensate.

With longbows, which may have little or no arrow shelf, the arrow has to "get around the bow." This design, along with soft fingers—even encapsulated in a leather glove or tab—releasing the bowstring, causes the string to swing a fraction to the side as it moves forward. It will want to swing back an equal amount in the opposite direction. Our long-dead friend Isaac Newton described this as a third law of motion: to every action there is always opposed and equal reaction.

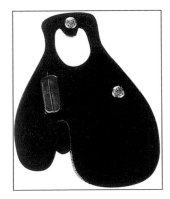

Glove and Tab. You could pull the bowstring with your bare fingers, which is fine with a lightweight bow in the backyard. However, as you become more interested in precision shooting or as you move into heavier bows, you will need a drawing cushion over your fingers. A glove or tab is customary around the world, typically the glove for hunting and the tab for competition.

Newton's law and the instantaneous loading of energy cause the arrow to wallow or fishtail. It bends during flight, sometimes horizontally when forces are left-right as they typically are when the string is released with fingers, and sometimes vertically when a compound string is released mechanically or when the nocking point locator is badly positioned. You can observe this primarily in its first ten yards, before the arrow stabilizes from the drag of the fletching and the equalization of energy along its length.

Imagine looking down on a fish swimming or perhaps a snake crawling (although the snake's manner of propulsion is different). As the fish tail pulses left and right, it moves in an "S" motion. It continues to move as long as its muscles apply force against the water.

Arrow fishtailing is particularly visible in slow motion photography. Unlike a fish, the side-to-side movement of the arrow indicates loss of energy—energy not directed toward the target and, hence, less speed and penetrating power. The illustration emphasizes the need for a crisp string release and for matching a correctly spined arrow—correct length, diameter, forward weight, and wall thickness—to the shooting system.

Most archers who shoot recurves without bow sights give credit to the "scooped-out" riser area above the recurve's shelf with helping them focus on the target. This area gives them visual perspective, even if they use pin sights or a scope-and-pin sight.

Finally, the deeper cut of the recurve grip raises the wrist and forearm into the shooter's peripheral vision. This gives some shooters yet another sighting-plane to aid in target acquisition and distance estimation. It is triangulation—your line of vision, the long straight arrow, and your arm—and triangulation, it is said, is seldom wrong.

The Reflex/Deflex Puzzle

It's like the brothers Tweedledum and Tweedledee. Hard for the person who isn't deeply involved to keep them straight or perhaps to care.

In reference to the limbs, it depends on the way they curve. Having the limbs made such that, until strung, the tips project or curve forward rather than backward is *reflex*. Having the limbs curved or curled at the base so they turn toward the archer when unstrung, thus reducing the strain on the limbs and also the energy stored, is *deflex*.

In reference to grip, handle riser and limbs at their attachment positions, the fades for a one-piece bow or the limb bolts for a take-down recurve, the reflex/deflex terminology has a slightly different referent. A *reflex* bow can be identified when the ends of the riser angle toward the back of the bow and away from the archer. This places the grip pivot closer to the shooter. With a *deflex* bow design, the ends of the handle angle toward the archer and the riser bends away from the shooter.

The reflex/deflex definition is interesting, a puzzle of sorts because brace height depends on position of the string relative to the grip point and the position of the string depends on the position of the limb tips to which it is attached. (Brace height is measured from the center of the bow grip to the bowstring at ninety degrees.)

And of course, recall that one style of longbow is the reflex/deflex . . .

The Greatest Bow of All Time

. . . was a recurve. And it was built and used by Godless, bloodthirsty savages. Or so they were called, though not to their face.

The greatest archery achievement of all time was not designing the compound bow or achieving an arrow speed of 400 fps. Those, after all, are products of the twentieth-century technological culture. The greatest achievement was the development of the composite recurve bow of the Mongols, 800 years ago. As an accurate, long-range individual weapon, it can be argued that it was not surpassed until Colt developed the rotating cylinder for his Paterson revolvers or Winchester developed the Model 1873, the "gun that won the West."

The Mongols lived with the bow almost from the moment of birth, although it was not their only weapon. They hunted with the bow, fought with the bow, and played games both on foot and on horseback with the bow. (Their twenty-first-century ancestors still practice archery skills in Naadam, the "three games of men": Mongolian wrestling, horse racing, and archery. Naadam festivals are held throughout the country during the midsummer holidays.)

A Mongolian soldier of Genghis Khan's armies typically carried two bows on horseback, one for long range and a second for close distance. He also carried five dozen arrows in several quivers, arrows for different types of assignments: anti-personnel or hunting arrows and arrowheads, armor-piercing heads of tempered steel for use against armored knights, incendiary arrows for setting wooden and thatch towns afire, and even whistling arrows for signaling and for causing terror among enemy troops.

The Mongol recurve was a model of complexity and sophistication; their long distance bow was smaller than the revered English longbow but, at a peak draw weight of about 160 pounds, easily as powerful. Effective range of the longbow was perhaps 250 yards, but the Mongol composite bow could hit a target at 350 yards or more. (Such distances are only best estimates as this must have varied with the stature of the archers and many other unknowns such as quality of wood, weight of the arrow, wind speed and direction, heat and humidity, etc.)

Construction of the composite bow began with a wooden backbone about sixty inches long, typically birch. The compression or belly side of the limbs was covered with thinned, elongated, and flattened sections of horn, which added resilience to the wood. A layer of sinew was applied to the opposite side of the limb, the side that would need to elongate and then snap back without breaking. Sinew has a peculiarly elastic quality of increasing in strength when subject to stretching. A layer of birch bark protected against moisture and was followed by more sinew. All of these extremely thin layers were held together with a special preparation of fish glue, made from extracting a protein substance from the swim bladders of freshwater fish.

Viewed from outside the group as opposed to growing up with it, the construction was a difficult and time-consuming process, but not altogether different in concept from the construction of the self bow described earlier. Here is a summary of the steps:

1. the wooden frame is cured,

2. horns (sometimes bone was used) are boiled to softness and applied,

3. sinew is prepared: tendons dried, crushed to a mass of loose fiber, and then mixed with fish glue,

4. the sinew is applied in a two-step process: too little leaves the bow weak and too much makes it excessively stiff,

5. the sides are glued together: the outer birch bark layers are boiled to softness and glued to the finished bow,

6. the bow is placed in a form to dry and harden and the bundle is wrapped tightly in ropes: this may take a year or more, and when it is unwrapped and tested,

7. the bow is now ready to be decorated or personalized by its owner and will be stored in a leather case.

The bowstring, incidentally, was made from animal hide: horse was preferred. The inner fat was scraped away and the hide was cut in thin strips, stretched and twisted taut. Animal intestines were also used but, being less water-resistant, were better suited to dry weather.

Birch was favored for a Mongol warrior's long arrows, which were between thirty and forty inches in length. Bird tail feathers, especially those of cranes, supplied fletching.

Taken together, the equipment became a system and a warrior shot with what was known as a "Mongolian release." Because his bow was powerful and the warrior was often seated on a short but hardy horse, the left hand (if right-handed) pushed the bow forward while the right hand pulled the string back behind the ear. This was not a position that one could hold for more than a few seconds, but the string was held by the thumb, the strongest human digit, and the thumb was supported with the index finger curling around and placed atop the outermost joint, exactly at the base of the nail. The other fingers were also curled, forming a fist. Even so, this was not enough and the Mongols used a special ring on which the string was hooked before release. This thumb ring, a cylinder that fit around the thumb and protected its pad from damage as the string was released, was sometimes made from jade or agate, but leather, metal, and bone were also used.

We mentioned that Mongol soldiers often shot accurately while sitting on the back of a galloping horse. This was apparently accomplished by timing shots to the moment when the hooves of the horse were in mid-air, thus avoiding disturbing the aim when the hooves hit the ground.

Now, Kiss Your Bow Every Day

Caring for a traditional bow is easy. It only takes a moment of mindfulness and it begins with stringing your bow.

Old-time bowhunters often use what's called the step-through method of stringing and un-stringing their recurve or longbow. They place the large loop over the top limb and slide it down the limb. Because the string will be loose at this point, they place the smaller loop over the bottom limb tip and into the string grooves. Then, bracing the bottom limb tip against the outside of their boot, they step between the bow and the string with the other leg. The final step is to bend the bow and simultaneously press down by hand on the top limb while slipping the top loop up and into the groove at the tip.

In this one instance, *do not* imitate your elders. The beauty of the step-through procedure is that it is fast and eliminates carrying a cord stringer. The dark side of the method is that it has ruined more bows, put out more eyes, and caused more injuries to archers than any other aspect of archery except perhaps falling out of tree stands when hunting.

Bow Stringer. *Always use a cord bow stringer to string and un-string your bow! Proper use of a cord stringer prevents the limbs from twisting dangerously and is safer for both archer and the bow. As you string a bow, you bring enormous force to bear on the limbs. One small slip and you can twist and crack the limbs, or they can spring upward and put out an eye . . . or worse.*

There are several different styles of cord stringers, essentially long cords with pouches at either end. These pouches fit over each end of the limb. (Some stringers use a pouch on one end for the small loop and a non-slip section of rubber on the other. They work equally well.)

Choose a stringer that fits your bow's length and limb nocks, because stringing the bow can be dangerous if you don't do it properly. To string your recurve, follow the steps below. (To un-string your bow, simply reverse the process.) It's like riding a bicycle. The instant you "get it," it becomes second nature.

a. Since the limb tip is smaller than the width of the limb below the tip, loops must be a bit larger. The largest loop of the string goes over the top limb, while the small loop goes on the bottom limb. This order is important because the small loop stays in position on the lower limb while stringing and unstringing the bow. The larger upper loop travels up and down the limb when stringing and unstringing.

b. The position of the bowstring is very important. The string's bottom loop must fit securely in the groove in the bottom limb. Before releasing pressure on the limbs, make sure both string loops are secure and straight in the grooves on the limbs.

c. To use the cord stringer, first hold the bow with the front face of the bow facing down. Grip the center of the riser with the hand that has the most control and strength. With the bow facing down, put the larger pouch over the tip of the lower or bottom limb. Now put the smallest pouch over the tip of the upper limb.

Make sure that both pouches are fitted securely over the tips. The stringer cord should now be hanging below the bow.

d.   Step on the stringer cord, approximately in the middle, using the same side as the hand used to hold the bow. Pull up on the riser; just enough to make the string taut, making sure that the lower end of the string is still secure in the grooves on the lower limb.

e.   While still pulling up slowly on the riser, guide the string into the notches of the upper limb. Watch that your fingers stay to the sides of the limb, making sure not to place them between the bow string and the face of the bow.

Useful Tips

Here are a couple more useful tips for a long and happy life in archery.

- A bow is not like a firearm, whose trigger you can pull without damaging the instrument. Never dry fire any bow. "Dry firing" means drawing and releasing the string without an arrow on the string. This may cause instant breakage and certainly induces structural fatigue.

- Don't expose your traditional bow to extreme heat. The easy forgetfulness is inside a vehicle—a car trunk, or even in direct sunlight coming through a window (which can reach 150 degrees F). This kind of heat may cause delamination. If you inadvertently subject your bow to high heat, let it cool before stringing it.

- The occasional application of a paste wax guards against moisture invasion, ensuring that the bow's finish continues to act as a seal.

- Don't leave your bow strung for long periods of time, not even in a cool place like a dark closet. This may cause a bow, which is under a lot of pressure when strung, to "take a set," lose its shape and poundage. Plus, it's unwise where children may find and play with it.

- When assembling a take-down bow, apply only enough pressure on the limb bolts to seat them snugly. Cranking down hard on the takedown bolt can force the washer into the face of the limb, causing cracks. Also, take-down bows are not meant to be disassembled after every shooting session. The take-down feature is for occasional easy transport and limb-switching.

- Use bowstring wax to retain string flexibility, even with synthetic strings. Check your string often for fraying and replace any questionable string before it breaks. Most experienced shooters change strings at least once a year.

* * *

UNDERSTANDING THE X-BOW

Why shouldn't the crossbow have a traditional side? Its history is just as convoluted as the vertical bow, though it is certainly thousands of years more recent. The earliest crossbow discovered in ancient literature dates from the Greek-Egyptian end of the Mediterranean about 2,500 years ago, but it was known in China as much as 500 years prior to that.

Early Crossbow. *A heavy siege crossbow (a wallarmbrust) used in defense of a city and belonging to Andreas Baumkirchner (about 1460– 1471) of Austria. It can be seen in the Museum of Fine Arts, Vienna.*

Crossbows appear to have evolved rapidly from handheld weapons to larger models for attacking city walls or breaking up concentrations of enemy troops. Our ancestors built some huge crossbows called "ballistas" (a Roman term after the Greek name), even chariot-mounted crossbows, as well as handheld weapons for attacking individual soldiers and hunting. A bit smaller crossbow called a "scorpion" (another Roman term) was a stand-mounted sniper weapon.

Unlike a vertical bow, which an archer had to stand up to draw, aim, and shoot, an archer could lie flat on the ground, under a bush or a blanket, and fire a crossbow accurately. More than two thousand years ago, the Chinese even experimented with a repeating crossbow and with crossbows that shot multiple arrows at once!

In modern design, and built with space age materials (impact-resistant plastics and exotic, space age metal alloys) and computer controlled methods (stamping, forging, cutting, molding), today's crossbow would nevertheless be recognizable by those early Greek and Chinese soldiers. Still, the modern crossbow has acquired an updated appearance.

Crossbow. In modern design, and built with space age materials (impact-resistant plastics and exotic, space age metal alloys) and computer controlled methods (stamping, forging, cutting, molding), today's crossbow, such as this Winchester Stallion, would nevertheless be recognizable by those early Greek and Chinese soldiers. Still, the modern crossbow has acquired an updated appearance and a low-power scope, and it launches a powerful bolt.

Rise of the Shoulder-Fired Bow

Early crossbows promised the delivery of a deadly missile at long distance even when shot by relatively unskilled hands. And therein one discovers the real key to their popularity: they were easy . . . sort of.

During the reign of Henry II of England (1154–1189), every man who earned two to five pounds per year had to own a longbow. And practice shooting was mandatory, on Sunday no less. At one time, the crown required churches to build and maintain target butts on their grounds for practice. There were even laws about practice distances.

Continual practice was necessary with the longbow of that era because draw weights were extremely heavy, heavy enough that over time they could disfigure the hand and arm drawing the string. From the wreck of Henry VIII's ship *Mary Rose* (sunk in battle with the French in 1545) came a treasure of period artifacts, including stores of longbows and arrows. The original draw weights of longbows from the *Mary Rose* averaged an astonishing 150 to 160 pounds at a thirty-inch draw length. The full range of draw weights was 100 to 185 pounds. (The thirty-inch draw length was used to measure draw weight because that is the length allowed by the arrows found in crates on the *Mary Rose*.) It took a very strong man to draw and shoot a 150-pound longbow, and to shoot it accurately required continuous practice.

The long, vertical bows required a lifetime of familiarity. This was certainly the case in pre-historic cultures where a man was at once a skilled craftsman and a hunter of big game. And so the benefit of the crossbow was that armies of slaves or peasants could bring formidable firepower to a fight without a lifetime of training, maybe with only a few hours of instruction. When the battle was concluded, the crossbows could be confiscated and any surviving peasants could be sent home without fear that they might own the tools and the skill necessary for the assassination of the ruler or his deer.

Cocking and Rate of Fire

Although some crossbows (both ancient and modern) cock using only the unassisted arm strength of the archer, one hand drawing back the string on either side of the barrel—*hand-spanned* is the technical term—powerful crossbows require some sort of mechanical device to help draw and reposition the string following a shot. A strong man can put one foot in the stirrup and cock a 150-pound crossbow repeatedly by hand—and in battle, adrenaline supplements one's normal strength—but even he will need help straightening his back and standing straight the following day.

Crossbow cocking mechanisms allowed the use of weapons with a draw force comparable to and sometimes in excess of the longbows of the day. There were pull and push levers, even a clever variation known as a goat's foot. Some of them used a hook fastened to a belt around the waist; after a shot, the archer knelt, placed the hook around the string, placed a foot through the stirrup, and stood up, guiding the string into the trigger mechanism by hand. Other devices used ratchets and pulleys, which would wind a string into the trigger, and while these could cock powerful bows, they were slow.

Few archery illustrations of the late Middle Ages survive, but the central panel of a church altarpiece from Cologne, Germany, illustrates the situation of longbows and crossbows at about the time Columbus first landed in the New World. Surrounding a suffering Saint Sebastian are six men wielding longbows (and a plague of officials and curiosity seekers). Another archer appears already to have shot and is rewinding a crossbow with a cranked rack-and-pinion device called a "cranequin."

Saint Sebastian. This image now hangs in the Wallraf-Richartz Museum in Cologne. In 288 CE, the poor Sebastian has already been shot an astonishing seventeen times at close range. (According to legend, he recovers in time to scream curses at the Roman emperor Diocletian, who promptly has him beaten to death and has his body thrown into the sewer.)

The benefits of the crossbow—a short, heavy killing bolt and a short learning curve, plus the ability to keep the bow cocked and ready to shoot—were balanced, however, by problems. Compared to the English longbow men, for instance, the Genoese mercenary crossbowmen employed by the French at the battle of Crecy

(1346) experienced several unforeseen and almost insurmountable difficulties. The range of their bulky crossbow was shorter than that of the longbow, and the time between shots was longer. Under pressure, the Englishmen may have gotten off five to ten shots a minute. The Genoese were lucky if they managed half that number.

Three additional difficulties arose, one before and two during that long-ago battle. First, the crossbow was more expensive to produce than the longbow. It might not have been more complicated to produce, but it had more moving parts, and in an age where nuts and bolts and screws and clamps were all built one at a time, by hand, this was always a problem.

Coupled with a relative ease of training, the craft factor made the crossbow ideal for use by wealthier town militias, the townspeople generally being more concerned with commerce than with warfare or hunting. There was an added advantage in that the less-intense training schedule for crossbowmen meant the weapons could remain in a city armory instead of being dispersed to the homes of individual militiamen. Thus, in times of civil strife, the authorities controlled the supply of deadly weapons. A fear of revolt at home seems to have been one of the reasons for the failure of French militias to make a go of their efforts to train longbow men.

At Crecy, a sudden thunderstorm prior to the battle soaked the Genoese crossbow strings, slackening them and decreasing their range and power. Strings of the era were strong fibers selected from materials that resisted fraying: whipcord, linen, hemp, twisted mulberry root, and sinew. Unlike the longbow, the crossbow could not easily or quickly be unstrung (the same is true today).

Another problem was the re-cocking effort, which we have already touched on. This required the Genoese mercenaries to crouch behind shields, kneel down, and draw the heavy string into the trigger mechanism as they prepared again to shoot. In other words, they had to turn their backs on their enemies . . . but they had neglected to take shields to the battlefield that day.

A final obstacle in this 1346 battle was the Genoese choice of paymasters. The mounted Frenchmen were members of a sullen and peevish nobility. It was frustrating enough for them to require the services of foreign commoners (in 1139, Pope Innocent II declared the crossbow to be an "evil" device that was "deadly and hateful to God and unfit to be used among Christians"), but when the Genoese found they could not match the English archers, they began to leave the field of battle. This angered their French allies, who charged forward, killing many of them. The French continued, racing impatiently onto the muddy field toward the English lines and annihilation.

The crossbow has always had strong positives and negatives. Early crossbows were heavy, bulky, and unwieldy. (Even today a traditional shooter could still claim this about any crossbow.) In unskilled hands, they could be frightening but were relatively inaccurate. Draw weights of the enormous, horse- or ox-drawn ballistas, which fired projectiles of great size at enemy fortifications or troop formations, could range from hundreds to several thousand pounds, but they were slow to fire, massively unwieldy and subject to the weather. The short draw length of a handheld crossbow was both a blessing, because it was maneuverable, and a problem, because it could not be un-cocked without firing the bolt. And to change the string while suffering a rain of deadly arrows and ducking the occasional thrust of a lance or swipe of a long sword, as the Genoese mercenaries discovered at Crecy, was impossible without a significant supporting cadre.

Nuts and Bolts and Arrows

Crossbow projectiles were formerly called bolts and averaged between twelve and eighteen inches in length. Made of heavier woods, ash and birch as opposed to poplar, which was light and easily shattered against a hard surface, they had a flat base or a shallow half-moon cut-out for the string. Medieval bolts were usually fitted with two vanes directly opposite one another, which may or may not have been arranged to induce spin. The fletching might have been of wood, parchment, leather, feathers, or even metal. Some bolts had no fletching at all. The bolt's tips were various, depending on their purpose. Armor-piercing anti-personnel heads were tough and sleek, while heads designed to cut ship rigging had a "Y" or a butterfly wing appearance.

Today, with growing acceptance in the United States—with states permitting crossbows to be used in their archery big-game hunting seasons—the projectiles are normally referred to with common archery terminology as arrows. Typically, the short but heavy crossbow arrows (twenty to twenty-two inches long) are fletched with three plastic vanes. The optimum weight for bolts (measured in grains at 437.5 grains per ounce) to achieve maximum kinetic energy varies depending on the power of the crossbow. In ancient times, the bolts of a powerful crossbow, although shorter, were several times heavier than arrows.

And, Today . . .

Today's crossbow is essentially a very short compound or recurve bow affixed horizontally to a stock that can be shot in the manner of a gun. It is shoulder-fired or braced, and the synthetic bowstring is drawn back toward the shooter into the trigger housing, where it engages an automatic safety. The string is released with a mechanical trigger, whereupon the arrow zooms down the flight rail. The bow (or "prod") mounts to and is held horizontally by a bolt on the fore-end of a stock. A crossbow shoots short arrows tipped with sharp broadheads for hunting. These head kill by causing hemorrhage. There will be some shattering of bone and tearing of tendon but suffocation due to blood loss (exsanguination) is the proper medical term.

Despite occasional rumors of secret experimentation and contrary to contemporary fantasy novels, the era of the crossbow as a military weapon is long past, even if some of our highland village allies, the Hmong, traditionally relied on them in Vietnam. Today, it is strictly a tool for hunting and for some minor competitive events. It can still be mastered far more quickly than the vertical bow, and it can be shot from a resting position, from ambush, seated, or lying down, like a gun. Although its draw length is shorter than a vertical bow, its arrows tend to be faster, with a slightly greater range and flatter trajectory, than a vertical compound bow. Neither does it require continual attention to tuning; nor is it as temperamental as a high-speed vertical bow. Men and women accustomed to shooting firearms are immediately comfortable with it, even though there is a natural but short learning curve. Older bowhunters too find that if a crossbow is equipped with a cocking-aid, a heavy strain does not tear their shoulders as much as would a heavy-draw-weight compound bow.

Today's crossbows are built both with wheels or cams (compound) and without wheels (recurve) at the end of the limbs. Proponents argue vehemently for the benefits of each style, but with only modest care each performs capably in the field. The speed of their arrows depends on draw weight, length of pull, and the resulting power stroke as well as matching the properly sized (length, circumference, wall thickness, and weight) arrow to the bow. Crossbows require little maintenance, can be equipped with a low power scope and carrying sling, and are tooled to accept a quiver with arrows.

Much work has recently been done in two areas of crossbow performance: cocking and silencing. Not long ago, crossbows were exceptionally noisy. Consumers, pro shooters, and manufacturers alike only shrugged, "That's just the way they are." Thus, in a hunting situation, the crossbow became a one-shot weapon, for if a game animal were not vitally hit, it became so alarmed that it ran away before the bow could be re-cocked and re-loaded, all of which requires much effort and movement. Now, numerous rubberized silencing devices can be attached to the string, the limbs, and the barrel to help dampen the noise of a shot.

Manufacturers have also addressed the re-cocking problem that has plagued crossbow shooters since the beginning. A heavy, 150-pound draw weight crossbow must be cocked—the string drawn from the forward position to the safety latch—carefully to ensure that the string is centered in the stock. If the string is off-center, it will apply unequal pressures to the arrow and the arrow will fly erratically. To cock a normal crossbow, one puts a foot in the stirrup, bends over, and manually draws the string back, one hand on either side, into the receiver. Not much different than a medieval Genoese crossbowman. To make this less arduous on the back, manufacturers have developed a variety of cranks and rope-devices, but in reality, cocking is little easier than it was a thousand years ago.

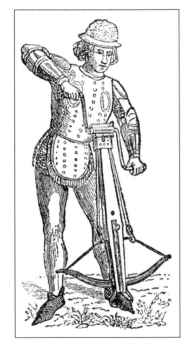 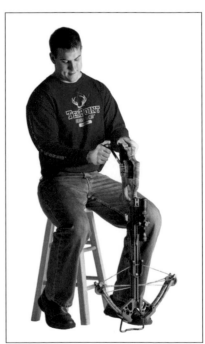

Cocking the Crossbow. *The windlass, a horizontal cylinder that is rotated by the turn of a crank, was used for cocking a crossbow in the Middle Ages. Today's windlass, as typified by the ACUdraw from TenPoint Crossbow Technologies, is not altogether different, though it is faster and mechanically easier to use.*

Commercial crossbows have terrific shooting characteristics in the hands of the average archer. They are easy to shoot, weigh about the same as a rifle (seven to eight pounds, fully equipped), have a *normal* effective range to sixty, possibly eighty yards, and have realistic top speeds upwards of 350 fps.

The number of crossbow enthusiasts—almost 100 percent hunters—is unknown, but the best guess is perhaps a quarter million. The number is surely rising rapidly as states open big-game seasons for crossbows. The "crossbow generation" is expected to increase in the next decade for two reasons.

- First, crossbow technology has taken dramatic steps forward in the past decade, and many of today's bows are available in the buff, paramilitary style that is currently popular.

- Second, the bubble of hunters from the baby boom generation is retiring. By their sixties, most men and women in affluent countries encounter the natural physical problems of aging: body parts ache, muscles weaken, second helpings of dessert beckon. If they want to stay involved in archery, the crossbow provides an acceptable opportunity to do so.

Wood is no longer the preferred building material for crossbow stocks and definitely not for bolts. In fact it is no longer easy to find a wooden-stocked unit. Wood was heavy and tended to swell with absorbed moisture. The new materials are lightweight carbon-impregnated fiberglass stocks and limbs with machined aluminum or molded fiberglass barrels and synthetic strings, catgut having long been out of style, if it ever was truly in style. The new crossbow is built with a Picatinny rail for a scope, low fixed-power or red-dot non-magnifying scopes being preferred because of the arrow's relatively limited range (relatively limited compared to a firearm). Arrows are specially constructed aluminum or carbon fiberglass tubes, and the front end is tipped with a modern broadhead that may weigh as much as 150 grains (about one-third of an ounce).

In short, nothing "traditional" remains of ancient crossbows, but everything remains: the general shape, the concept of shooting, the difficulty of cocking, and the memories.

THE COMPOUND BOW: OUR STORY . . . AND WE'RE STICKING WITH IT

The most recent incarnation of the bow is the compound or cam bow. You can spot it immediately at any shoot or in a pro shop because it looks so weird. Unlike classic, elegant stick bows and recurve bows or even the crossbow, the invention and subsequent development of the compound bow is precisely dated.

Let's cover the compound as we did the crossbow. Sometimes understanding what one is doing and shooting is best understood in contrast with what one is not, or the opposite.

History

In the 1960s, Holless Allen sawed the ends off a conventional recurve bow and then added pulleys to each end. He applied for a patent on June 23, 1966, and US Patent 3,486,495 was granted to him on December 30, 1969. He thus became the official inventor of the compound or modern bow, although much of his work was aided and improved upon by California bow maker Tom Jennings.

Today, Allen's designs and, indeed, the bows he personally manufactured seem horribly antique, but they were the foundation for modern cam bows. Hundreds of patents have since been awarded for refinements to the Allen concepts, improvements and innovations that have resulted in a shooting and hunting tool that is ingenious, marvelous really, but certainly not traditional.

Gyro-Tec. Even without a bow quiver full of arrows the modern compound bow can be a formidable shooting instrument. When the archer draws the string and the cams roll over, you will hold as little as 20 percent of a modern compound's draw weight. But is it archery? Doesn't it make you proud to shoot a recurve or a longbow?

Impact and Numbers

Since the sixties the compound bow has become the principal bow in the United States and Canada. Here, archery is dominated by hunting and hunting-themed shooting events. Today, the lion's share of North America's three million bowhunting archers shoots a modern compound bow. This number is based on counting the sale of US state and Canadian province archery hunting licenses, where available, and coming up with an estimate for the rest.

The number contrasts vividly with the number of people shooting traditional gear, although no state segregates its license sales by type of bow except to single out the crossbow. According to best industry estimates, a few hundred thousand people shoot longbows and recurves, and this includes a lot of kids in school and at summer camp. And that statistic is threatened by a cam bow called Genesis that Mathews Archery developed for the specific purpose of introducing young people to archery.

The Genesis System eliminates let-off and there are no specific draw-length requirements. The result is a bow that fits virtually everyone (fifteen to thirty inches) and that a young person can't outgrow. A Genesis bow, set at twenty pounds (it's adjustable from ten to twenty pounds), stores and releases energy comparable to that of a thirty-five-pound recurve, the manufacturer says. Plus, with zero let-off, it has the holding weight necessary to pull the string from your finger, making it easy to shoot.

And for years the archery industry has recommended that the best learning platform is a lightweight recurve. Is nothing sacred?

Companies in a free market rarely share sales data, and therefore it is difficult to know how many compound bows are manufactured outside North America. The modern bow competes against other modern bows in International Field and some sanctioned FITA (Olympic) events, just not in the Olympic Games.

Several non-US manufacturers sell compound bows on the world stage—Cartel/Doosung and Win & Win in South Korea, Petron and Merlin in England—but most of the world lacks an extensive and sophisticated infrastructure of support. The modern compound is, after all, a complex system of cables and pulleys, and it requires an array of arrows and other accessories (plastic fletching, sights, stabilizers, complex arrow rests, mechanical release aids). Modern archery depends on a strong commercial and informational support system. In North America, this system is present in thousands of sporting goods stores and pro shops as well as a highly developed information system of magazines, books, specialty television programming, and Internet sources.

Why Shoot a Compound—I

As previously noted, the compound bow is much easier to shoot effectively than a traditional bow. The entry-level learning curve is shorter, and the requirement for continual practice is lessened.

From an engineering point of view, a compound bow is a fancy lever using a system of cables and pulleys in the shape of eccentrics to bend the bow limbs and store energy. The action part of compound limbs are exceptionally short and stiff compared to traditional limbs, and yet they are still flexible. They store more energy than recurves or longbows and store it in a more efficient manner. Traditional bows store energy, in a sense, in a cooperative arrangement with the archer's muscles: the back, shoulders and arms, hands, and neck. But when the archer draws a string that is attached to a cam, the cam rotates and the archer gains mechanical advantage over the stiff but now bending limbs.

More readily available energy typically means one shoots a faster arrow a greater distance with increased energy delivery. This results in a flatter arrow trajectory and presumably greater penetration into a target, whether it is the steel breast plate of a charging knight or a trophy bull elk.

Why Shoot a Compound—II

The draftsman's description of a bow's draw cycle (pulling the bowstring from rest to full draw) can be pictured by what is called a draw-force curve. The curve charts draw weight in pounds on the vertical Y-axis, against draw length in inches on the horizontal X-axis. The area beneath the curve represents the kinetic energy available to the arrow. Even an efficient compound bow does not deliver 100 percent of its potential energy to the arrow. Some energy remains in the system as friction, noise, and vibration, but generally, for every foot-pound of energy delivered, a modern cam bow actually harnesses 1.5 pounds, so about one-quarter to one-third is lost in friction.

For a stick bow, the draw cycle approximates a gently curving line rising at about forty-five degrees. The greater distance the archer pulls the string, the greater the energy stored, but the stiffer the resistance and the more difficult it becomes to hold at full draw.

For a compound bow, the chart resembles a bell curve with a short tail. One draws the bowstring at first with increasing effort to the bow's peak weight, but then the pulleys (cams or wheels) rotate or roll over at the top of the bell curve and the effort to hold at full draw is instantly reduced. This is the bow's let-off.

Today's cam bows generally allow the archer to pull against "the wall." Once the cams roll over, one can feel that point of hold at which resistance increases, whether the string is drawn further or the string is let down. This is "the wall."

(And letting down a compound bow without shooting the arrow is much different than letting down a traditional bow. Choosing not to shoot and letting down—relaxing the string—with the arrow on the string means the archer relaxes the recurve or longbow, making sure the string doesn't slip. Letting down a modern cam bow requires you to move once again up and over the peak effort of the bell curve, and it thus calls for the archer's full attention and strength.)

What this all means is that, at full draw, a modern cam bow makes the archer hold far less weight than a comparable traditional bow. Pull a sixty-five-pound longbow to the corner of your mouth and at full draw you are holding sixty-five pounds, which you will inevitably strain to hold for more than a couple of seconds. Pull a sixty-five-pound cam bow—usually these days with a mechanical release aid held in your hand or strapped to your wrist—to the wall and you hold far less than sixty-five pounds. If the modern bow comes with 65 and 80 percent let-off (the drop in holding weight after the pulleys roll over) modules, you have a choice, but you only have to hold a weight of either twenty-three or thirteen pounds, respectively. And you can hold that all day—or at least much longer than you can hold sixty-five pounds! This modern bow advantage gives the archer the ability to regulate his breathing, estimate distance, and concentrate longer on aligning his sights with the target.

About Materials

Much like the various lifesaving and high-tech gadgets introduced at the beginning of James Bond 007 films—exploding briefcases, satellite communication built into a wristwatch, surfboards with hidden panels, X-ray vision eyeglasses—as the compound bow evolves, its component materials evolve.

Compound bows built between Allen's patent and the early eighties were often built with wood risers, laminated for strength. Browning, American, Jennings, and most other companies built with wood. Even the limbs were made from wood laminates. Use of wood was natural. Bowyers understood wood and stresses, and so it was to be expected that they would begin building compounds with the components they understood before moving forward with research and discovery.

Something else happened in the early years of the compound era—something fundamental. As the designs of new bows became more extreme, as new materials replaced wood, the old bowyers gradually retired from or were fired by the large commercial manufacturers. They were replaced by college-educated, certified engineers.

The old tradition of craftsmanship, the tradition of building one bow at a time, by hand, disappeared . . . only to come alive in custom bow shops. Today, a self-taught man like Fred Bear or Earl Hoyt or Ben Pearson would be an oddity in manufacturing circles, perhaps could not even get a job with the companies named after them.

So as engineers built more powerful compounds, they realized that metal handles (called risers) were more effective at bracing for the heavier, multi-directional stresses of compound shooting. Laminated wood handles were gradually replaced by cast magnesium. Then, in the late 1980s, when computerized, automated machining allowed the use of aluminum billets, magnesium was relegated to less expensive, often entry-level compound bows and eventually phased out entirely.

For a compound, aluminum is a superior riser material to magnesium, and certainly to wood. Aluminum is roughly one third heavier than magnesium and four times as heavy as wood, but it is corrosion resistant, cannot rot, and has a much higher tensile strength than either material.

CNC-machined risers dominate the market today, even for commercially produced take-down recurves. In modern CNC systems, end-to-end component design is highly automated, using computer-aided design (CAD) and computer-aided manufacturing (CAM) programs. And so, modern compound bows can be programmed and built practically untouched by human hands.

It took longer for mass manufacturers to realize that wood was not the best choice for limbs on compound bows. Although laminated wood limbs were things of beauty, especially when molded under great heat and pressure into a recurve shape or with interior laminates of colored fiberglass, the countervailing stresses of modern high-energy, hot-shooting bows are simply too great for the structure of a laminated wood limb. Today's limbs on a compound bow, whether solid or of split design, are inevitably fiberglass, often called carbon, and either extruded or compression molded. They are short, strong, and durable.

Wildlife Successes: Saving America's Wild Places

A significant attribute that allowed archery to grow in North America since the end of World War II has been a heritage of game management. Settlement of the continent, the free rural lifestyle, raced ahead of the rise of great cities and smokestack manufacturing. With the devouring spread of twentieth-century commercial agriculture, however, often planting "centerline-to-centerline" in response to market pressures, the continent was knit together by roads and rail systems. A century ago, no one could have predicted whether moose and geese, deer and antelope, and coyotes would survive. They have, and their populations have thrived, but only because

American hunter conservationists fought for them and forced politicians and bureaucrats to set aside wild lands and preserve them from development.

The North American wildlife success story is unique in the world. In most societies, the average person has been a peasant or small shopkeeper, barred from the king's lands and game animals and barred from possessing powerful weapons of any sort, guns or bows. In North America, the average person is expected to fend for himself, and on this most recently settled continent, a tradition of hunting and fishing has persisted. It is a miracle.

So it is safe to suggest that in the world at large, a world that cannot support game populations or the right of average citizens to own guns or powerful bows, traditional style shooters may far outnumber modern compound shooters.

CHAPTER THREE

THE TRADITIONAL ARROW

The bow gets the spotlight, but many toxopholites argue that the arrow is the true marvel of archery. Will Thompson, whom some consider the father of modern archery, at least in the United States, reported that an Indian once told him: "Any old stick for a bow, but an arrow should be perfect." In truth, the two sticks are interdependent variables of a powerful shooting system. If one part of the system is eliminated or is an improper fit or is damaged, the entire system falls apart.

It is the arrow that flies—true or errant—to the target. It is the arrow that delivers the potential of the bow to the destination in the mind of the archer. And it is, after all, intention plus action that makes archery such an admirable pastime. If the bow is the meditative element, the arrow is the action element, and thus the yin and yang, sun and shadow, are interconnected and complementary. Working independently they have no life, but together, interdependent, they become transcendent.

An arrow is a word, a handshake, a token of exchange, a contract. It is the element that connects the subject with the object, and in this manner it is the same as the ones and zeros that make up binary code. It is communication.

Like any programming language, the arrow requires the careful assembly of multiple parts of speech to work properly. From one tip to the other, the arrow is a complex system and it all must work together, speak the same language, to fly true and strike the target with force.

Today's modern arrow is in all ways similar to and different from the traditional arrow. In fact, many archers who shoot traditional stick bows choose to shoot modern arrows . . . and many others do not. Let's find out what that's all about.

IN THE BEGINNING, A FEATHER

The idea of the arrow begins with a single bird feather. Without feathers on the butt end of the arrow, an archer would rarely hit his target. It is the feather that makes the short-range thrusting spear into the superior atlatl and then the accurate long-range arrow, which changes the equation of grazing animals consuming forbs and legumes into steaks and chops.

How did some primitive man realize that the rear end of an arrow needed feathers? It is impossible to know, but at some point an early genius realized that friction at the back end of the arrow helped the front end fly properly.

The feather concept was probably transferred to the arrow from the atlatl dart (and continues, for example, with the fins on the base of rockets). Perhaps an early man saw the arrow wobble and made the connection to the dart. It could have required a long process of experimentation independently over many cultures, or it could have been a single moment of inspiration that spread, hunting clan to hunting clan, around the world like wildfire. However it developed, the application of feathers to the shaft was an astonishing technological step in man's long prehistory.

Applying feathers to the rear of an arrow shaft ultimately provides stabilization to the arrow by causing turbulence (friction) in the air. Friction is necessary because of the way the arrow is loaded with energy. As the bowstring shoots forward, it takes the potential energy stored in the bow and transfers it into dynamic energy in the arrow. Because the arrow is a long, thin cylinder—either hollow carbon or aluminum, or solid wood—and although loading the energy is *practically* instantaneous, the transfer is uneven along its length. Becoming energized, the base of the shaft in effect wants to move forward on its own. It is the job of the feathers to slow it down, give the energy time to transfer forward.

The key word is "practically." It takes a fraction of a second for the energy to distribute through the column of the arrow, but in this fraction of a second, the feathers begin to work. When they "grab" the air, they begin a rotational pattern of one full rotation every five to six feet. (For non-engineers, it is a puzzle like the idea that different points on a wheel rotate at different speeds. The inner section is faster; the outer section slower.)

High-speed photography demonstrates that the initial force of movement, the initial air resistance, causes the feathers to lie down flat. But they recover quickly, in a fluttering manner. This flutter is important because it creates resistance, which gives the energy the moment it needs to begin stabilizing the head and steers it toward its intended destination.

Feathers control the back of the shaft by providing friction or drag in equal quantities around the shaft, in all 360 degrees. They thus provide "rotational stability." Again it was some unknown early thinker, a tinkerer with excellent vision who realized that a rotating shaft was more stable in flight than a non-rotating shaft.

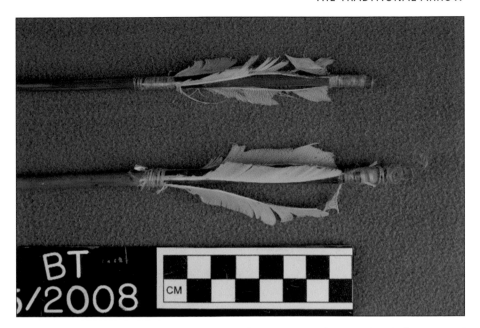

The Discovery of Fletching. *The discovery that fletching—the feathers on the end of an arrow—helped it fly straighter and strike with greater force was a giant step forward in the development of bows and arrows as effective weapons for hunting and warfare. These arrows are attributed to the displaced Modoc Indians in Oklahoma and were built about a century ago.*

FLETCHING

Anything attached to the butt end of the arrow to provide directional and rotational stabilization is called *fletching*. Modern arrows typically use cheaper plastic vanes instead of feathers because the plastic—cut into shapes resembling feathers—tends to be quieter, is arguably more durable, and does not absorb moisture. Feathers, contrarily, are durable and even, to some extent, self-healing.

Plastic vanes can gain or lose flexibility depending on extremes of heat or cold and are measurably heavier. But the last thing you need on the butt end of the arrow is more weight. This means that arrows fletched with feathers are ever-so-slightly faster—a few feet per second—than those fletched with plastic vanes.

So should your traditional bow use arrows fletched with plastic or feathers? If you shoot off the shelf, off your fist, or off what is called a "shoot-around" arrow rest—these are all elements the fletching actually comes in contact with as it zooms forward—feathers are undoubtedly better because they are more "forgiving." When a properly mounted feather hits something inflexible, it is built by nature to fold down; when it passes by that object, the bow riser, for example, a feather rises back into shape. A plastic vane on the other hand, is less forgiving because it cannot fold so easily out of the way. So any physical contact between the fletching and the bow throws the arrow off track, but feathers tend to throw the arrow off course much less than do vanes.

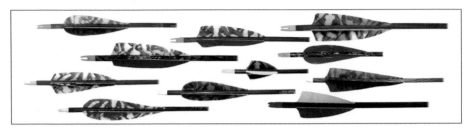

Camo Feathers. *If you shoot traditional, regardless of the type of shaft, feathers such as these from Trueflight Manufacturing work better than plastic vanes. Using feathers results in higher arrow velocities, greater stability, better guidance, higher accuracy, and more forgiving flight.*

Among archery aficionados, there is noisy debate about fletching, but none of this noise is terribly important in the general sense. (It reminds the author of the comment made by a former anthropology professor about argumentative colleagues disputing the proper techniques for diagramming social kinship systems. The professor described them as "guppies licking excrement off the bottom of fishbowls.") Nevertheless, in order to be informed, what follows is a sense of the structure of those arguments.

NUMBER OF FLETCHING

Most archers have settled on three per arrow. Three feathers or vanes evenly spaced around the shaft give plenty of steering and control for smooth flight. Some archers prefer four fletches, but this only adds weight, not better control. The best configuration is an individual decision depending on an archer's style of shooting and equipment set-up. If you fletch your own arrows, three is easier than four; if you purchase arrows, they are less expensive. And remember, cock feather out—pointing away from the bow.

SIZE OF FLETCHING

Length and height of the feathers or vanes are dictated by the draw weight the archer is shooting, the type of bow, the type of arrowhead, and the length and size of the arrow, but something in the four-inch-long range is usually just fine. Some traditionalists swear by five-inch vanes, but they are noisier and naturally provide more steering for heavy arrows than does smaller fletching. A five-inch vane is fine for very close shooting, maybe out to thirty yards, but beyond that the speed and energy of the arrow drops dramatically.

The size and type of fletching impacts weight and something called FOC, forward of center, which we touch on more fully later. Remember that fletching weight, though slight, is concentrated at the rear of the arrow, so heavy fletching requires more tip weight to maintain an acceptable FOC. Fletch with four-inch feathers and you add more than eight grains to the arrow's tail, whereas plastic

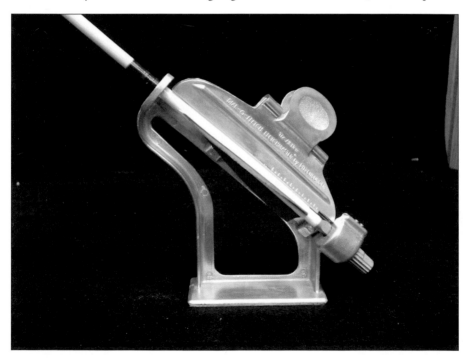

Bitzenburger. The classic Bitzenburger fletching tool is indispensable for those who wish to build their own arrows. It can be configured for left- or right-hand feathers (or vanes) and can position them securely in almost any position. Large dials at the top and bottom of the magnet holder make it easy to adjust your angle of fletching within seconds, to fletch straight, offset, or true right or left helical.

vanes add twenty-four grains; with five-inch feathers, you add eleven grains, but with five-inch vanes, it is three times that weight. More surface area gives more air resistance in flight for quicker stabilization, but increasing the surface area cuts into arrow speed. Recreationally, field points stabilize rapidly and a four-inch feather is probably fine. For hunting heads, the larger five-inch feather is better because the arrowhead's weight distribution is extreme, and the wide blades will want to react to air friction or to wind-plane and will throw the arrow off course.

STYLE OF CUT FOR FLETCHING

Since we rarely hunt today to kill birds and pluck their feathers for the arrows we make, we have numerous commercial choices. Is a "shield cut," where the back of the feather is slightly scalloped, better than a smooth "round cut"? This, like color of the fletching, makes no—zero, zip, nada—difference.

MOUNTING THE FLETCHING

The style of mounting or placement and twist of fletching on the shaft also affects an arrow's flight.

A helical mount is best overall for broadheads. It gives consistent flight and accuracy, although it slows arrow velocity a few feet per second, and clearance of the fletching around the bow riser needs experimentation. Some archers claim that left-hand helical fletching promotes loosening of their field points . . . but in reality it doesn't.

The offset mount is good for broadheads. It provides less air resistance in flight than does the helical mount and works with most arrow rests. To medium distances, it provides stable flight profiles. There will be some (minimal) fletching clearance issues and two to three feet-per-second loss of arrow speed when measured against a bare shaft.

The straight fletch is the fastest flying vane configuration, providing the least amount of air resistance. It works with any arrow and gives little in fletching clearance problems once set up, but at medium to long distances, it is notably less stable than helical or offset. Straight mounting is not recommended for large hunting heads without carefully tuning your set-up.

POSITION OF FLETCHING

It is a rule, whether you shoot the most primitive longbow or the most modern cam bow, that fletching applied in a manner such as to cause smooth spin or rotation is best. This means, for best flight, gluing—animal intestines or silken threads were fine for attaching feathers in the old days—the fletching in a helical or slightly non-linear manner to the shaft. The rear of the feathers should be far enough forward of the string position at the base of the nock to clear the shooter's fingers (or if shooting a modern bow, the release mechanism) when holding and releasing the string. For finger shooters, this is usually 1 to 1 ½ inches. The fletching should also be far enough forward so that its bases can be securely attached to the shaft, not to the nock or, in the case of some aluminum arrows, any nock insert.

RIGHT-WING OR LEFT-WING

You can successfully shoot feathers from either wing. Arrows do not noticeably promote rotation until they are well clear of the bow, between five and ten yards. Left-wing feathers will rotate the arrow counterclockwise, and right-wing feathers will rotate clockwise (as viewed by the shooter). Whichever you choose, be consistent in the application.

ARCANE TERMINOLOGY

An antique archery term that is today used primarily in the Old World is *cast*. It is the ability of the bow to shoot an arrow quickly and cleanly; sometimes it also refers to the distance over which it is shot.

AN ARROW CALLED FLU-FLU

A specialized type of arrow fletching, the *flu-flu,* is designed for very short-range shooting, recreationally at flying targets or when hunting targets in trees. Because flu-flu arrows fly short distances, it is easy for an archer to recover their arrow whether they hit the target or miss it. Without the large flu-flu fletching to apply the brakes, an arrow might otherwise travel hundreds of yards and either become lost or become a real danger. (When you shoot, elemental safety says, always know what you are aiming at and what or where the arrow will stop if you miss your target. Arrows that fly out of sight will be almost impossible to find. So when you hear, "I shot an arrow into the air and where it landed I know not where," think "Knucklehead!")

The flu-flu is quite a bit larger than the fletching typically used on an arrow and is cut in a ragged manner or even left uncut. Whereas a typical arrow has three or four feathers (or vanes) on the shaft base, a flu-flu might have six or might even spiral, untrimmed, entirely around the shaft. Either way, the excessive fletching generates more drag (turbulence and friction) and slows the arrow down rapidly after a short distance (about thirty yards). Recreational flu-flus sometimes use large rubber points

Flu-Flu. *The design and color of flu-flu fletching varies with the builder—and you can do this at home—but the idea is always the same: to slow the arrow, to limit its flight. A spiral wrap flu-flu is useful for bird hunting, for example, where you can shoot into the air but don't want the arrow to fly a quarter mile and become lost or a danger to others.*

called "blunts" to increase forward weighting; this spreads the power of impact but reduces or eliminates penetration. This forward weight gives the arrow a forward thrust—so it doesn't fly erratically—and keeps the flight slower.

When bird hunting with arrows fletched with flu-flus, predominantly pheasants because they are a sizable bird and relatively slow on take-off, an archer must learn to lead the bird—like a shotgunner might lead a flying duck or goose—and release the arrow in anticipation of the bird's path. A variety of special points, from Judos to wide, looping wire Snaro, are used when bird hunting.

HOLDING ON

You have to hold the arrow on the string and you need a dependable spot to draw the arrow so that force is applied consistently shot to shot. Only then can you aim and predict the arrow's flight path and only then will the arrow fly consistently. Shooters of every kind of bow, except a crossbow—and even the crossbow string must be consistently drawn straight back into the receiver before it is locked into the safety—will use a bowstring with a nock-point locator attached and an arrow with a plastic nock affixed to the butt end. The nock snugs around the string and positively positions the arrow beneath and against the nock locator in the deepest, tightest spot of the drawn string's angled "V."

(Split finger and recurve shooter Darrell Pace won an Olympic gold medal in Los Angeles in 1984. Olympic-style archers use a split-finger draw and release because it facilitates a more solid anchor, either at the corner of the mouth or beneath the line of the jaw. Pace said he "had to learn to shoot like a machine." In other words, consistently, without *thinking* about every detail of the shot process.

This state of mind-body synchronization was achieved by—watch the wording here—"mind-numbing" practice, literally.)

The nock locator may be nothing more than a small knot tied in position and covered with a drop of glue. It may also be a cushioned brass "C," cushioned because the metal can otherwise crush and damage strands of the bowstring. The nock locator gives a permanent position or at least a ready-reference point for placing the arrow. Usually an arrow is placed below it, but this probably does not matter as long as you position it the same way every time. Below the locator is the deepest part of the "V" formed by the pulled bowstring.

Whether the locator is a metallic button or a tied-on (archery jargon calls this "served-on") string, frequently a knot of dental floss covered by a drop of glue to bind it in place, is a matter of preference. If you change arrow types or weights of heads or size of feathers or the full-draw location from corner of the mouth to below the jaw, however, the nock-point locator on the string will need to be adjusted up or down for best flight, because all of these adjustments effectively change dynamic arrow spine. This is because the arrow responds to the force and "moment," or direction of the force, delivered through the string, and unless it is centered in such a manner as to fly over the rest in the same manner each shot, the forces will be irregular, and different application of forces each time means different arrow flight.

The "thing" holding the arrow against the string may be nothing more than a slight notch cut into the base of the arrow, but because so much pressure is applied in such a short moment, arrows cut in this manner—unless they are specifically treated or reinforced with sinew tightly wrapped and glued around the base—tend to split from the base forward. Thus, a molded plastic nock designed to fit the bulk of your bowstring—and numerous brand names are available—is an excellent way to position an arrow consistently.

Nocks sized on the arrow are usually glued on the base of a shaft and rotated so the cock feather points out, away from any possible contact. The ideal fit on the string is snug, not tight. Pinching the string too tightly will cause the nock to stick or fail to loosen at the right moment, and this retards arrow flight. Yet, too loose a fit defeats the object of holding an arrow in place and will allow the arrow to slide down the string, even fall off, the moment you take your fingers away.

Nocks can be either slipped over the flat rear end of a prepared arrow shaft or fitted over a taper cut into the wooden dowel or aluminum tube. A taper tool for wood is inexpensive and nothing more than a type of pencil sharpener. The point taper is five degrees while the nock taper is eleven degrees.

GETTING THE SHAFT

The traditional arrow—at least during the last century in the United States—was built from a wood called Port Orford cedar. You can build an arrow from practically any material that is straight, consistent in quality, and has the correct weight, straightness, and stiffness (called spine) for your set-up. Cedar is straight and very durable, but fine arrows can also be built from Sitka spruce, ash, redwood, slow-growth pines, and a variety of other materials.

Arrows, arrows, arrows. No matter what type of arrow shaft you choose, they are adaptable to traditional shooting: carbon, wood, aluminum, or even some combination!

SPINE

Spine is the most important part of arrow shaft equation and it is difficult for the average archer to determine. Arrows need a consistent spine to fly consistently and to group in a target. The measure of spine is established with a twenty-nine-inch arrow placed on two posts that are twenty-eight inches apart. A two-pound weight is hung in the middle of the shaft and the measure of deflection, how far the arrow shaft drops, gives a static (non-moving) spine.

If you hear about *dynamic spine*, know that it is a measure of arrow flex when moving after being shot. It too needs to be consistent or at least manageable for your set-up. Stiffer is better than weaker for best shooting results. Too stiff favors arrows flying left. Too weak favors arrows flying right.

We discuss arrow spine a lot in this book because it is the single most important concept in good arrow flight. Get the spine right and everything else falls into place.

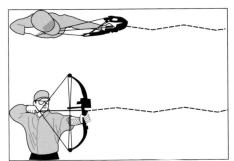
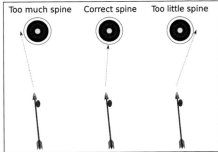

Archer's Paradox. Every arrow bends as it leaves the bowstring. It naturally wobbles or fishtails as the energy of the shot distributes through the shaft. Understanding what has become known as "archer's paradox" and how it affects your bow-and-arrow set-up can be simplified by finding the correct spine, or stiffness, of your arrows. Proper arrow spine may not cure all ills, but it cures many of them in archery.

WEIGHT

You should purchase a grain scale. They cost less than $50, but here is a tool that will last forever without wearing out or going out of style, so go high end for another $50. If you decide to begin building your own arrows, you will use it 10,000 times. The scale will help you work with consistent parts: the arrow shaft, nocks, points, and fletching. How much variation is too much? Does it matter if your completed arrows are two to four grains different in weight? If one ounce equals 437.5 grains, we really have to assume that a couple of grains either way is insignificant and will not affect the flight of the arrow. Other factors such as wind or the smoothness of your release will be far more critical. Wood arrows are normally spined for a twenty-eight-inch draw. Spine decreases by five pounds for every inch over twenty-eight and increases by five pounds for every inch below twenty-eight. The general rule for wood arrows is to select approximately 8.5 to 9.0 grains of weight for every pound of bow draw weight. A sixty-pound bow thus takes an arrow that weighs around 500 to 540 grains.

STRAIGHTNESS

Manufacturers of modern arrows promote straightness tolerances as if this were the most critical factor in hitting a target squarely. Carbon Express, for example, advertises their Heritage 250 shaft (for fifty- to seventy-pound draw weights) with straightness ± .005-inch maximum and weight tolerance ± 2.0 grains (eleven grains per inch, .373-inch spine, and .305-inch diameter). Carbon Express says these carbon shafts are "for the hunter who wants the look and feel of classic cedar with the high-tech performance and toughness of carbon composite. This perfectly spined shaft is ideal for recurve or longbows."

Leek for America. The Archery Trade Association blog says, "Miranda Leek has the sweetest smile but, when her bow is at full draw, her face is a study in intensity. While she looks like the quiet piano player she is, her competitive spirit sits just below the surface. . . ." Leek shoots with all the toys: tab, chest protector, finger sling around the riser, competition arm guard, and carbon arrow. (Photo courtesy of Archery Trade Association)

For top-ranked international competitors, straightness is probably critical, to a point. They are, after all, shooting recurves at nearly 100 yards and hitting a target that, at that distance, their pin sight entirely obscures. For the average archer, this is one of those horseshoe-and-hand-grenade moments where close is good enough. You want to shoot a nice, straight arrow, but wood is not a product designed by nature to be perfectly straight or perfectly consistent. If this is crucially important to you, perhaps the choice of a carbon or aluminum shaft is better than wood. Unlike the wood shaft, which is solid, the manufactured shaft is a hollow tube. Carbon bends but, unlike aluminum, does not take a permanent bend.

ABOUT PORT ORFORD CEDAR

It's really a cypress, not a true cedar. Alternately, it's called Lawson's Cypress, and it is native to the Klamath Mountain valleys of southwest Oregon and northwest California. In the wild, it's a large evergreen conifer that may grow 200 feet tall with trunks from four to six feet in diameter.

The wood of Port Orford cedar/Lawson's cypress is light yet strong and rot-resistant. The untreated wood has a detectable aroma of ginger, which, digging into the trivia closet, gives it substantial commercial value for coffins and shrines in Asia, particularly Japan.

The wood also possesses a straight, tight grain that is great for arrow shafts and stringed instruments. Its fine grain, good strength, and tonal quality are highly regarded for soundboards in guitar making.

It's anyone's guess how long Port Orford cedar will be with us. In the wild it is threatened by a root disease thought to have originated in Asia named *Phytophthora lateralis*. This disease kills the trees, and there is no known cure.

As far as Port Orford cedar shafts are concerned, here is a typical advertisement:

Premium Port Orford Cedar Arrows and Shafts

Hand-spined, walnut-stained, clear-lacquer-dipped, and crested for lasting trueness and classic good looks. Helical fletched with 5" left-wing shield, barred cock feathers, and solid-color hen feathers. White snap nocks installed. Full length and uncut. Per 6. **Made in USA. Available in packs of six - $59.99. Specify weight range:**

45–50 lbs.
50–55 lbs.
55–60 lbs.
60–65 lbs.

THE FOOTED SHAFT

A wooden arrow shaft made of two different types of wood spliced together is called a *footed shaft*. Footed arrows were used by both early Europeans and Native Americans, and they are both instruments of beauty and highly effective as arrow shafts.

Footed arrows typically consist of a short length of heavier hardwood near the head of the arrow, with the remainder of the shaft built of a softer wood such as pine or even cedar. By reinforcing the area most prone to break, the arrow is more likely to survive impact while maintaining overall flexibility and lighter weight. Most footed arrows also consist of a reinforced nock.

A "footed shaft" or "footed arrow" should not be confused with the practice of footing an arrow, although the purpose is similar. It is sometimes useful for traditional shooters to foot their carbon shafts because carbon tends to crack or "blow out" at the advanced end if an arrow hits something hard. Simply glue a short piece of aluminum shaft tubing—not more than an inch or so—over the forward end the arrow, using the insert in the shaft for a visual marker. This makes the arrow stronger and more durable on impact. It prevents the insert from crushing the carbon shaft if you hit something hard and doesn't significantly change the FOC (forward of center: see below) of your arrow. (Some shooters also reinforce the back of the arrow.)

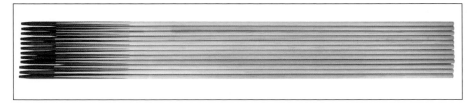

Footed Shafts. *There are no more beautiful arrow shafts in the world than a matched set of footed shafts. Two types of wood are spliced together, a harder wood on the fore-end (the darker end) and a softer wood on the rear.*

AIN'T ALL JUST "BUBBA"

Arrows are complex and fascinating. Learn arrows and you have a true insight into the mechanics of archery.

With a modern carbon or aluminum shaft, a small aluminum (sometimes plastic) sleeve or "insert" is glued into the forward part of the arrow. The insert provides a threaded hole in which to screw in a variety of "arrowheads," although that term is somewhat antique now. Archers talk about the arrowhead or tip in terms of a field point for practice, a broadhead for big-game hunting, or a blunt for small-game hunting or backyard shooting fun. These different types of tips are glued onto wood arrows.

Many archers, both traditional and modern, enjoy "cresting arrows," which means painting the rear section in a personalized pattern of colors. This may be an ancient tactic for identifying arrows shot while hunting or in games or on the battlefield, but it is today an art that enhances the appearance of arrows.

Basic Bamboo. *Each time one of them appeared skittish, Kapara would slap the ground with the palm of his hand, imitating the thumping noise that a wallaby would make. His arrow was a short bamboo spear with a forged metal tip.*

ISSUE: "ARCHER'S PARADOX"

This is one of those terms that gets nitpicked by archers who perhaps study too much and shoot too little. Apparently, Robert Elmer coined the term in the 1930s when everyone shot wooden recurves or longbows. He said that in order to strike the center of the target, the arrow must be pointed slightly to the side of the target, and he named this observed phenomenon "archer's paradox."

Elmer realized that arrows needed correct spine to flex out of the way of the bow riser, to deform upon being shot, and then return, or straighten, to the correct path after they left the bow. Incorrectly spined arrows fly erratically, he observed, and if they hit the side of the bow upon a shot, they can't fly accurately.

Bows with light draw weights typically require arrows with less spine because the energy they transfer is less than that of heavy bows. On the other hand, powerful bows need stiffer arrows with more spine, as the bow will have a much greater bending effect on the arrow as it is accelerated.

An arrow with too much spine for the bow will not flex sufficiently. As the string comes closer to the riser, the arrow will be regularly forced off to one side of the target. Too little spine results in an arrow deforming too much and being propelled toward the opposite side. In extreme cases, the arrow could break before it accelerated, but might also whirl or even fly sideways, and if it hit the target—if you were very close—might hit at a radical angle and would barely penetrate, if at all.

In modern times, with vastly upgraded—or at least more complex—equipment, the term "archer's paradox" has simply come to mean the natural bending of the arrow as it is loaded with energy and leaves the bowstring: wallowing horizontally side to side when released with fingers or porpoising vertically up and down when released mechanically.

ISSUE: FORWARD OF CENTER BALANCE

The flight of your arrow will be most stable when the weight or mass forward of the center of the arrow is heaviest. This idea, FOC or "forward (front) of center" balance, has recently gained a great deal of attention from archery engineers and those who love to estimate the number of grains of sand on a beach. They say a high FOC, something like 16 to 18 percent, flies well, but has a premature loss of speed and trajectory, while a low FOC, maybe 5 to 8 percent, holds trajectory but can fly erratically.

Unless your arrow spins in flight like a merry-go-round or hits the target at a weird angle, don't worry about FOC. Standard components on either end of the arrow will give you good shooting. It's only when you choose an odd combination—a super-heavy head and super small fletching, for example—that you will experience problems. Nevertheless, if some evening you are bored with television and want to think about absolutely maximizing arrow flight, consider FOC. Usually, a finished percentage between 7 and 15 percent is acceptable. As you can see, there is no magic number.

Check the balance of a raw shaft, one without any attachments. It should balance in the middle, which is considered zero FOC.

You are putting a heavy head on the shaft, though, a heavier head than the fletching and nock on the back end so your finished arrow balances forward of the middle.

Here's how to compute FOC:

Measure the distance between the arrow's physical center to the point it actually balances. With a thirty-inch raw shaft, the balance should be at fifteen inches.

Now balance your finished arrow, the arrow you will shoot in competition or when hunting. If it balances three inches forward of the actual center, its FOC is $^3/_{30}$, or 10 percent. If your twenty-nine-inch arrow balances 2 ½ inches forward of its actual center, the FOC would be $^{2.5}/_{29}$, or 8.6 percent, and you might want to experiment with either a slightly heavier head or slightly smaller fletching.

Some students of archery claim that FOC should be replaced by "EFOC," or Extreme Forward of Center, certainly with traditional equipment. To EFOC and ultra-heavy broadhead advocates, 20 to 25 percent is not too much (instead of the standard 10 to 15 percent) to maximize penetration on big game. Arrow penetration expert Dr. Ed Ashby finds that an arrow with extreme FOC—an arrow with the large heavy heads that he manufactures and sells—shot from a lighter bow out-penetrates the standard arrow from a heavier bow by almost half. Of course, shooting an arrow with EFOC requires a close-range shot, so it is certainly an issue to discuss and experiment with before hunting season. (We will touch on FOC again in the next chapter.)

CARBON

Carbon arrow shafts are constructed by rolling very thin layers of carbon sheeting into perfectly straight tubes (imagine rolling up a big map or hand-rolling a cigarette). Once wound, the tubes are heat-treated to bond the layers together. When the tubes cool to room temperature, they are cut into sections as raw shafts. At some point the tubes are coated with a finish, both to seal the porous raw carbon sheeting and to provide a more visually appealing and slicker surface.

Some of the shafts, particularly those that come from the center of the roll, retain ±.001 inch straightness. Other sections distort slightly from the heating/cooling process. Small variations in the daily manufacturing environment (humidity, pressure, air convection patterns, etc.) along with tiny deviations in the characteristics of the raw materials ultimately determine the straightness of the finished product.

Arrow shafts are graded by straightness, and the straighter they are advertised, the more they cost. But what's realistic or necessary for a traditional archer?

Most standard-grade carbon arrows have an advertised straightness of ±.005 to ±.006 inch. These shafts are usually sold to hunters and beginning archers. For big-game hunting and general target shooting, standard-grade shafts are great. A human hair only measures .004 to .006 inch in diameter. Thus, a basic carbon shaft

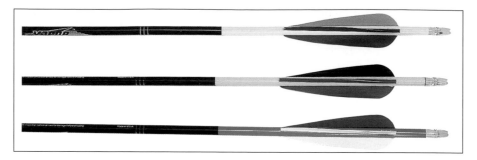

Carbon. Prepared with care, carbon shafts will work well with a traditional set-up, although you should consider fletching them with feathers instead of plastic vanes. Carbon shafts are rugged and useful for all shooting and hunting situations. Are these high-tech shafts "traditional"?

of .006 inch straightness is fine, and certainly straighter than you could possibly perceive without specialized equipment.

But is carbon even a good arrow choice for a traditional archer?

CARBON TECHNICAL

Arrows have tubular shafts because, for a given mass of material, tubes are stiffer than solid rods. (Solid fiberglass or aluminum arrows are sold for bowfishing where shot distance is very short, maybe ten yards, and the arrow must punch down through the dense water to its target.)

For a given mass of material, larger diameter tubes with thin walls are stiffer, but they are also mechanically weaker than narrow, thick-walled tubes, so there is a trade off.

Bowfishing. Besides wood, the only other completely solid shaft is the solid fiberglass shaft for bowfishing. Shooting distance is very short, because the arrow is attached to the bow, or a reel mounted on the bow, by a heavy Dacron line. The arrow must punch into and through the water and carry a heavy head that penetrates and holds a fish. The head must then reverse mechanically so that it can be withdrawn. A recurve is the perfect bow for bowfishing because the draw is smooth and steady and the shooting can be very fast.

Being stiffer and lighter than aluminum, a carbon shaft's overall diameter can be thinner (thus more aerodynamic) and the arrow lighter (thus faster) for a given stiffness.

An interesting variation is carbon fiber bonded over aluminum tubing. Easton builds a set of these shafts, which are also slightly "barreled" so that the wrap of carbon is very slightly stiffer in the middle than at the ends, like an old-fashioned barrel. The premium design and construction of these shafts makes them quite expensive. (English archery enthusiasts proudly point out that the best longbow arrows of the medieval period, all wood of course, were also barreled.)

Beman, which styles itself "First in Carbon," begins its shaft selection chart with a choice of compound or recurve, recurve being on the right-hand side of the page. Draw weight in pounds with a finger release is noted in five-pound blocks. Beman notes that measured arrow lengths in increments of an inch should be "rounded up" to the next inch. Thus, a 28½-inch arrow would be considered twenty-nine inches. Moving left from the recurve column on the first chart to the twenty-nine-inch column designates arrow group "E." Dropping to Group E arrows in the following chart gives the correct arrow size (Beman 400), the spine (.400), a choice of arrow models—MFX Bone Collector, ICS Hunter, etc.—and notes about the weight by model in grains per inch.

In a way, this is much simpler than choosing an aluminum shaft. For that, you have a choice among numerous arrow styles. The MFX Bone Collector, for instance, advertises straightness of ±.003 inch, weight tolerance of ± two grains, and weighs nine grains per inch. A number of other features for inserts, nocks, and adapters are specified.

ABOUT ALUMINUM—ARROWS THAT IS

Was it intuitive that a hollow aluminum shaft was the next step up from a wood arrow? After all, no other metals were suitable: bronze, copper, iron. Yet aluminum is plentiful, relatively lightweight, and easier to work than many other metals.

Today, aluminum arrows are synonymous with the Easton family of California. Their experimentation with aluminum began in the thirties, when everyone shot a traditional bow, drawing and releasing the string by hand, and it has not ended today. It was James D. "Doug" Easton, delivery truck driver and archery pro shop entrepreneur, who realized that a combination of factors—length, tube thickness (weight), and outside diameter—were instrumental in determining the spine of the shaft. Compared to the wooden shafts previously used by archers, his aluminum shafts provided superior consistency of weight, balance, and arrow flight.

In 1946, Easton Aluminum produced the first trademarked arrows, model no. 24 SRT-X, offering them for sale to the general public. In 1955, the popular XX-75 arrow shafts were added to Easton's arrow line. Then, for sixty years, practically from the time of their development, aluminum arrows dominated the arrow market. In the eighties, Easton was selling sixteen million shafts a year.

Today Easton offers several lines of aluminum and is even is wrapping aluminum shafts in carbon. Easton has cornered this shrinking market segment but, a dozen years ago, bought into the expanding carbon arrow market by purchasing Beman—and aggressively filing lawsuits against any aluminum competitor for more than a generation.

Aluminum's superior strength and consistency make it an ideal element for arrows. When a longbow string is released to travel forward, the string applies a steady amount of energy to the arrow. This is unlike the modern cam bow, which almost instantly applies maximum energy to the arrow. Thus, when the highly adjustable compound bow came along, the number and types of shafts exploded in complexity.

Easton uses a four-digit number to identify their aluminum shafts. This number is actually two 2-digit numbers; the first number indicates the outside diameter of the arrow shaft in sixty-fourths of an inch, and the second number indicates the wall thickness of the shaft in thousandths of an inch. In this system, a 2215 shaft is $\frac{22}{64}$-inch in diameter with a wall thickness of 0.015-inch.

Many traditional archers shoot aluminum arrows. They grew up with aluminum; they are familiar with the shaft selection charts pioneered by Easton. Aluminum is relatively cheap and it is now easy—at least now that the mechanical processes are understood and proven—to take a rod through the steps to become a fine arrow shaft. The knock on aluminum is that they are pretty easy to damage. In many ways they are not as durable as wood arrows or the current market leader, carbon. In practice, if one launched arrow hits an arrow already in the target, the earlier arrow or perhaps both will sustain damage. If a launched arrow hits a hard surface, a rock or a tree, it will bend, and while a variety of arrow straighteners are commercially available, you should never again have confidence that this arrow will fly true.

Easton has two selection charts for its aluminum arrows, one for hunting and one for target. If you know your bow's draw weight and the length of arrow you want, finding arrows with the correct spine is easy. Easton has two sets of columns on its two-page chart, one for Recurve Bow and one for Modern Longbow. Select the bow, then select the weight of the broadhead in grains: seventy-five, 100, 125, or 150. Next, drop down to your "actual peak bow weight" in that column. Move across that bow-weight row horizontally to the column indicating your correct arrow length. Note the letter at the intersection of the arrow-length column and the bow-weight column.

For example, if you have a twenty-nine-inch draw and shoot a 125-grain broadhead with a sixty-five-pound recurve hunting bow, the intersection gives a letter "J." Checking the key for J gives you a range of sizes, spines, weight in grains per inch, and weight at twenty-nine inches. It blocks out arrows in the following categories:

- lightest and fastest
- medium weight, offering good speed and durability
- heavier weights for excellent durability and penetration
- aluminum/carbon and carbon

In the example above, Easton's chart recommends a 2219 shaft ($^{22}/_{64}$-inch diameter with .019 inch wall thickness). The spine is measured at .337 and the weight per inch is 13.8 grains. This indicates a 400-grain shaft at twenty-nine inches (or about 600 with a 125-grain head plus the inserts, nocks, and fletching) and the chart recommends either an Easton Super Slam or an XX75. The chart also suggests that the 2315 ($^{23}/_{64}$-inch diameter with .015 inch wall thickness) Super Slam or XX75 is a good second choice. At 11.7 grains per inch, the 2315 is slightly lighter, though its .340 spine is actually greater than the first choice of shaft.

MEASURING AND FITTING ARROWS

The draw lengths of the archer and the bow need to match. Determine yours first because that will tell you the size bow that fits. A simple measure of your draw length is to stand naturally against a wall with your arms spread out, palms facing out or forward. Have a friend measure from the tip of one middle finger to the other. Then simply divide that number by 2.5. The quotient is your approximate draw length (in inches) for your body size.

There are several other means for measuring draw length and you may want to try them as well. For instance, stand straight, extend your arms to the front, and bring your palms together. A yard stick placed between your palms and against your breast bone will read your draw length at the tips of your middle fingers.

Most adult archers will have draw lengths from twenty-eight to thirty-one inches, and the tendency is to go on the long-ish side. You want to be sure that you don't buy or cut arrows that are too short, so that any tip you attach interferes with the bow's riser or shoot-around rest (if you use one). Neither do you want an arrow that is too long because that adds useless weight and interferes with the dynamics of arrow flight, so get this right. A little longer is better than a little too short, though.

Unlike a modern compound bow, a traditional bow can be drawn to almost any length. So to find the arrow that's right for you, draw your bow—or a lightweight bow with an arrow scaled in inches permanently attached (available in most archery pro shops) because you can hold it for five to ten seconds—and have the pro shop manager or a friend measure from the string (technically the bottom of the groove of the nock) to the pivot point of the grip. Now add 1¾ inches, an accepted standard for distance to the outer edge or back of the bow's riser.

If you're strong enough (weight increases as you pull), you can draw a long-bow or recurve past your comfortable and natural draw length, even pull the arrow straight back off the rest or the shelf. If you find this happens more than once, you have cut your arrows too short and you should make an immediate change. (The practice of shooting excessively short arrows became popular in the early years of the "speed craze" era of the nineties. Compound shooters who wanted short, lightweight arrows to maximize arrow speed equipped their bows with overdraw shelves, but then discovered all manner of tuning and shooting problems. Not the least of these problems were several well-publicized accidents caused by arrows being pulled back too far or falling off the overdraw shelf. The archers ended up shooting themselves through the arm and wrist, an extraordinarily painful, crippling, and life-threatening injury.)

To avoid real safety problems, never buy or cut arrows that are too short. Some archers or pro shops cut arrows to the minimum in order to minimize weight and maximize speed. Your health is not worth an extra two or three feet per second of arrow velocity. An arrow that lodges behind the rest or continually falls off the rest or shelf (this means you are twisting the string as you draw—be conscious of your finger placement on the string) is an obstructed path shot, and a splintered arrow can hurt you. Badly.

So remember that at full draw you want an arrow to extend a minimum of an inch beyond the front of the bow. This length should be sufficient for both safety and to maximize arrow performance.

If you order shafts by mail or via the Internet, you may purchase them to a precise length or uncut. The "measure twice, cut once" rule applies because once you order cut and trimmed arrows, wood, carbon or aluminum, they cannot be returned. Besides, carbon shafts can't be cut successfully with the hacksaw in your tool box. Carbon arrows should only be cut with a high-speed abrasive-wheel saw; a pipe cutter will cause the carbon strands to split and crack. For best results trimming aluminum shafts, use a small handheld rotary pipe cutter, as the home hacksaw tends to leave the shaft ragged and even bent at the tip.

Determining your draw length and matching it to the bow and the arrows— actually the other way around—means that you will be shooting efficiently and that your gear will also be efficient and effective.

For draw length, correct measurement to within a half inch is fine for archers interested in hunting and recreational shooting. Depending on how you feel or whether you are smiling or frowning or perhaps have a sore shoulder, your draw will vary slightly from day to day. Plus, some strings stretch as they age, and so maintaining a precise draw is almost impossible.

SEXY BOW TUNING—NAKED ARROWS

It is actually called bare-shaft tuning. The idea of tuning a French horn or a violin is easy to understand. To produce beautiful symphonies, an instrument must play in harmony with the other instruments. Archery is the same way, and by selecting the properly spined arrow for your set-up, you have gone a long way toward "tuning" your traditional equipment. Each part, from arrow rest, if any, to fletching to the bow's draw weight, is important to the archery symphony, and they have to play well together.

Traditional archers are finger shooters and so have individual variations of form that require fine tuning of arrow stiffness and bow set-up to produce the perfect arrow flight. A manufacturer's arrow chart will get you close, but you may have to tweak point weight slightly (or possibly arrow length) for ideal arrow flight with your set-up.

Bare-shaft tuning is a step in the process of getting arrows to fly straight, and you can do it with any type arrow: wood, carbon, or aluminum. It begins with a fully set up full-length arrow, less fletching. Three arrows are preferable so you can observe how they group in the target.

Place a nocking point on the string using nock pliers, which are designed to squeeze the nock around the string evenly. Place the bottom of the nock about ⅛ inch above the arrow shelf as measured with a bow square. Attach it tightly enough to hold in place but not so tight that you can't slide it up or down in small, incremental steps.

Shooting the long, fletchless arrows from a short distance will almost certainly result in them sticking in the target with their butt- or nock-end high. You can gradually trim fractions of an inch off the arrow down to the proper length as you go, which increases arrow spine (stiffens the shaft), until the arrow sticks fairly straight in the target.

First, while standing fifteen to twenty yards from the target, shoot three arrows for a group using fletched shafts and mark the center of the group. Next, from exactly the same spot, shoot a group of bare shafts and mark this center, also. If both groups have essentially the same center, your bow is acceptably well tuned for finger shooting purposes. If the bare shafts plane off-line, however, and have a noticeably different group center, you will want to make corrections.

You are going to make adjustments based on where the groups are in relation to each other, not on whether the nocks are kicking one way or another. Ignore the angle of the shaft. Concentrate first on vertical, up/down alignment, as this is a nock-point location issue. Remember that the nock follows the point of impact: too low, lower the nock and too high, raise it.

- Too low: If the bare-shaft group is below, move the nock point down—perhaps ¹⁄₁₆ inch or less—and check fletching contact with the shelf or rest.
- Too high: If the bare-shaft group hits high, experiment with moving your nock point up the string very slightly and shoot again.
- Left: If the bare-shaft group is to the left of your fletched shafts, the spine is too great. Try using a more flexible shaft, increasing point weight, switching from a Dacron string to a DF-97 or Fast Flight, or perhaps increasing your bow poundage by giving the string an extra twist (which brings the limb tips closer). Many traditional archers shoot 150-grain heads, and some shoot broadheads as heavy as 190 grains. Another option if you have a thick side plate on your arrow shelf in the sight window is to reduce the thickness of that side plate, moving the arrow closer to centershot.
- Right: If the bare-shaft group is to the right (or if they won't group and tend to scatter), the shafts are too weak; try switching string material (from a DF-97 or Fast Flight string to Dacron, for example), making the shaft a bit lighter (even trimming it very slightly if you have length), producing a lighter point, or, if possible, reducing your draw weight. You might even build out the side plate on your arrow shelf to move the arrow away from center.

For a properly tuned set-up, bare shafts and fletched shafts will group together, even out to seventy yards or more. Expect your groups with bare shafts to be larger than the fletched groups, for obvious reasons. The better your form, the better your release, the tighter the groups, and the farther away you can maintain good groups. In the end, the most forgiving arrow will actually show a slightly weak/slightly high nock-point indication. In other words, at twenty yards, bare shafts grouping a little low and to the right is excellent because fletching makes a shaft react as if it were slightly stiffer.

Bare-shaft tuning is a process of experimentation, and you have many tools available: length of the arrow shaft, arrow spine, nock-point position, weight of the arrow point. The point is to go slowly, varying one thing at a time, and learn, because the more you play with the tuning elements of your traditional bow, the easier and quicker it will be in the future whenever you buy a new bow or change arrows or broadheads. The point is to have fun.

THE WORST SUBJECT OF ALL

Velocity. Arrow speed. It's been all the rage in modern compound bow circles for twenty years. A lighter, faster arrow reaches its target quicker with a flatter trajectory, and that makes distance estimation somewhat easier. Indeed, some advertised arrow speeds have climbed above 400 fps, although the average archer probably shoots in the 250 fps range—perhaps the 175 to 200 fps range for traditional shooters. Increased speed is good, but only to a point.

Speed means beefed-up bows and lighter arrows. The speed craze isn't all bad, even though it doesn't necessarily apply to traditional shooting. The moment an arrow is released, it begins to lose velocity. As it succumbs to gravity and air resistance, its flight path (trajectory) changes and the arrow eventually begins to drop. Light, fast arrows hold trajectory better than slow, heavy arrows. Thus archers who shoot lighter, faster arrows have less need to adjust for distance. Their margin of error is greater. Faster arrows, it is said, add a little "forgiveness" to your shooting.

For bowhunters, a fast arrow gives game animals less opportunity move out of position. Because sound travels at about 1,200 fps, it is much faster than the arrow and a deer, for instance, hears the sound before the arrow arrives. Its natural reaction is to crouch in preparation for jumping away from the noise and what it perceives as a threat. Archers traditionally call that "jumping the string" and so miss the deer when the arrow flies a little high.

The difference between a 200 fps arrow and a 300 fps arrow, however, is measured in micro-seconds. Statisticians can work out the timing and distance, but a 200 fps arrow travels thirty yards in about half a second (0.471 seconds), whereas an arrow that is 50 percent faster, 300 fps, gets to the thirty-yard target in about a third of a second (0.314 seconds). You just have to ask yourself if this length of time is critical to success and the answer is invariably no!

A light, fast arrow will reach its target quicker and give you a bit of a margin of error in distance estimation, but when it reaches its target it is going to carry a lot less energy than a heavier, slower arrow. This means its ability to penetrate is diminished, an important factor when hunting big game. Then too, lighter, faster arrows are almost always noisier. If you are a hunter, you will take some natural steps to silence your shot with rubberized elements perhaps woven into or wound around the string and attached to the bow limbs and quiver. A faster shot makes silent shooting difficult to impossible because the arrow absorbs less energy and that energy dissipates as noise and vibration and continual jarring occur in your elbow and shoulder.

Dangerous Game. *Brown bears—huge, temperamental cousins to the grizzly bear—make a living catching migrating salmon in Alaska and British Columbia. In a world where such omnivores—who will eat anything that does not eat them first—exist, the bow and arrow must have been welcome at early human campfires.*

No one rule fits every archer. Noise and penetration are of special concern only to hunting archers. If you don't hunt, bow noise isn't a serious concern. And for competition 3D shooting, where noise and penetration don't make a difference in scoring, lighter arrows with flatter trajectories may definitely be better, but fat shafts that might cut or even nudge a line are in demand. As a traditional shooter, never imagine that competition is less intense because you share an ethic!

If speed is critical, shoot a rifle and you can fire a projectile at ten times the speed of the arrow. If the experience, fun, and camaraderie with other archers are more important to you, enjoy the moment.

THE BEST SUBJECT OF ALL . . .

. . . at least for a hunter. A competitor's arrow only needs to stick in the target, and an inch or two might be sufficient. A bowhunter needs an arrow that penetrates, some say passes completely through, his or her prey animal, because an arrow kills by causing its prey to bleed copiously and thus expire quickly, essentially from suffocation, because blood carries oxygen.

All things being equal, your recurve will have more kinetic energy and penetrating power when you shoot heavy arrows. A factor in learning to shoot and enjoy the traditional bow is learning the arc of the arrow's flight, learning to judge distance and wind. If you want fast and straight, a shot with greater certainty and less challenge, take up the compound bow. Or is the light arrow/heavy arrow discussion an argument with little foundation?

Kinetic energy is a measure of the energy of motion. All objects including arrows carry kinetic energy, and it is measured in foot-pounds (ft/lb). The energy an arrow carries depends on its mass and speed. As one or both increase, the energy package increases by this formula: KE = ½ MV2. The hidden factor in the equation is that at any given propulsive force (draw weight), as mass increases, velocity decreases and vice versa.

Here's an example. Shooting a light 400-grain arrow gives you 52 ft/lb. Increase the weight by half to 600 grains and the KE increases to 54 ft/lb. It sounds good, but to achieve that increase of two foot-pounds of kinetic energy costs upwards of 20 percent in speed. Perhaps to a hunter after ultra-fast pronghorns or black-tail deer, speed is required, but to hunt bison or elk, the heavier arrow with greater penetration is better.

Let's perform a sample calculation. The kinetic energy of an arrow is found by $KE = (mv^2)/450{,}240$ where m is the mass of the arrow in grains and v is the velocity of the arrow in feet per second. The 450,240 is a constant converter changing feet per second and grains to foot-pounds. So if you shoot a 500-grain arrow at a respectable 200 fps, your actual kinetic energy—think of it as knock-down power—is:

$$KE = (mv^2)/450{,}240$$
$$KE = [(500)(200^2)]/450{,}240$$
$$KE = 20{,}000{,}000/450{,}240$$
$$KE = 44.42 \text{ ft/lbs}$$

How much KE do you need? A target archer will easily find the amount in the example above is sufficient, as will a small and medium game hunter. The larger the animal however, the more careful the archer must be to pick a spot and make a good shot. Arrow placement always trumps speed.

The Joy of Archery. *The look of passion an intensity on the face of the girl who has just loosed an arrow from a lightweight recurve says so much about the possibilities inherent in archery. The bow and arrow become a lifetime obsession for thousands and carry the elements of sport, technical development, competition, and a network of friends. Bowhunting can put food on the table, while competition archery can fatten the wallet. And it always retains some element of mystery, with more to learn and understand.*

CHAPTER FOUR

THE ARROWHEAD

Your arrow is tipped with a specialized head. Perhaps the first arrows, many thousands of years ago, were simply sharpened shafts held over a fire to evaporate the moisture, making them brittle and hard, but even then, probably not. After all, the earliest archers already had thousands of years of experience with spears and atlatl darts. Innovation cascades; development breeds development. Arrows for hunting and war were simply too hard to manufacture, straighten, and prepare; one would not use them casually, and without a weighted point they would not have flown in any manner to damage or even hit a target.

The head of the arrow has always been detachable. An archer switches points depending upon the use. For hunting big game like bears, a broadhead is required—wide and very sharp. For hunting very small game like rabbits, a specialized blunt point is called for. For target shooting or practice, a variety of small heads, today called field points, is available to help the arrow fly true with the least interference from wind. An archer who wants to hunt deer in the morning and then practice with friends near home later in the day has always been able to switch heads and even the arrows. Today you simply unscrew the hunting head and replace it with a target point . . . much easier than relaxing the sinew and rewinding or waiting for the fish glue to dry. Changing tips only takes a few seconds, even being careful not to get cut from the sharp blades of the hunting head.

Learn what archers have always known. Never shoot an arrow of any type without a proper tip. Doing so will almost certainly destroy the arrow, at the very least causing dangerous cracks in shaft structure that the naked eye cannot see. Plus, when it hits a target, an improperly constructed shaft will probably shatter or ricochet in some unexpected direction.

EARLY ARROWHEADS, EARLY ARCHERS

The earliest arrowheads were almost certainly sharpened bone used for fishing or flaked stone points for hunting. It took thousands of years and superior advances in metallurgy to build a metal head . . . and even then it wasn't guaranteed to be better—sharper, straighter, more durable—than flaked flint or obsidian.

The purpose of the earliest arrow was the same as the lion's fangs. To survive. To stab a game animal, an antelope or a monkey, for the hunter and his family to eat. Not to kill meant they went hungry unless berries and other fruits and roots were in season, but sooner or later the man had to make a kill or scavenge from a carcass. Early road kill (unappealing as that sounds) stolen when the leopard was sleeping. Thus, early archers quickly learned—because it meant the difference between life and death, eating fresh meat or fighting the hyenas and wild dogs for some lion's scraps—the secrets of the arrow and the arrowhead.

Hunting for Food. *A common misconception is that an arrowhead (or the head for a dart thrown by an atlatl) was a large shaped stone, but the archeological record indicates that true flint or obsidian arrowheads were very small. The larger blades were invariably knives, scrapers, or heads for thrusting weapons such as spears. (© Libor Balak, Antropark, Czech Republic: with permission)*

Early archers learned that the size of the head had to be much smaller than the head of a spear, smaller even than the head on an atlatl dart. The head had to cut deeply into the animal though, as the deeper it penetrated the more certain it was that the family would eat. Deep penetration of a sharp cutting head meant that the hit animal—or another person in case of a feud between clans over hunting territories or stolen women—would bleed copiously. This gave the hunter a blood trail to follow, and these men were expert woodsmen, so a well-hit animal rarely escaped.

It may also be the case that hunters dependent on killing big game for survival took no chances with blood trails and smeared their arrowheads in poison. This makes practical sense—although the use of any type of chemical is verboten in modern bowhunting—and numerous cases have been documented from cultural pre-history and, indeed, are still in use in Equatorial societies today.

Elephant. Traditional archery gear is sufficiently powerful to bring down any game animal on Earth. This elephant was taken in Tanzania in 2006 with a two-blade broadhead on a heavy carbon shaft. Thick-skinned game—elephant, Cape buffalo, hippopotamus, etc.—require heavy bows to deliver as much striking power as the archer can manage as well as careful shot placement. The ancients perhaps used poison-tipped arrows, but no nation allows that for big-game hunting today.

From the earliest writings come tales of poison arrows. The Greek hero Odysseus from Homer's *Odyssey* poisons arrows with juice from the plant hellebore, or Christmas rose. In Norse mythology, Baldr, the second son of Odin, is slain by an arrow (or spear; the sagas are ambiguous) dipped in poison. The Chinese and some Native American groups and African tribes have used various poisons.

In the famous ethnographic film *The Hunters* (1957), anthropologists follow Bushmen of the Jul'Hoansi tribe into the Kalahari Desert. After several days and many miles on the trail, the small hunters eventually stalk a giraffe and shoot it with arrows tipped with poison. Their objective is to kill the animal with the poison rather than blood loss from a deeply penetrating, broadhead-tipped arrow, as is the case in modern bowhunting. Due to the great size of the giraffe however, the tiny amount of poison on their small arrows is insufficient to kill the animal. When the Bushmen have exhausted their arrows, the cameraman, in a heavily edited scene, shoots it with a rifle, whereupon the animal falls and the Bushmen—by this time exhausted and out of food and water—butcher it and return to camp with fresh meat.

Early archers also learned that the arrowhead added weight that both was needed to help the arrow fly properly and caused problems if the head was too large; after all, their primary experience was with the thrusting spear, which can carry an enormous point, and to a lesser experience the atlatl dart. Without a weight-forward head, the rear of the arrow—the first section to receive energy from the string—would tend to fly sideways, and the archer would never hit a target. Thus, the first arrow was a little different mechanically than those shot today.

Those first warrior-hunters also learned that the head should have as low a profile as possible, what we might call a sleek, aerodynamic profile. They immediately recognized that wind affected arrow flight, too, and learned to account for wind drift, pressure against the shaft, the feathers, and the head. Of course, as consummate hunters they understood about wind (and odors), so the application of their knowledge to the arrow was an easy step.

They learned head size, shape, and weight depending upon the material used. They learned to match the head to the arrow and the arrow to the bow. They learned about binding the head to the shaft; the first heads set in a split shaft with binding wound around the base to hold them tight. Eventually, they learned about glue—perhaps fish glues—and experimented with the best way to hold the stone head on the stick. They also passed their learning to their children, and in this way small—or large—innovations compounded. Knowledge grew. The clan and the family prospered.

LITHIC REDUCTION: EVERYTHING IS POSSIBLE

Experts like to make things hard. It's what makes them "experts." Making an arrowhead out of a stone is the perfect example. The idea of "lithic reduction" is to take a certain kind of rock and pound the daylights out of it; take away everything except the sharp arrowhead. It's like Michaelangelo saying he imagined the image inside the marble block and then simply removed everything except the Pietà or the David captured inside.

Lithic reduction began when some early hominid picked up a rock and realized the sharp edge would help hack a piece of meat off a dead zebra. He could use the sharp edge in his hands to trim a flank steak and thus chew while keeping his head up to watch for hyenas or leopards. He could eat standing up rather than kneeling in the dirt and chewing right from the carcass like the other wild predators did.

At some point, perhaps lacking a pre-sharpened rock, a man began to pound one against another, hoping for a sharp edge, and, *voila*, civilization was born. Maybe at that point all of humanity came into being. That act probably wasn't accompanied by orchestral music as it was in the 1968 Stanley Kubrick movie *2001: A Space Odyssey*, but at that moment a couple million years ago, composers began writing symphonies and inventors developed the internal combustion engine. That act released man from the shackles of tooth and fang. At the moment the first man broke a rock, found and used an acceptable flake, and taught someone else how to do it, everything became possible. Men became birds and flew; became fish and dove to the bottom of the ocean; became gods and left Earth for deep space.

In general terms, chipped stone tools are nearly ubiquitous in all pre-metal-using societies because they are easily manufactured, a tool-quality stone is usually available nearby, and stones are easy to transport and sharpen. Not every rock will make a sharp edge, though. Only certain types of chert, flint, or obsidian break away in flakes and make a sharp point for needles or arrowheads or give a sharp edge for a scraper, a sickle, or a knife.

Ancient as it is, this technology is alive today and a few archers even build their own heads—the process is today called "knapping"—from stone or glass. It is rough on the hands and makes a giant mess of smashed rock, but a skilled artisan working in stone can produce numerous finely shaped arrowheads in one day.

Knapping. *Making an authentic-looking tool out of stone is called knapping, and it can be an incredibly complex art that can require years of experience to create beautiful and functional tools. In its simplest form, however, it is banging two stones together, causing one to fracture and create a sharp edge. You can learn to make a simple tool in hours, but for a truly complex and beautiful point, you might spend years of apprenticeship to a master.*

Paying the Tradition Forward. *Knapping is the art of chipping and flaking a useful tool out of stone, a tool such as an arrowhead or a knife blade. It is an especially traditional craft with no other usefulness today than perpetuating an ancient art, but when it can be combined with a learning experience in the company of your youngster, it is a valuable experience for both generations.*

So, here is a little-known fact. For specialist purposes, glass knives are still made and used today, particularly for slicing thin sections of tissue for electron microscopy in a technique known as microtomy. Freshly cut blades are always used since the sharpness of the edge must be extraordinarily great. These knives are made from high-quality manufactured glass, however, not from natural raw materials such as obsidian. Surgical knives made with obsidian are still quietly used in some delicate surgical techniques, even though the medical establishment frowns on the unregulated material.

Knapping is a side passion but is allied to the shooting of traditional bows, as is atlatl making or the amusing but lovely art of pumpkin throwing with a modern trebuchet. Nevertheless, almost 100 percent of traditional archers use modern, commercially made heads. We seven billion people simply do not live in an era when it would be practical to close the computer, grow a garden, build a cutting head, and hunt for game as if our lives depended on eating what we killed and using the inedible parts for tools, shelter, and clothing. Such a state will never happen on Earth again, at least not for *Homo sapiens* . . . and thus the reason to keep ancient technologies alive is to connect us with our roots, our ancestry.

THE SPECTACULAR STONES

Obsidian. Volcanic glass. Dragon glass. The names sound earthy and yet swarthy, even magical, as if the material is the product of a magic forge in Richard Wagner's classic Ring Cycle operas, *Der Ring das Nibelungen*, or was secreted away by a dragon or dwarves in J. R. R. Tolkien's timeless saga, *Lord of the Rings*. (Both works prominently feature archers.)

Perhaps because it is black, a complex, naturally occurring substance, yet shiny and opaque, men found obsidian desirable and soon enough found it useful. It is hard and brittle, and it is available all over the world. It fractures easily when struck on the oblique, and its flakes have incredibly sharp edges. For more than 25,000 years, men have shaped obsidian into knife blades and arrowheads.

There is little chance that your surgery will be performed with an obsidian scalpel, since the substance is not approved for use on humans by the US Food and Drug Administration, but perhaps it should be approved. At about three nanometers thick, the cutting edge of a fractured sliver of obsidian is many times sharper than even the highest quality steel surgical scalpels. Even the sharpest carbon steel scalpel, its blade coated with Zirconium nitride to increase its sharpness, has a grain and a jagged, irregular edge when viewed under a strong enough microscope; but, when examined even under a scanning electron microscope, the cutting edge of an obsidian blade is very fine.

Flint. A recently knapped stone head tied to a bamboo shaft with Dacron string material. Once, carefully worked stone heads were necessary to sustain life; today, they may still be wonderful artifacts with strong teaching value and internal character.

Obsidian and flint fracture in the perfect way to produce sharp edges. The expert term is a "conchoidal fracture." This means that when it breaks, the break does not follow a natural plane of separation. In other words, it can be shaped, split, hammered, even pressured to produce a design that originates in the imagination of the artist or toolmaker. The resulting shape is controlled only by the stresses applied, not by some predetermined orientation of the material itself.

Unlike obsidian, the more widely available flint (or chert) is actually a sedimentary rock. It also has the properties of conchoidal fracturing and so it also was highly desirable for stone heads and tools. Flint may have been in use—at least for primitive tools such as the hand axe—for as long as 2.5 million years, but let's skip forward . . .

ABOUT FOC

FOC means front or forward of center of the arrow. We touched on the subject in the chapter on arrows, but let's review because it is primarily determined by broadhead weight. FOC affects arrow flight and it can be measured and adjusted. It is an especially important consideration for distant shots with wide broadheads.

FOC is the percentage difference between an arrow's measured midpoint and its balance point, compared to the total length. It really is a basic concept and is easy to understand. (The great secret is that FOC may be an essentially meaningless concept for the average archer, but for the sake of those who measure out sheets of toilet paper per visit to *el cuarto de baño*, let's plunge ahead.)

The moment you release the bowstring, the arrow jumps forward. It leaves the string within six or seven inches, in any case, before brace height and long before the string serving area reaches the face of the bow. At this instant, the arrow carries the maximum kinetic energy (or momentum), and by the time the nock end of the arrow flies past the back of the bow, the fletching has already begun correcting the arrow's flight, right in the midst of its natural wallowing or fishtailing. At about a dozen yards, the fletching has corrected and straightened the arrow's flight; the energy is well distributed in the shaft.

Any imperfection in the initial launch of the arrow, however small—shooting with fingers, sloppy release, a poorly tuned bow, twisting (called "torquing") the riser—will cause the arrow to flex, even leave the string a bit crooked. As air flows over the fletching, causing drag during flight, this gradually self-corrects, because the arrow rotates around a center of pressure and spins and stabilizes. That "center of pressure" is the point along the shaft where aerodynamic forces are balanced.

Fletching steers best when the center of pressure is farther behind the center of gravity and when it has a long way to fly.

If the center of gravity and center of pressure are too close together, or worse, if the center of gravity is behind the center of pressure—if the arrow is tail-heavy—the arrow will become unstable. As an example, try to throw an arrow backwards. It does not work very well.

For best penetration, a larger FOC value is needed. Hunters want a higher FOC so that as the broadhead enters the game, the distance from the front of the arrow to the center of gravity is lower, making it more difficult for the arrow to flex or deflect. Any flex or deflection of the shaft upon entry means that energy is being lost or expended somewhere other than directly along the center of the shaft, lessening overall penetration.

A larger FOC is best for long-distance shots where crosswinds affect flight. The same applies to shooting broadheads, because the larger surface area of a broadhead is more greatly affected by launch imperfections as well as crosswinds. Broadheads move the center of pressure closer to the point and tend to steer an arrow (which can sometimes have a negative affect that the fletching must fight to overcome).

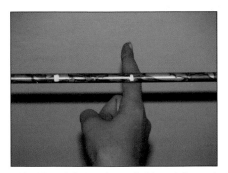 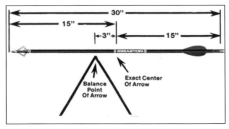

FOC. FOC stands for Front (Forward) of Center balance point. This measurement results from the relative weights of the components used in the arrow: shaft, insert, head, fletching, and nock. It is generally agreed that the optimal FOC percentage balance for an arrow is 7 to 15 percent and is easy to measure.

Calculate your arrow's FOC like this:

1) Measure the length of the shaft from the throat of the nock to the end of the shaft, excluding the insert. This will be your length, *L*.

2) Using a sharp or a narrow edge, balance the arrow (with the point attached) and mark the balance point.

3) Measure the distance from the throat of the nock to the balance point. This will be the length *B*.

4) Input *B* and *L* into the following formula: FOC% = (B/L − 0.5) x 100.

Recommended values for FOC vary depending on the application. Target arrows (field and practice points) ought to be in the 8 to 11 percent range, hunting or broadhead-tipped arrows a little higher, perhaps in the 10 to 15 percent range. Olympic and longer-distance shooters will often aim for a 12 percent FOC, even though they are using field points, because of the long distances involved, out to ninety meters for men, seventy meters for women (women typically shoot a bit lighter draw-weight bows).

Note, however, that some traditional shooters with heavier broadheads—sometimes very heavy broadheads like the ginormous 315-grain Ashby Nanook—and larger sets of fletching than is needed for compound bow shooting, set up for a much larger FOC, what they call EFOC or Extreme FOC. With a heavy bow, an FOC of 25 to 30 percent might enhance penetration on very large game animals, but this is probably not a formula for shots beyond forty yards—perhaps not even thirty yards, depending on your set-up. Experiment with this at your shooting range before making a decision.

PRACTICE POINTS

A practice tip, like the ubiquitous field point, is simply a metal tip for your arrow. Reliable. No surprises. Unexciting, like dating the next-door neighbor you have known all your life. And yet there is a need for such a point—and there are several minor variations in style—because it flies true, with little wind planing. Practice tips, whether target or field points, are cheap and pull cleanly out of targets. In effect, they are indispensable, and over the course of your archery career this is probably the point you will shoot the most. It won't even be close for blunts and broadheads and other types of points.

The trick with practice points, whether they glue on the wooden shaft or screw into a lightweight metal insert, itself glued into the carbon (or aluminum) shaft, is that you want them to weigh the same. You want, in fact, each arrow to weigh as close to each other arrow as possible. If your arrows are structurally identical you remove one factor in errant flight and erratic point of impact. They won't ever be exact, of course—feathers absorb moisture despite dusting with a desiccant powder, arrows are dinged, heads are scratched—but tinker with them until they are close. If your arrows are 100 grains apart in weight, get to work; if they are ten grains, ignore the difference and concentrate on your shooting form—a clean string release, for instance.

Close in weight at the tip, especially, means one crucial archery flight consideration is overcome.

BLUNTS—NOT THE CIGARS

In the old days, a blunt might simply have been the brass casing of a handgun cartridge glued over the end of an arrow. That works, but not everyone has a handgun or an empty shell casing, and even then it might not be the right size.

Manufacturers stepped into the void quite a while ago, because using blunt-tipped arrows for what was formerly called "roving" was very popular. Roving was simply taking your recurve or longbow and blunt arrows—remember that an arrow has to be tipped or it may shatter or bend on impact with a hard surface—and wandering through fields and forests shooting at stumps or rocks or flowers or even small game. It was fun. It was harmless. It was often a social event with friends. The blunt delivered high-impact energy, stunning without penetrating, but roving was doomed . . . at least in the heavily populated eastern United States.

Blunt. A heavy plastic blunt designed to screw into an arrow for use hunting small game or in recreational shooting.

The advent of the compound bow in roughly 1970 coincided with a lot of social and economic conditions that put an end to that archery pastime. Landowners became increasingly passionate about nailing "No Trespassing" signs to fences and trees, perhaps concerned about lawsuits should anything at all happen to archers or gun hunters while on their property. Urban sprawl had also begun to limit available land, both for archery and for gun hunting, and governmental jurisdictions, at least east of the Mississippi River, began to frown on the roving, closing vast tracts to men and women who formerly went into the field for fun. Thus the need for blunt-tipped arrows declined.

As people in the United States lost the opportunity to wander their neighborhoods with bows and arrows or BB guns, with those neighborhoods becoming increasingly civilized, the casual use of blunts became more of a pastime for specialized target shooting inside or in the backyards of archers. The other option was small-game hunting.

A popular blunt was invented by the Zwickeys in the seventies and was named the Judo Point. It solved a problem with roving, which was that spent arrows were often hard to find. They passed through worn sections of hay bales or targets and scooted into the weeds and under the grass, often becoming invisible. It was common to see archers take their shoes off and "feel" the grass with their feet as they walked, hoping to discover the shaft they could not see with the naked eye. Obviously, this was problematic and was out of the question in areas where sandspurs grew or if one was shooting broadheads.

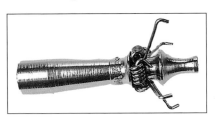

Judo! The unlosable Judo point, with springy wires on each side, was designed to deliver a strong punch to small game and yet avoid the frustrating tendency of arrows tipped with field points to become lost when they zoomed into the grass. Often imitated, the Judo has proven its usefulness to several generations of archers.

The Judo Point was a stylized head that had wire twisted around it in the shape of spring arms. The wires extended out the side, and it was small enough that at relatively short distances for small-game hunting or field shooting, it flew quite well and could deliver a lethal punch to a rabbit or squirrel. Most significant, however, the tips of the wires would catch on grass and the arrow would flip up, making it much easier to find. In fact, they were marketed as "the Unlosable Miracle Point." Judos were cheap, effective, and are still in the quiver of every archer, though now they are available in a variety of weights for different set-ups.

CUTTING TO THE CHASE—BROADHEADS

The earliest archers were content with flaked stone heads. And why not? They worked. At some point, however, as the population increased; as individuals adopted permanent specialized roles: farmers, bakers, weavers, and a plague of warriors; as metal tools became more common, pre-fabricated metal arrowheads began to replace the individually produced stone heads. It must have been due to the decline of big-game populations as human populations spread and to the rise of mass warfare. Armies in the tens of thousands required weapons in the tens of thousands and a single archer might shoot dozens of heads in a battle.

Whatever the reason, heads of bronze and iron were the classic tips of arrows and they could be adapted to a wide variety of purposes. Heavy iron tips sometimes

132

referred to as bodkins were ideal for punching through lightweight armor and the heavy padding used by those who could not afford the highest grades of steel plate. Bodkins were used in conjunction with the wider broadhead, sometimes with specially hardened edges. The broadheads were more often used against lightly armored men or light cavalry than against a heavily armored adversary. Inventive in the ways of war, men even developed wide, sharpened heads shaped in the form of a crescent moon and shot them to cut the rigging of wooden ships.

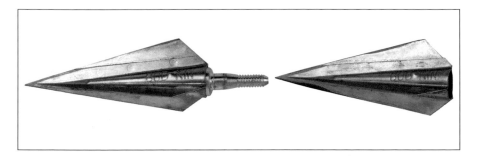

Bodkin. *The ancient bodkin point arrowhead was useful when fired at men in light armor. It is questionable whether or not it would punch through expensive armor plate worn by the noblemen of the Middle Ages. The modern bodkin point is much less aerodynamic, its three sharp blades designed mainly to penetrate big game, causing profuse bleeding and rapid expiration.*

Eventually, as firearms developed, archery languished. Indeed, it almost disappeared, although numerous small cultures persisted in using the bow and arrow in their survival arsenal well into the twentieth century. When archery began to emerge from its long slumbers, the single-piece broadhead was the style everyone used for hunting. The style was almost infinitely varied in blade angle—both of the blade itself and the angle of the sharpened edge—width of the blade cut, whether or not it carried a detachable "Bleeder Blade," and, of course, weight.

With the rise of the compound bow in the seventies, though, and the spread of new materials and new opportunities for commerce, the archery industry in the United States flourished. Dozens of individuals began experimenting with heads. Eventually this led to the idea that continual sharpening could be eliminated—enthusiasts argued that the average archer probably did more dulling than sharpening when he sat down to hone broadheads with a file—if pre-sharpened blades direct from the factory were used. These blades were readily available and relatively cheap from manufacturers of replaceable blades for safety razors. The application transferred directly from shaving to hunting. Once blades became dull, they could simply be removed from the ferrule, thrown away, and replaced with new, sharp blades. Hence the term "replaceable blade head" to contrast with the older "fixed blade head."

Following the success of Duke Savora and a few other inspired men, dozens of broadhead patterns flooded onto the market. The "rise of the broadhead" initiated wonderful and never-ending arguments among archers, such as which style head is better for hunting—those with blades that extend to the tip (called cut-on-contact) or those with a tough, pointed tip (called punch-cut). (The cutting tip has a very slight advantage.)

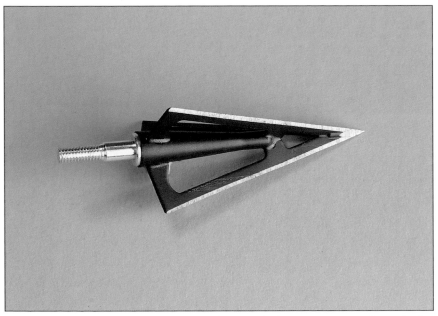

Snuffer. Snuffer three-blade broadheads come in four sizes for traditional archers: 125-, 150-, 175-, and 185-grains. They offer file-sharp, cut-on-contact penetration that puts big holes through big game. Snuffers fit all carbon and all aluminum arrows; the head is also available as a glue-on for wood shafts.

By the late eighties, archers were seriously experimenting with mechanical heads. A mechanical head is a broadhead that flies with its blades folded into the ferrule. This minimizes wind planing because the blades of the head, which act like small wings, are tucked away prior to impact. Upon striking a target, blades deploy to their full extent and, in theory, penetrate as well as any fixed-blade broadhead because they have saved energy in flight for penetration.

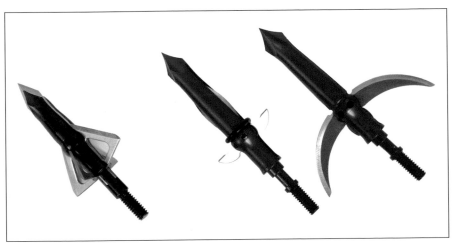

Broadheads. *The modern hunting broadhead comes in two basic styles: fixed and mechanical. The fixed-blade head on the left has four replaceable blades and a cut-on-contact tip. The mechanical broadhead on the right—shown closed for flight and open for penetration—has a chisel tip and two blades and presents a much lower flight profile for wind planing. In theory, it will fly with greater accuracy because its tucked-away blades cause less friction in the air.*

The early generation mechanical heads were heavily criticized, perhaps correctly, because they sometimes did not open when they hit a target, especially a distant target where the arrow had lost a lot of kinetic energy. At times, the arrows were recovered only to find that only one blade had deployed or with blades snapped off, perhaps from hitting bone or even a branch on their flight toward a deer. By and large, present-day mechanicals are so well designed and constructed that they overcome these objections, and they are certainly suitable for traditional shooting, though very few recurve or longbow enthusiasts use them.

OPTIONS

A huge range of broadhead options is available today. In any mass merchant or sporting goods store that sells hunting supplies, you can purchase heads with sharp, cutting edges on both sides of the blade so that if an animal tries to pull an arrow from a failed pass-through shot, the blade cuts as it comes out. There are heads with two, three, and four blades; heads with blades inserted straight and heads with blades that are slightly offset to promote rotational stability; mechanical heads with blades that open front-to-back and others that open back-to-front. Numerous styles differentiate their mechanical mechanisms by using small rubber "O-rings," which snap on impact and allow the blades to open and penetrate at their widest angle. For bowhunters, a complete pass-through arrow allows blood to leak or spurt out of holes on both sides of a game animal. This makes a hunter's visual trail, the blood trail, easier to follow, and quick recovery of the animal is practically certain. (Conversely, a minority of hunters argue that an arrow should remain inside a big-game animal where it will continue to cut as the animal runs. This would surely promote additional cutting and bleeding.)

All of these arguments are interesting because of the way an arrow kills—and if you are not interested in hunting, skip right by the next few paragraphs. An arrow hitting a deer will slice inward with great, though rapidly diminishing, power. A deer or a bear hit hard by a broadhead-tipped arrow dies from blood loss, from hemorrhage. Blood pressure falls, less oxygen circulates into the vital organs (heart and brain), the lungs may fill with blood, and the animal collapses. In a sense, it is the same as the bite of a tiger or a shark. Such a collapse and final kick may take only a few seconds or it may take several minutes, in which case the archer may attempt—without spooking his prey—to hit it with a second arrow, ensuring that it dies quickly, with the least amount of suffering. Animals in North America—indeed, most of the world—collapse quickly, often in less than a minute, after being hit hard by an arrow in the vitals. A very large animal, an elephant or a hippopotamus, for example, may take several hours to expire due to their sheer size and, hence, the volume of blood. (An adult African elephant has about 100 times the amount of blood as an adult human, roughly 450 liters to 4.5 liters.)

An arrow cuts, unlike a gunshot wound, which is technically referred to—perhaps to keep the gory details at arm's length—as "ballistic trauma." The immediate damaging effect of a high-power bullet is typically bleeding, and with it the potential for what is known as "hypovolemic shock" from inadequate delivery of oxygen to vital organs. Not only is there usually significant blood loss, but gunshot wounds typically involve a large degree of nearby tissue destruction due to the physical disruption of the projectile.

A gunshot also produces hydrostatic or hydraulic shock. This phenomenon produces remote wounding and incapacitating effects in living targets through a hydraulic effect in their liquid-filled tissues, in addition to the local effects in tissue from direct impact. There is scientific evidence that hydrostatic shock can even produce remote neural damage and produce incapacitation more quickly than blood-loss effects. Human autopsy results have demonstrated brain hemorrhaging that was apparently caused by a fatal gunshot to the chest.

Hence the difference between the arrow's cut and the bullet's shock. An arrow traveling at 250 fps may crack a rib or even a leg bone, but it kills by causing hemorrhage. The effects of a bullet traveling at 2,500 fps are much wider in scope, and this can be seen in high-speed photos demonstrating the effects and penetration into ballistic gelatin. Many bowhunters have described deer shivering when an arrow passes through their body; then continuing to munch on acorns or Virginia creeper for ten or fifteen seconds until they suddenly collapse, kick once, and lie still.

Other discussions you will hear regarding hunting broadheads are about how sharp they must be or what kind of steel is best or even what the proper blade angle should be. Many archers believe that blades must be "razor sharp," or as sharp as they can possibly make them, and will demonstrate by shaving hair from their forearms.

Other archers, now in the minority, but clustered in the camp of traditional shooting, suggest that blades must be sharp, but also need a rugged and even a slightly ragged edge to cut properly through hair and hide, but leaving a wound that does not easily close and seal. They note that famous successful archers of the past used files to sharpen their arrows, perhaps finishing the edges with a few whacks with a ceramic stick or leather strop. Depending on the blade angle, modern three-blade heads can be drawn across several grits of sandpaper and then polished with a counter stroke of steel wool to remove any loose and jagged edges.

SO, WHAT IS TRADITIONAL?

On the one hand, what you define as traditional and for your enjoyment need only satisfy you. On the other hand, we recognize the power and the pressure of our social group. Thus, most traditional shooters of longbows and recurves rely on wide, heavy, fixed heads with two blades. These heads are occasionally designed to carry a smaller sideways-sitting "bleeder blade." The bleeder in a head, such as the traditional Bear Razorhead, provides a slight perpendicular cut and is so small that it is not affected by wind. (Never shoot into a target with a removable bleeder blade in the head. The bleeder blade will inevitably fall out or break inside the target and cause problems for some unlucky archer at a later date. Shooting into fixed or foam targets, the bleeder will contribute to the early demise of the target without contributing in any positive manner to your performance, and they are banned from competition shooting.)

Many in the traditional hunting camp believe that single-bevel broadheads are by far the best choice for longbows and recurves. Unlike standard double-bevel heads of any size or style (fixed, mechanical, or replaceable blade), a single-bevel head is sharpened only on one side of a blade; and these heads only come in traditional two-blade styling.

Dr. Ed Ashby has studied broadhead effectiveness for years and believes the single-bevel head style is superior because it continues to twist or rotate even after penetration. He claims this is an advantage if the blade hits bone and, upon dissecting his own hits, claims that a heavy single-bevel head has a "clearly noticeable increase in tissue damage over a double-bevel head." Ashby's single-bevel heads may weigh up to an astonishing 315 grains. For extreme big game—elephant, water buffalo, or hippo—this requires a push from a heavy bow and an arrow that is easily twice as heavy as a conventional arrow, more than 1,000 grains.

The Single-Bevel Head. What is the best edge for a broadhead? A standard V- or saber-grind, sharpened on both sides, is sharp and durable. The single-bevel head, however, has many adherents in the traditional community.

A chisel-ground blade has only one side ground down. The other side is flat. Culinary knives from Japan often feature this grind, and they are considered sharper than the V-grind. These knives, and chisel-ground broadheads, come in left- and right-hand versions.

Todd Smith of Alaska Bowhunting Supply sells predominantly to traditional bowhunters. Big heads on heavy arrows have arcing trajectories but carry lots of kinetic energy (and momentum).

"The solid one-piece forged Ashby single-bevel broadheads," Smith says, "are amazing, especially for the biggest of the big game. We have taken literally dozens of Cape buffalo, Asiatic buffalo, several hippo, and probably fifteen to twenty elephant so far with it. These heavy, single-bevel heads are tempered to 58 Rockwell so they will not bend or curl. The edges of single-bevel broadheads must not curl or they lose the leverage they need to split the biggest bones."

You will treasure a wide, heavy, fixed blade head because it completes the traditional arrow. Looking at the arrow from nock forward, the sharp head or field point is the last element in the required shooting equation. Now you have the important items. Everything else is just talk . . .

A STRAIGHT-SHOOTING NOTE

It is easy to make sure your arrows are straight and balanced, and that your components—inserts, nock, fletching and broadhead—are in line with the centerline of the shaft. The old way, which you will still see at bowhunter gatherings, was to place the tip on your thumbnail; while holding the shaft upright between the thumb and middle finger on the opposite hand, blow on the feathers and watch for arrow wobble. Sometimes that worked and sometimes it didn't because so many things affect an arrow's straightness: a tiny deviation as you build the arrow, gluing in (or on) nocks and inserts, deflecting off a branch during a shot, or pulling it out of a target at a slight angle.

The better way to check straightness is with a tool, such as the Arrow Inspector from Pine Ridge Archery. With low-friction, precision-cut steel axles and aluminum wheels,

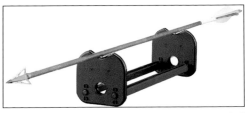

Arrow Checker. The Arrow Inspector is a precision instrument built to a simple design that will help ensure smooth and accurate arrow flight. If they don't spin right, without any detectable wobble, they won't fly right! The Arrow Inspector will check arrow shaft straightness, broadhead balance and straightness, nock alignment, and vane and feather balance. It features low-friction, machine-cut steel axles and precision-cut aluminum wheels to detect even the slightest bend in an arrow shaft or unbalanced arrow.

the Arrow Inspector detects even the slightest bend in an arrow shaft or an unbalanced arrow. It's cheap and easy to use. Place your arrow on the wheels and give it a spin. If the shaft is bent, it will come to a stop and then roll backwards a little. If any part of the arrow appears to wobble, it isn't straight and won't fly straight. This is your chance to fix it before a tournament or before a weekend hunt.

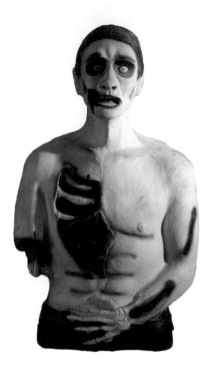

Practice, Practice, Practice! *Thus, a long-lasting foam target such as Undead Fred from Delta (about $75) will keep traditional archers in practice and is also a fun target to shoot . . . especially in preparation for the Zombie Apocalypse!*

CHAPTER FIVE

THE MECHANICS OF SHOOTING

Archery is a highly individual activity. It is not a team sport, although you can join a team or shoot in leagues, and international competition features both individual and team events. But the act of shooting a bow and hitting your target is entirely personal. You can hire a coach and take instruction (that is, in fact, recommended, especially if you aspire to better-than-average shooting), but when it comes to releasing an arrow, it is only you, yourself, on the line alone. This is why we have said that archery is about you, and only you.

Performing at your best, hitting the target, requires that you have equipment that is matched specifically to your personal taste, your body style, and your comfort level.

Many novice archers start with hand-me-down bows or equipment that is "just like Dad's." Good shooting gear certainly is not cheap, but unlike a .22 rifle, for instance, which can be passed down the generations or around the club and shot successfully by dozens of people if they tweak the sights a little, a bow-and-arrow set-up has to be matched to you personally: to your dominant eye, to your draw length or how far you will pull the string, and then to your preferred draw weight, which is a function of your strength and the bow's design.

YOUR DOMINANT EYE

Bows are built to fit right-handed or left-handed individuals, but your choice of a shooting instrument could be based on eye dominance . . . not, it will surprise you to learn, on hand dominance. Just as we write, brush our teeth, or eat with a fork right-handed or left-handed, we also have a dominant eye, sometimes called our master eye. For most of us, hand and eye dominance are the same—a left-handed person will be left-eye dominant—but sometimes a right-handed person will have a dominant left eye or vice versa. This issue applies equally to traditional and modern shooters.

There are two ways to determine your dominant eye.

METHOD ONE

With both eyes open, point your index finger at a distant object. Now, close your left eye. If your finger still appears to be pointing at the object, you most certainly have a dominant right eye. If your finger appears to shift to the side when you close your left eye, you probably have a dominant left eye. For confirmation, point again with both eyes open and then close your right eye. If, when you are looking with your left eye only, your finger still points at the object, you can feel certain that your left eye is dominant.

METHOD TWO

An optional method which some people find less optically confusing uses both hands at the same time. First, place your hands together at arm's length from your eyes, palms facing out so you are viewing the backs of your hands. Now, touch the tips of your thumbs and forefingers and swivel your hands together so that the "V" between your thumbs and your forefingers forms a hole. Pick out some object on the far side of the room and center it in the hole. Slowly move your hands together so the hole becomes smaller and smaller and, while you are doing this, bring your hands—and the hole—back to your face. You should end up with the hole circumscribed by your hands in front of your dominant eye.

Your Dominant Eye. Demonstrating Method Two, this will help determine which of your eyes is dominant. Finding out which eye is dominant is crucial for successful shooting.

Hand-eye coordination is simplified if your dominant eye matches your dominant hand. If this is the case, simply choose a bow configured for your dominant side. For example, a right-handed person with a dominant right eye will choose a right-handed bow: you will grip the bow with your left hand and, with your right hand, pull the string back to your right or master eye. Vice versa for a lefty.

If your hand and eye dominance are mismatched however, you should select a bow based on eye dominance rather than hand dominance. A right-hander will almost certainly feel awkward at first, shooting a left-handed bow, but in the long run, you will shoot better and more comfortably this way.

Most successful archers sight with their dominant eye. Hand dominance in archery is simply performing the manual operations called for by the brain. This allows aiming with both eyes open, which allows better depth perception for distance estimation and a better "feel" for the shot. To aim with your weaker eye, you need to close or cover your dominant eye.

STEPS IN LEARNING TO SHOOT

The steps in shooting well, hitting your target consistently, and having fun at it are essentially the same whichever bow you choose to shoot . . . to a point.

STANCE

Begin by facing your target and then turning your feet to one side, some say as much as forty-five degrees: counterclockwise or right shoulder back for a right-hander and clockwise or left shoulder back for a left-hander. This is the classic open stance. It offers several practical advantages both for hunting and competition. First, it helps move the bow and string slightly away from your arm and chest. This is doubly important because a few slaps of the string on your bare forearm can be enough to make a strong man squeal with pain. Second, if you are layering or wearing a down jacket on a cold day, the string is less likely to hang up on your clothes. If it does hang up on the zipper or some fold of clothing, you will not hit what you are aiming at.

The open stance allows hunting archers to shoot down from their tree stand without bumping their leg against the bow's lower limb. The limb will naturally bend between your knees no matter how steep your shot angle becomes.

Traditional shooters, especially those shooting heavy bows, typically find themselves gravitating toward a more closed stance. This gives them more power by aligning the bones, muscles, and joints with the pull of the string, but it has the disadvantage of bringing the bowstring close to your chest and clothing. A chest protector is sometimes worn by women or by either sex if they have difficulty with string clearance.

GRIP

How you pick up the bow is important every time you shoot. Recognize that this stick is going to come alive in your hands, moving from a state of passivity to become an active partner in making a good shot.

Bows have different cross sections at the grip area, and traditional bows, especially, have more or less configuration, curvature, and bulk. The most common way to grip the bow is a *low-wrist grip,* and archers with all bows use it because it aligns the strength, the bones and muscles, of your hand, wrist, and arm behind your draw. A low-wrist grip lets your whole hand, the web of thumb to the heel, brace the bow steadily as you draw. The flat grip of a longbow is especially suitable for a low wrist grip.

Most recurves, however, have a differently sculptured grip area. Lay a recurve side by side with a longbow and you notice that the recurve handle is stylishly curved. This is much more accommodating for the medium- or even the high-wrist grip, which spots the pressure in the web between the thumb and forefinger. Here, the palm of the hand points down and the wrist rises.

The *high-wrist grip* is preferred by international FITA competitors. They say this hold turns the four inches of palm pressure on the bow grip into possibly an inch of contact, thus moving from area pressure to point pressure. The valley between the thumb and forefinger thus acts like a pivot point that cannot impart torque to the bow. These archers also wear wrist slings and learn to let the bow to leap forward after a shot.

Whether you choose a higher or lower grip style is not as important as that you are consistent, gripping the bow exactly the same for every shot whether you are kneeling behind a rock in a cold drizzle or standing on the target line in a public park. It's called habit or muscle memory.

Because the bow comes to life in your hand and will tend to move of its own volition as you place an arrow on the rest, draw, and shoot, the tendency will be to grip it tightly. After all, you don't want to lose control. But imagine that you are holding a child's arm in traffic. Keep a firm control, but not so much that your hand twists the bow. Twisting the bow applies torque, it rotates the riser, and it causes the string to move in a circle. Pick up your bow at the grip and hold it lightly in your bow hand—now squeeze it hard. A right-handed shooter will be able to see the bow twist, usually clockwise. This twist will be transferred through the string to your arrow and throw it off course.

The bow knows. When you pull, it wants to slip out of your hand and hit you in the face. When you release the string, it wants to jump forward, especially in the tip area.

Your job is to recall the child's arm in traffic. Grip tightly enough to maintain control but not so tightly that you have a death grip on the bow. Recognize that when the bow comes alive with energy, it has a mind of its own, but remember who the adult is—control with love.

Canting the Bow. *Most traditional shooters—other than international FITA competitors—cant the bow slightly when they draw. If you hold your bow arm out in front without correcting or twisting for its natural "lean," you will find that your grip is not vertical. Thus canting the bow helps the arrow stay on the rest or shelf and gives the shooter a natural stance.*

SHOULD YOU USE A BOW SLING?

When you release the string, the bow will naturally jump forward. Because its stored energy is released and directional, it wants to follow the path of the arrow. There is nothing especially wrong with this except that a lot of archers hold the riser too tightly, so afraid are they of losing control and dropping the bow. (It may be heresy to say so, especially if you have paid a thousand dollars or so for a custom bow, but dropping your bow, unless it is into a fire or over a cliff, is probably not going to hurt anything. Attend enough tournaments or visit enough hunting camps and you will eventually see a well-known champion throw their bow in disgust at making a poor shot. A bow is more delicate than a golf club, but all in all, it is a robust tool and can take a bit of abuse. A bit. And the champion's poor shot—hint—it wasn't the bow's fault.)

Many archers, though not longbow shooters, use a bow sling to help control the bow following the shot. The theory of the sling is that by gripping the bow, even lightly, you impart torque to it (twist it), and this is somehow transferred magically to the arrow and thus throws the arrow off course. Perhaps the magic happens if fletching hits the riser. Perhaps it is all a bit of a myth . . .

If you are shooting a lightweight competition recurve, a bow sling perhaps makes sense. Styles vary from full wrap-around slings, which are anchored in the stabilizer bushing on the back of the bow, to very lightweight finger slings that loop around your thumb—which is on one side of the riser—and around the index or middle finger on the opposite side of the bow. With a sling, you will be able to use a fully relaxed grip and allow the bow to move naturally. When it jumps forward, it will encounter the sling and the tip will rock forward and down, but the bow will remain in your hand.

Experimenting with a sling makes sense, but it is one of those sly elements in archery that is more of a mental buffer than a true, practical aid. If you end up bowhunting, moving through the brush or hunting from a tree stand, a sling will quickly become a nuisance, something unnecessary to worry about when a big deer suddenly walks into your shooting lane. In competition, when you have time to relax and consider the distance and think about your shooting form and sip from your Gatorade and take a deep, relaxing breath, fine. Otherwise a bow sling is simply a bother and it would be best to avoid it. Simplify. Grip your bow lightly but securely, practice, and have fun. And if you do drop it, pick it up, wipe it off, and shoot again.

DRAWING THE STRING

It may seem that no explanation is necessary for drawing the string, but ask your piano instructor if hand position above the keys is important; ask a batting coach about stance in the batter's box and gripping the bat. Archery is no different. Small things matter.

MEDITERRANEAN

The Mediterranean draw is most common in Europe and America. It is the standard way to pull the string when shooting FITA or Olympic archery, too. With this draw style, the index finger wraps around the string above the arrow while the middle and ring fingers wrap around below the arrow. With the nock on the back end of the arrow snugged against the nock point and held between the fingers, you have a stable pull. The string rests in the first crease of the three fingers.

When you draw, technically with the muscles of the back rather than the arm, the hand and wrist should remain relatively flat. The idea is not to make a fist. Let your hand become a hook, it's only influence being to draw the string straight back and then to let go with the fingers at precisely the same time so that the string moves straight forward. Of course, we know that, propelled by the energy stored in the system, the string moves very rapidly, faster than the fingers, and so makes a bit of a loop around the fingertips. Your job as an archer is to minimize that rotational or circular movement of the string.

After you have shot a while, you may discover that you are holding the string less in the deep crease and more out on the fingertips. This is fine, because the idea is to obtain as close to an instantaneous release as possible, smooth, without jerking backward. Simply opening your fingers. Of course, you want to settle into one consistent spot, not move around on the fingertips.

Variations of the Mediterranean draw might be two or three fingers under; three-under is popular among traditional shooters. This brings the arrow closer to the eye, facilitating "point of aim" and instinctive shooting, and it allows the archer to use what is called the "string walking" aiming technique. This might actually allow for a cleaner release, although the pressures are different.

OTHER WAYS TO DRAW

The pinch draw grasps or squeezes the end of the arrow between the thumb and index finger. It is an easy method for young people who are starting on very lightweight bows. The release is clean because at some point the force of the bow overcomes the tight pinch of the fingers and the arrow is loosed. Although this draw method dates back thousands of years, it only works with very lightweight bows (or a person with very strong fingers).

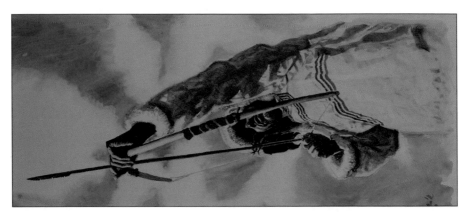

Pinching the String. There are several different ways of drawing a bowstring. The pinch draw squeezes the end of the arrow between the thumb and index finger. Most people use this draw naturally when they begin shooting. The release is clean because when the pull reaches a certain point, friction can no longer hold the arrow. This release prevents the drawing of a stiff bow, though, unless the archer possesses great strength in the fingers. It was widespread in traditional archery; the arrow may be placed on either side of the bow. (© Libor Balak, Antropark, Czech Republic: with permission)

A variation is to pinch the arrow between the thumb and the bent forefinger, sometimes wrapping the forefinger around the string along with the middle and ring fingers. One of the enjoyable aspects of archery is to read such details, understand that such a draw method appears in early Assyrian reliefs and perhaps on Greek pottery, and then try to imitate it in the backyard. It's a personal connection with history, because in reality, some of those men and women were your ancestors.

The Mongolian or thumb draw uses only the thumb, the strongest single digit, to grasp the string. Around the back of the thumb, the index and even the middle fingers reinforce the grip. The thumb draw is traditional across Asia and the horse cultures, from the end of the forests and across the barren steppes to the Pacific Ocean. Ishi, the last of the Yana Indians in California, used this string hold on the short bows he made, and so it was widespread in the Americas as well.

The Positive Anchor. *Khatuna Lorig shows a positive anchor—tip of nose, lips, chin—while shooting for the US team at the London Olympics. (Photo courtesy of Archery Trade Association)*

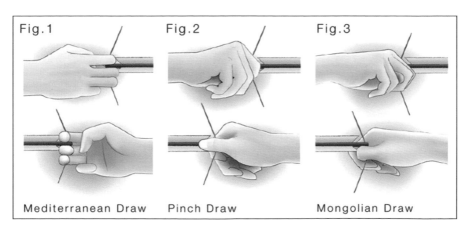

Main Methods of Drawing Bows. *Three methods of gripping the string and drawing the bow.*

PROTECTING THE DRAW

A tough hand probably means a tough man, and he can pull the string with an effort denied to most of us. Pulling it repeatedly, however, calls for some protection for the delicate fingers drawing the string back, no matter how strong you are. You need a glove or tab not only to protect your fingers, but also because they allow you to release the string smoothly.

For the Mediterranean draw, the fingers may be protected with shooting gloves or by finger tabs. A shooting glove is a three-fingered glove that goes on the string or primary hand of the shooter. Models range from full-finger leather to gloves that only cover the tips of the fingers. Today these gloves are used mostly by traditional and bare-bow shooters. (Twenty years ago, before engineers became so obsessed with hyper-fast, hyper-powerful bows—when, you might truly say, archery was more fun—compound shooters often used them.)

Finger tabs are pieces of material, now often layered, that are attached via leather straps or holes to the middle finger. Professional and FITA shooters use elaborate tabs that include metal ledges to touch a spot on their jaw or cheek, but for newbies, a plain, multilayer tab made of leather with a cushioning rubber layer is simple, cheap, and still highly effective protection for the fingers.

Thumb rings or leather thumb tabs are used by archers practicing the Mongolian release. Most of them cover and protect the skin of the thumb only. The Japanese *yugake* is a reinforced glove with a special ridge that holds the string.

A note about mechanical releases. Don't. A release aid is designed within the scope of forces of modern compound bows. It improves the shooting of a modern archer, but it may very well cause a traditional bow to shatter. The smooth and instantaneous ease with which it releases the string neither works in concept nor in theory with traditional shooting. Admire the modern release aid but stay away from it. Besides, release aids are not allowed in a traditional shooting environment.

TARGET PANIC AND SNAP SHOOTING

Everyone gets the flu at some time in their lives. You cough; you sneeze; you run a fever; you can't carry on. To archers, regardless of the bow they shoot or the game they play, the flu is called "target panic."

Perhaps it is not literally true that "everyone gets it." Like "writer's block," target panic is a result of pressure to achieve. It is a natural psychological problem. Bowhunters who are serious about taking big game get it. Olympic archers get it. It was almost assuredly a problem for hunters in millennia past when they faced, at relatively close distance, the Irish elk or a snorting bison. They locked up.

Target panic is a shooting problem, a problem with the brain coming between the hand and the eye. At Civil War battlefields, many men facing extreme fear, if not outright panic, double and triple loaded their black powder muskets, leading to devastating explosions when they finally did pull the trigger. That was a variety of target panic. The second baseman (the New York Yankees' Chuck Knoblauch) who suddenly cannot make the throw to first base, the tour professional who cannot sink a short putt (Ben Hogan or Lee Trevino), or the basketball star (Shaquille O'Neal) who cannot sink a free throw—they all had a variety of this common syndrome and it is no respecter of sex: men and women suffer equally.

The result of target panic can be curious and maddening. Some have difficulty releasing the arrow at all, begin to shake, and ultimately shoot wild. Others release as soon as they see the target without aiming.

The first sign of target panic may be anxiety and denial, blaming the equipment. An archer can't release the string properly. He blames the bow or the arrow or the mother-in-law. She twitches endlessly, shuffles at the target line, or hesitates when the shot is clear.

And the problem with target panic—other than the fact that it is a universal affliction—is that it recurs. Just when you think you have it under control, bingo! It comes back.

Some sports psychologists believe that target panic is actually a neurological disorder known as focal dystonia. Musicians are apparently prone to the disorder. It's an affliction caused—or so it is believed—when the neurons that guide a particular repetitive movement become worn from overuse. Sort of a psychosomatic repetitive motion syndrome. As if the body says, "I've done this so often, I'm sick of it."

Neurological or psychological, target panic feeds on itself. The more it manifests and you worry about it, the more it manifests . . . and the more you worry. Of course, perhaps the words themselves are to blame. Perhaps if it were only "target concern" or "target worry," it would not be as severe.

So, if you get it—and target worry is not usually a difficulty for novices—what do you do?

Several options are available to cure target panic, although in truth, it may be more akin to an illness that can't be "cured," only managed. Archers are no different than any temperamental or high-strung athlete who will go to great lengths to change equipment or change style or grip if they believe doing so may help them shoot even 1 percent better. They will turn to positive reinforcement and creative visualization or meditate and practice square breathing. Some look for an archery coach, either a professional or a mentor whom they admire. Others remove the aiming points from their practice target and begin to rehearse the basics, simply shooting into a blank target.

If you find that you are suddenly having trouble staying focused or are perhaps snap shooting, the important concept to keep in mind is that this is natural. Since the dawn of the bow and arrow, archers have experienced it. You can overcome it and be successful. So relax, breathe, and work through it.

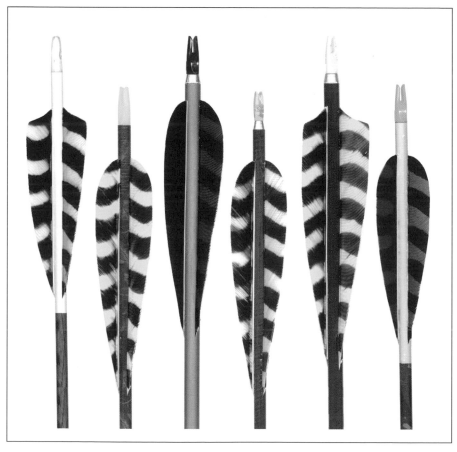

Use Feathers. Traditional shooting with the longbow or recurve requires that your arrows be fletched with feathers. Feathers are much more forgiving of an imperfect release.

Snap shooters are most commonly traditional archers. Snap shooters release the bowstring early, before they get to full draw. It is a form of target panic, perhaps caused by the dramatically increasing weight of the bow and the registration of this strain in the muscles of your arms, back, and, eventually, the sensory triggers in your brain.

The problem with snap shooting is that the arrow, not being fully drawn, does not have a chance to be aimed well, not even for a split second. Accuracy suffers and the arrow does not have a chance to absorb all of the kinetic energy it would absorb if pulled to full draw. The result is often poor arrow flight and poor penetration. Successful snap-shooting archers like the famous Fred Bear just learn to compensate through a great deal of practice, some good luck, and, occasionally, a guide behind them with a high-power rifle.

THE FORCE-DRAW CURVE

Remember that a force-draw curve is a two-dimensional graph that plots a bow's draw weight or force in pounds on the Y or vertical axis against its draw length in inches (inches in the United States but perhaps centimeters in Europe) on the X or horizontal axis. It is measured at regular intervals, usually every one or two inches, for the entire draw stroke of the bow.

Unlike compound bows, which have let-off, some of them as much as 85 percent, neither recurves nor longbows have cams. Consequently, their force-draw curve is a curving line rising at something like a forty-five degree angle, rather than a bell curve. The gently curving line means that the more pressure or strength you exert, the greater the weight you hold, and the greater the effort required to draw your bow further; it is a compounding process.

All bows are not created equal. With a typical sixty-pound, 65 percent let-off compound bow, you reach peak weight about halfway through the draw; then the weight drops until you are holding about twenty-one pounds; with 80 percent let-off—now standard on modern bows—you are holding a mere twelve pounds. With a sixty-pound recurve or longbow, you pull to sixty pounds at your draw length, say twenty-eight inches; draw beyond that—and most archers do—to say twenty-nine to thirty inches, anchoring at the corner of your mouth, and you will actually be holding sixty-five to sixty-seven pounds. You could bench press that weight all day, but with archery gear, you can't hold that weight much longer than a quick breath.

For studying traditional bows, archery manufacturers have established a draw length of twenty-eight inches as the standard at which all adult bows can be compared. A force-draw curve for a traditional stick bow will have a steep but short initial slope in the neighborhood of four or more inches of draw, easing to a slope of about two pounds per inch. For a smooth-drawing, non-stacking characteristic, the two to three pound weight per inch of draw slope will be maintained in a linear manner through the twenty-eight-inch standard draw length to thirty inches or beyond.

The force-draw curve tells you more than just the energy transformation you are going to experience when you pull the string back. If you chart the X-Y curve on graph paper, it can also tell you exactly how much energy the bow stores at any given draw length. The area under the force-draw curve corresponds to the stored energy of your bow.

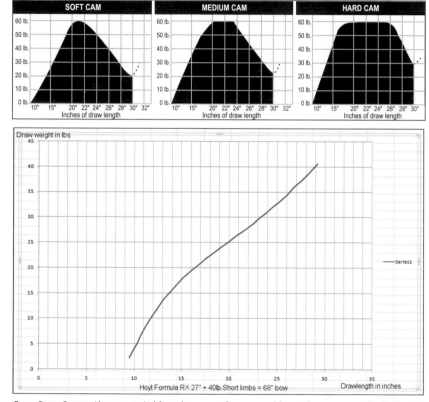

Force-Draw Curves. *Above are typical force-draw curves for compound bows. These curves graphically illustrate the amount of energy—the dark areas beneath the curves—stored by this modern bow style. These curves also show the dramatic point of let-off typical of a compound or cam bow. The lower graph illustrates the force-draw curve for a Hoyt recurve bow. The farther one draws a recurve or longbow from brace height (x axis), the greater the effort required to hold (y axis). Total stored energy is that area beneath the sloping line from brace height to the archer's full draw. (Layer graph courtesy of ArcheryTalk.com)*

We are accustomed to discussing energy as foot-pounds, but a chart is calibrated in inches and pounds, hence inch-pounds. Each square therefore represents one or two inch-pounds (depending on how the chart is laid out—and there is nothing holy about it in any case) of stored energy. Simply count the squares, including an estimate for the partial squares (there is surely a mathematical way to do this), under the force-draw curve and you can determine the approximate stored energy of the bow. Count from the brace-height measurement, usually six to seven inches, to your draw length; add the squares and divide by twelve to convert inch-pounds to foot-pounds.

An interesting measure, when you have time, is to identify the efficiency of your bow. You only need to do one more simple division. Divide the kinetic energy of the arrow by the stored energy of the bow.

The draw-force curve for the recurve bow is quite different, showing a gradual but steady increase in energy—that area beneath the sloping line from brace height to your full-draw position—and suggesting the further you draw, the more power is required to hold the string.

ABOUT KINETIC ENERGY AND MOMENTUM

When you pick up your bow it ceases to be an inanimate stick and becomes something with living potential. You participate in a transition from possible to actual, potential to vibrant. You make the difference between a runner at the blocks, tense and waiting, to the burst of speed that vaults onto the track and over barriers.

This leap between potential and actual is what archery is all about. Thus, energy is an important concept in archery, especially in bowhunting, because it is one of our few relative measures of penetrating ability. Some argue that it is an arrow's "momentum" rather than its kinetic energy that is most important, and that may indeed be true, but we have conventionally considered arrow kinetic energy to be the measure of a good set-up for many years, and we will stick with that terminology or idea in this book. Penetrating ability is extraordinarily important, because without it you simply have no ability to take home and eat a big-game animal. Penetration with a broadhead-tipped arrow means slicing and bleeding, and that means a blood trail and big game that expires in less than a minute with a good clean shot through the heart-and-lung vitals.

It is no longer arguable whether you want a broadhead to pass completely through an animal or to remain inside it. In the old days perhaps, in 1914 when Ishi was teaching Dr. Saxton Pope to hunt deer with the bow and arrow, the knapped flint heads remained inside the animal because Ishi's bows were not powerful enough to drive the shaft completely through. Thus, many primitive hunters—not Ishi, as far as we know—have used poison-tipped arrows because their arrows lacked sufficient kinetic energy to kill an animal like a deer, much less a giraffe or a big kudu, by hemorrhage alone. It is different now. The idea that a broadhead should remain inside an animal and continue to cut and chew up its insides as it runs is no longer accepted by experienced big-game hunters, unless the animal is one of the truly big game: a hippo or a water buffalo or maybe a brown bear.

The North American penetration standard today is an arrow tipped with a super sharp broadhead that passes cleanly and completely through an animal, although the percentage of clean, pass-through shots is unknown and unknowable. Nevertheless, complete pass-through shots give the hunter an entry and an exit hole, both leaking blood. Because most big-game animals are taken when shooting from tree stands, it is important to have a lower exit hole for blood to drain out, as more blood will typically pour out of the lower hole than from a hole higher on the body.

There is no universally accepted standard for determining how much kinetic energy (or "momentum," if that is your preferred measure) is sufficient for bowhunting. Hunting archers believe, however, that the larger the game the greater the energy required for a quick, clean kill. For deer, forty to fifty foot-pounds delivered from a forty-five-pound traditional bow will do the job, though it is a minimal standard. Less force is generally acceptable with precise arrow placement (although "precise" is rarely possible when the wind is blowing or it's snowing or you're shaking from adrenaline or shooting at an odd angle). For larger, heavier animals like elk or caribou, you need to step up your energy output. If you fly to Alaska for Kodiak bear or take a safari to Africa—at least a safari that involves thick-skinned game such as Cape buffalo or even a big antelope species like eland—a dramatic increase in force is required.

On the face of it, the idea of kinetic energy is relatively simple. The formula for calculating kinetic energy in foot-pounds is speed (in feet per second) squared, multiplied by total arrow weight (including the arrowhead, in grains), and this number divided by 450,240, a gravitational constant. A foot-pound, by the way, is the energy required to raise one pound one foot against gravity. Under controlled laboratory conditions, an arrow with fifty foot-pounds of energy will penetrate twice as far as an arrow with twenty-five foot-pounds, at least through a uniform substance like ballistic gelatin.

Studying the formula, some archers are led to believe that a fast, light arrow gives them greater energy. In a sense, the formula is deceptive and the poetic idea of balance comes into play. A light arrow might be quicker out of the bow, but it absorbs less energy than a heavy arrow, carries less momentum, with the balance dispersing through the system—the bow, the elbow . . .

Here is an example. You are shooting 250 fps with a 500-grain aluminum shaft, the 100-grain broadhead included, but switch to a 400-grain carbon arrow, dropping down to a seventy-five-grain head. You will pick up about ten fps, but the heavier projectile hurtles toward the target with 69.4 foot-pounds of energy while the lighter arrow only gives you 60.0 foot-pounds. The lighter projectile has 16 percent less energy at chronograph, or point-blank, range than the heavier projectile. At close range, say ten to twenty yards, this may not be a significant difference, but as the shot distance increases, the lighter arrow loses energy faster than the heavier arrow. The same 500-grain arrow will have much more energy at forty yards than the 400-grain arrow. All things being equal, that may mean an additional six inches of penetration, the momentum of the heavier arrow overcoming the resistance force, and it is significant in terms of recovered game.

We know from years of study and a half century of modern bowhunting experience and testing that for deepest penetration, you want your arrow's energy and hence its momentum directed straight down the centerline of the shaft, because when a flexing arrow hits game, the shaft tends to whip to one side. This diminishes the energy package available to drive that shaft through your quarry. A perfectly flying arrow puts all its energy behind the broadhead.

Walking or running animals sometimes cause arrows to lurch sideways on impact. The broadhead enters, the arrow slows dramatically and the shaft whips to one side. Penetration suffers. For best penetration in game, always make a conscious decision about whether you want or need to shoot at a running animal. Lightweight arrows, never.

Kinetic Energy (foot-pounds) of Your Set-Up	Suitable for Hunting
Less than 25	Small game: rabbits and squirrels
26–41	Medium game: pronghorns and deer
42–65	Large game: black bear, elk, and wild boar
66 and higher	African game and the great bears (brown and grizzly)

SIGHTS AND AIMING TECHNIQUES

Bow Sight. *Page 12 of the 1961 Bear Archery catalog featured two bow-mounted sights. These early sights, the Muller Bo-Sight and Hoyt Line-O-Sight, could be taped onto or screwed onto the back of the wooden recurve bows of the era.*

You have picked up the bow and laid an arrow against the shelf. You have snapped the nock onto the string and lifted the bow, and even drawn it back. Now what? Well, now you aim at your target, release, and follow through.

We can begin this chapter with a man named Fred Bear, the founder of Bear Archery. His early bows did not look like anything special. Just a nice take-down recurve and before that a longbow that he made himself. Still, with it in his hands, he won dozens of competitions in Michigan and the northern states in the 1930s and 1940s.

But Fred was a snap shooter. He looked at a target, made a mental calculation, drew the bow to whatever elevation or spot he felt was right and let fly an arrow. It's one thing to do this with a traditional bow and quite another thing with a compound, but by the time compounds became popular, Fred was more than seventy years old. He said he experimented with compounds, but was too old, too established—loved his recurve and his legacy—to switch to the new technology.

By his seventies, Fred had already survived many battles in archery. One of them cost him . . . and still costs us . . . money, but Fred realized the end result was worth it. He argued for having archery equipment included in the list of taxable sporting goods items included in the Federal Excise Tax. As a result, 11 percent of the price of most archery (and firearms) items we purchase is funding for the Pittman-Robertson Act and is dedicated very specifically to four outcomes: basic research, wildlife restoration, hunter education, and the development of shooting ranges.

An earlier battle—smaller, but just as vicious as the one that inevitably cost archers and manufacturers millions of dollars—involved bow sights. The question: should bow-mounted sights be legitimate equipment in competitions sponsored by the NFAA (National Field Archery Association)?

In the sixties, when every archer shot a recurve or longbow, sights were primitive, at least by today's standard, and there were perhaps 100,000 archers or less in all of North America. Fred did not use sights on his take-down recurve, although his first employee and subsequent inductee into the Archery Hall of Fame, Frank Scott, vividly recalled Fred taping a wooden match stick onto the front of the bow on days when he felt he needed just a wee bit of help getting the distance down.

Evidence of bow-sight use in antiquity is marginal. By the middle of the twentieth century, however,

Modern Sights. Today's bowsight is a far cry from the sights of the fifties when bowhunting pioneer Fred Bear taped a wooden match to the back of his bow to use as a reference for aiming. Sights with fiber optic cables (and many with optional sight lights) allow bowhunters to see the sight pins clearly in all lighting situations. The question when you begin shooting a traditional bow is what accessory is important. Many excellent traditional shooters use no sight at all.

as men and women generally spent increasing time indoors in front of the television, sights began to appear in archery publications. The Folberth was a simple plastic strip with an adjustable reference spot that glued onto the recurve's riser. Folberth's and those of Earl Hoyt and others were often delicate, fingertip-adjustable, aperture-style single pin sights.

Then came sights built in to the wood risers. The high-end Bear Tamerlane recurve cost just $125 in 1964, but it was constructed with an innovative, vertical nylon cutout in the center of the riser. The arrow rest attached to the bottom of the plastic plate, and for an additional $19.95, the Premier Bowsight could attach to the plate directly above the rest. Fred's catalog that year promised that for the first time, "technically perfect arrow flight is now possible."

At Rest. *The weather-resistant Martin Dura-Flip Right Hand Rest features durable, plastic, self-adhesive foam backing. It can be used with a cushion plunger, although the one shown in the picture is not. Some will argue that the rest, if any is used, is the most important part of accessory gear, since it is the last element that touches an arrow or its fletching before it hits a target.*

Today's sights are marvels of engineering and imagination. Depending on the price you want to pay—and there is no reason you could not use one on a traditional bow that has drilled mounting holes with tapped brass inserts on the off-side—they incorporate features that archers a generation ago could hardly imagine. They use light-capturing fiber optic cords to give aiming points, rather than steel pins that needed to be dipped in white ceramic paint to be visible in low-light situations. Several sights use an encapsulated radioactive tritium dot for continual light. And although there is a bias toward metal and against plastic, they use a variety of impact-resistant polymers (there are hundreds of types of "plastic") to lighten the load.

Sight styles come and go. For instance, the pendulum sights popular with tree-stand hunters a generation ago have by and large been replaced by faster and faster compounds. Pendulums were only effective to about thirty yards, and today's hot compounds will shoot that distance, with no more rise in elevation than a breath.

The fun of traditional archery is paring down, though, learning that we do not need every available twenty-first-century electronic gadget and time-saving device that only seem to eat up our time, prevent concentration. You do not need (or want) to hunt and text, your bow in one hand and smartphone in the other, and yet there are a few things we might like, and for a bowhunter, a bow sight is one of them. Here's why.

In competition, you will join dozens of other traditional archers shooting at targets. You might shoot at a known distance or with your foot against a stake. You will wait in line, take your time, and normally shoot from ground level a relatively horizontal shot. The shot may not be easy, but the target will not move. You will shoot during the best hours of daylight, 10:00 a.m. to 4:00 p.m. Bowhunting is totally different.

Hunting is all about the unknown. The deer comes from an unexpected angle when you have just coughed or spilled your coffee. Your heart pounds, your breathing is irregular, your hands sweat and shake. If you make any careless mistake, the deer will see or hear you and race away. Game is most active in the early morning or late evening when ambient light is dim. You are probably hunting from a tree stand, in which case you must judge angle and distance quickly, and the deer will not wait for you. If you are hunting from the ground, chances are you will be inside a ground blind, and while you will be less visible to the deer, your own vision will be restricted. You must move carefully, but purposefully. For all of these reasons, a simple pin sight may fit your recurve and may enhance your hunting. You may also need to develop a tough skin to prevent the kidding from other traditional shooters, especially the men and women shooting longbows who would not be caught dead with a sight on their bow.

And so it is especially peculiar that the epitome of target shooting, FITA or Olympic competition, requires some of the most expensive and specialized sights for the recurves used. According to the rule book for a sight for an Olympic bow:

11.1.5. A bow sight is permitted, but at no time may more than one such device be used.

11.1.5.1. It shall not incorporate a prism, lens, or any other magnifying device, leveling, electric or electronic devices nor shall it provide for more than one sighting point.

11.1.5.2. The overall length of the sighting circle or point (tunnel, tube, sighting pin or other corresponding extended component) shall not exceed 2cm in the line of vision of the athlete.

11.1.5.3. A sight may be attached to the bow for the purpose of aiming and which may allow for windage adjustment as well as an elevation setting. It is subject to the following provisions:

A bow sight extension is permitted;

A plate or tape with distance marking may be mounted on the sight as a guide for marking, but shall not in any way offer any additional aid;

The sight point may be a fiber optic sight pin. The total length of the fiber optic pin may exceed ¾ of an inch, provided that one end is attached outside the athlete's line of vision at full draw, while the part within the athlete's line of vision does not exceed 2cm in a straight line before bending. It can only provide one illuminated aiming spot at full draw. The fiber optic pin is measured independently of the tunnel.

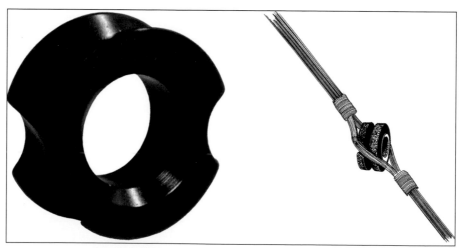

Peep. The peep sight serves into the bowstring and functions as both a rear sight—imagine front and rear iron sights for rifles—and as a check on your anchor point. You may want to experiment with the size of the aperture or hole (in inches) as peeps commonly come in ³⁄₁₆, ¼, and ⁵⁄₁₆, and they may even have a tiny, removable magnifier lens.

This of course is just a sample of the international rules. There are more. Altogether, FITA has researched and published six books of constitution, rules, and regulations, just for archery. We can guess that the objective is not to have fun.

To perform internationally at such a high level in archery (or in golf or soccer or chess) requires excellent equipment, 100 percent dedication, exceptional loyalty, and a grueling training regimen beginning before the teen years and lasting for a dozen or more. We respect those who commit to that, but let's face it: they're not having any fun. Their work-out is not part of a well-rounded life. Perhaps the best quality of life and the most enjoyable opportunity traditional archery can afford is to avoid this type of high-level and high-stress competition altogether.

STRING WALKING

An aiming technique known as string walking lets you use the arrow point as an aiming reference. It is an easy technique to practice but may be harder to master. With the arrow securely on the string below the nock-point locator, the archer moves his fingers down the string for a given distance estimation. Touch your arrow point to the center of the target, and if you are spot-on at forty yards, it is easy to see that the farther from the nock you slide your fingers, the closer the distance with the point of reference. For example, slide your fingers down a half inch and you will be golden, point-on, at thirty yards. Following this logic, if you slide your fingers a full inch down the string and away from the arrow's nock, you will be point-on at twenty yards.

To determine distance from the nock and, hence, impact point, a practiced string walker may count the serving strands, having determined in advance that sixteen strands, for instance, equals a half inch. Some who like this technique learn to replace the serving that comes on a commercial bowstring themselves with a tightly wrapped monofilament that is easier for the thumb nail to enumerate as it slides down. It can become a favorite aiming method because it lets you keep your arrow point on or around the target. It allows for a consistent anchor and a fairly precise and consistent finger position for a given distance. As a fairly primitive sighting technique, it is like having a movable pin sight.

The act of string walking may be fairly simple, but the mechanics are not, because moving one's holding point down the string actually changes the loads on the limbs and the arrow is drawn a slightly shorter distance. Move your fingers too far down the string and the string angle may become so acute that the arrow nock loosens and the arrow falls off the string. In addition, the arrow spine is also subject to change as your hold changes, and so many archers who practice this skill say that it helps to be in the middle of the spine range for your arrow since dynamic spine varies as you move your fingers.

Few people use string walking effectively in hunting. It simply takes too long. The game animals typically don't cooperate at walking slowly in a straight line or standing broadside while you calculate the distance and move your hand carefully down the string. Plus, the addition of a heavy broadhead to the arrow will change the dynamics of the shot entirely.

If this style of aiming appeals to you, check to see that it is allowed in your favorite traditional competitions. It would be useless—imprecise—in FITA competition, and it is not allowed in traditional competition in IBO or ASA, except perhaps in the barebow subdivision.

GAP SHOOTING AND DISTANCE ESTIMATION

It is not easy to learn to hit a target with an arrow, especially a moving target. It is a skill best learned with continuous practice. The more you do it, the more the spacing between shot arrows becomes tighter (or groups), and the more your knowledge of the capabilities of your tools—and yourself—become instinctive.

Some archers aim with a technique called "gap shooting." They focus on the spot they're shooting at and in their peripheral vision see the arrow and its tip. The trick is to learn to match the gap with the tip of the arrow. Some archers calculate the distance as if it were on a flat screen: two inches of gap for a shot of twenty yards. If the shot distance is longer, the gap decreases; if it is shorter, the gap increases.

To be proficient with this method, you must first find the best full-draw position, one you can repeat precisely for every shot. For instance, it might be string in the center of your chin with the arrow nock touching a precise spot below your chin every time you draw. Then you must learn to estimate distance to your target, and this, in itself, is a skill. How do you learn to measure distance?

Modern archers use handheld laser rangefinders that cost several hundred dollars each and are accurate from plus-or-minus one yard to over a thousand yards, far beyond the distance you will ever want to shoot. The now obsolete coincident rangefinder used two hands to manipulate an internal system of mirrors and an exterior knob that brought the mirrors into alignment. (The same type of system was used to focus a camera "back in the day": when the image went from fuzzy to sharp, the focus was correct.) Once in alignment, a scale read the distance. These rangefinders worked fine to fifty yards; that is, they covered the distance an archer would reason-ably shoot. Perhaps because they worked well, were inexpensive, and non-electronic (no batteries required) they went out of style. The modern laser is a marvel, but it requires batteries. If you are pronghorn hunting on the plains of Wyoming, stalking along gullies to sneak close to a buck, or hunting caribou in northern Canada, a laser rangefinder can be a definite aid, but once you are close to the animal, you have to put it aside and focus. That's when gap-shooting skills come in handy.

So how do you learn distance without an electronic aid? The same way you get to Carnegie Hall. Practice. Measure your paces for distances of ten and twenty yards. Then take a walk through the neighborhood or the local park. Notice landmarks such as a mail box or a tree trunk and estimate the distance; then pace the distance and divide by your paces per 10 or 20 yards. The more of this casual learning you do, the better you will get. Soon enough, you might be able to walk a hunting preserve or state land, carefully shooting at clumps of grass or stumps (they used to call this "roving") to try your distance estimation and your gap-shooting skills.

At first, gap shooting requires that you match the gap between your arrow tip and target with a set of memorized distances, but this is difficult to measure precisely, so it becomes a matter of experience, of training the eye. At some point, if you are a consis-tent student of archery, an instinctive style of aiming and shooting will become natural.

Shoot, Jake! *Jake Kaminski shoots his recurve with great form at the 2012 Olympics.*

CHAPTER SIX

A DOZEN THINGS TO KNOW . . .
AND BUY (OR NOT)

Archery is a hobby, but it is also an active lifestyle sport. For many enthusiasts, it becomes a passion and maybe a lifetime interest as well. If that is the case, your knowledge and abilities will deepen over the years in the way that an old aviator jacket softens, conforms to your body, becomes a treasured and indispensable item of clothing.

The bow, the arrow, and the broadhead need a supporting cast of smaller, though nonetheless important items. Let's review them. You may decide that the barest possible load of gear is right for your interests and move deeper into the traditional mode, becoming what many consider a "primitive archer." Or you may want to experiment and have fun before settling into the groove that's just right for you. Like few other active hobbies, with the possible exception of golf, archery offers a ton of accessories to complement your shooting.

THE QUIVER

Almost as soon as there were bows and arrows, there were quivers. Whether you are a hunter or competitor or strictly a recreational shooter, you need a quiver to carry your arrows. Yes, you could carry them in your hand and risk bending them or stabbing yourself, but even if you chose to do this, most clubs and ranges would not permit it.

Depending on your archery interest and the type of bow you shoot, quivers can be very different. Generally, three types are available. Quivers either attach to the bow or can be worn on the hip or over the shoulder on your back, and the elaborate nature of the design and quality of material can be immensely variable.

BOW QUIVER

If you are a hunter, you will have already considered this quiver. Most recurves and some longbows have pre-drilled risers with brass inserts tapped to mount a quiver on the off-arrow side. Typically a bow quiver will hold four to six arrows. You don't have to screw a quiver to the side of the bow however, as some attach via wire arms, one wrapping around the limb slightly above the riser and one slightly below at the fades.

The market is saturated with fine quivers, from standardized mass offerings to custom arrow holders designed just for your bow. Each style comes with its own positives and negatives, but one important consideration: cover any broadhead blades completely. In the old days, a quiver lacked a hood or had only a partial hood and it was easy to get cut. Plus, the open heads caught on clothing and brush, so this style of quiver was at best a dangerous nuisance.

You want a bow quiver that you can adjust for silence. One problem with bow quivers is arrow rattle in the hood as interior foam wears out or fletching brushes against fletching. This sounds minuscule until you are fifteen yards from a deer or a coyote—then the noise sounds like hurricane-force wind.

Another element to watch or listen for, especially as your quiver ages and you have pushed and pulled arrows in and out of the gripper(s) many times, is a secure fit. You want an arrow gripper that holds arrows snugly. Should you switch back and forth from aluminum to wood or even carbon when you change archery games, between recreational shooting and hunting, for instance, you may need to change grippers. Most commercial quiver companies are sensitive to this and sell replacement grippers. The last thing you want is loose arrows in a quiver.

Upon arriving at a stand, many bowhunters remove the quiver. This makes the bow more maneuverable without the added three to four inches wide by 2½ feet of "stuff" hanging on the side to brush against the stand or the fabric of the blind. An important consideration is to practice in the same manner that you hunt. If you hunt with the quiver off, practice that way, because a quiver and full complement of arrows can weigh half-a-pound and this weight attached to the side of the bow, even balanced roughly at the center of the grip, will definitely affect your draw, release, and point of arrow impact. Of course, most traditional shooters cant or lean their bow to the side, moving the center of force closer to the center of mass, and so the effect of the quiver and arrows may actually help some shooting styles!

A recent quiver design has emphasized moving the mass of the quiver and arrows toward the centerline of the bow. While the marketing is primarily directed at compound shooters, because there are so many more of them, it is probably of greater importance to the traditional shooter. After all, a traditional bow weighs about a pound, whereas a modern compound, even a short thirty-one-inch axle-to-axle bow with an aluminum riser, cams, and cable guard, weighs 3½ pounds, and so the offset weight is much more significant for traditional shooters.

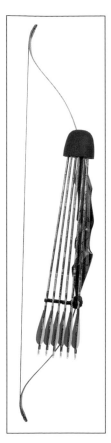

The Traditional Quiver. A bow-mounted quiver ensures that your arrows are always ready and can be quickly pulled out and set on the string. For hunting, a bow quiver provides secure carry and easy access.

Hunt and shoot the way you practice, because weight affects arrow flight—although we traditional archers get a break in this department because most of us cant the bow slightly. So if you hunt with the quiver and arrows attached, practice that way. If you remove the quiver when settling into a ground blind or tree stand, practice that way.

HIP QUIVER

Lots of shooters prefer a hip quiver. Generally it hangs from the belt in such a manner that arrows can easily be drawn forward and out. Typically, the hip quiver is used by recreational shooters with field or target points; manufactured quivers are wonderful for shooting a 3D range where noise is not a problem and come with clips for score cards and pockets for pencils and arrow pullers. (An arrow puller is a rubber tool that helps you grip the arrow, even if it is wet, and pull it straight out of a target without twisting or bending the shaft.) Some hip quivers even have separate tubes for arrows, similar to the tubes for clubs in a golf bag.

Several styles of hip quiver are available for bowhunting, but they are rare in the woods because the broadheads must be secured and the arrows must be held in such a way that they are silent, even when stalking through brush or descending steep hillsides. Hip quivers are fastened onto the belt and may be strapped around the leg to prevent flopping as one walks. Thus, most hip quivers used for hunting are used west of the Mississippi River.

BACK QUIVER

Shades of Robin Hood, the back quiver literally shouts "Traditional!" Yet it may offer more problems than it solves. You have to be careful reaching over your shoulder or behind your back and pulling an arrow tipped with a broadhead out of the quiver. A nasty slice to the neck is no laughing matter, especially when you are miles from your vehicle, and often, in the deep deer woods, a cry for help from a cell phone will not get a quick response. ("Let me get this straight. You're lying against the old oak tree with the broken limb? Where is that, exactly?")

With a back strap around the shoulders, back quivers, which are often made of leather, can be heavy and hot, and they must still perform the basic quiver function of holding the arrows silently and safely. Plus, if you are leaning forward and checking a blood trail or just looking for something you have dropped, the arrows will tend to slide out, over your head. Duck to go under a limb and you'll literally have to squat or crawl to keep the arrows from catching on the limb over your head, and you have to keep this in mind constantly as you walk or stalk through the brush.

 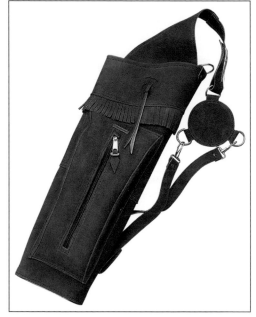

Quivers: Back and Hip. Some traditional shooters prefer a hip quiver to carry arrows; others prefer a back or a bow-mounted quiver. Depending on their style, hip and back quivers may allow your arrows to rattle or even fall out if you bend over to follow a trail under a branch. Although they are beautiful and traditional, on a hot day these fine leather quivers are going to prove heavy and will make you sweat.

Practically speaking, a bow-mounted quiver is the best all-around choice for bowhunting, and a hip quiver is excellent for a day at the range.

STRING SILENCERS

Be glad, be very glad you are not shooting a modern compound bow. Not only do traditional archers have more fun and enjoy a deeper connection to archery and to archers, but you don't have to worry so much about the noise of a shot. The longbow has a modest and pleasing "thrum" when it is shot. A modern compound, and certainly a crossbow, can be extraordinarily noisy delivering a "whack" that sounds like a hammer hitting barn siding. Consequently, a whole industry has grown up around developing silencing techniques and accessories for modern bows.

With a traditional bow—whether you are shooting a ½-pound bamboo longbow or a 1½-pound aluminum-handle recurve—a simple pair of rubber string silencers works just fine. Cat Whisker bow-string silencers have been one of the most popular silencers with traditional bowhunters for a quarter century. Tie a set on the string about a quarter to a third of the way from each limb tip, and you're good to go. Alternately, you can separate the bowstring bundle and inset the rubber whiskers into the string, tying (or "serving") them tightly in place with green dental floss (this

Shhhh . . . Quiet as it is compared to a modern compound bow, a hunting recurve will benefit from a bit of noise reduction, and it is easy to fit a set of silencers into or onto the bowstring. Set one above and one below the rest, each about a third of the distance along the string from the bow tip. Depending on the type you use, you may want to serve them into place as a traditional bow, and string should be relaxed at the end of a day's shooting.

looks a lot better). Just pull and snap or cut off the tips of the rubber strands, and the strands will separate. These lightweight rubber silencers do an excellent job of diffusing the "thrumming" noise of a shot, breaking up the string wave vibration (and shooting a traditional bow can be hard on your elbow). The all-rubber construction is waterproof and sold two strips to a bag in green, brown, or the traditional black, a pair should last for years. Plus, they only cost a couple bucks and are available in every pro shop, sporting goods store, and mass merchant.

CLICKER

You'll rarely see a clicker on a bow other than a recurve. A clicker allows a competitive shooter to know when they have reached full draw by giving an audible "click." In theory, on hearing that sound, the archer releases the string. A clicker is useful because it gives you—with a great deal of practice, of course—a positive release point and this gives, all other things being equal, consistent arrow performance.

The clicker is a lightweight armature of tensile spring steel (usually, though it could be a carbon/fiberglass arm) about ¼ inch wide by three inches long. It is screwed at its top into the sight window of a riser in front of the arrow rest. The archer places an arrow between the clicker and riser so that at full draw, the arrow point is pulled from under the clicker and the metal strip snaps back against the riser with an audible "click."

At higher levels of competition, archers may watch the clicker as they draw, checking to position it near the tip of their arrow—a delicate move they will have practiced thousands of times. After that, their visual focus switches to aiming and they use back tension—"back tension" being the fabled perfect way of drawing and holding among tournament archers—to move the final fraction of an inch to click and release. Many FITA shooters use a clicker, but finger shooters in 3D bowhunter-class competitions are usually not allowed to use clickers.

Clickers also help some archers who develop "target panic." Learning to use that little strip of metal properly discourages premature release, called "anticipation," because it builds a positive shooting habit, usually with demonstrable results.

KISSER BUTTON

A kisser button is a small plastic disc weighing about a dozen grains and measuring about a quarter inch in radius. Attached to the bowstring, it is positioned so that at full draw, it will touch the archer's lips or the tip of the nose. The purpose of

The Kiss-Off. A kisser button is mainly used on recurves as a competition accessory.

the kisser is to provide another position point of reference for the anchor position. Mainly it is used on recurves, not on longbows, and it is a competition, not a hunting, accessory.

Note: It is rare to see a kisser on a compound bow because modern compound shooters prefer a peep sight, a string mounted disc with a hole or aperture that gives them, in essence, a rear sight close to their eye. Plus, anything attached to the string, except "speed buttons" positioned near the cams, slows down arrow speed, even if only by one to three fps.

THE BOW CASE

Traditional archers need bow cases. The very best will be a hard-sided case that lets you stack it in the back of the truck with the duffle, tent, stove, and cooler for a cross-country trip. Many cases are available for take-apart bows, longbows, and recurves, but it is harder to find cases for long single-piece bows.

What to look for in a case is no different than if you were transporting some other valuable, fragile gear. After all, a cross-country drive or around-the-world trip

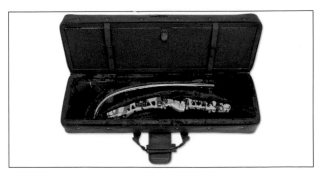

Bow Case. Barring some disaster, a quality hard-sided bow case will pay off for many years. This is one accessory that is a no-brainer necessity. Spend as much as you comfortably can, because when your bow and accessories are inside, the peace of mind you will have from using a rugged bow case will be worth whatever you pay.

to hunt Cape buffalo in Mozambique or red deer in New Zealand, or even for an IFAA international tournament, is very expensive. Some things you want to buy, use, and toss—early season cotton camo clothing might fall into that category because it tears and colors fade. But not bow cases. Buy the best case you can afford. The momentary pain of spending an additional hundred dollars for a truly durable case will forever be outweighed by the peace of mind knowing that your gear is protected.

In theory you want a travel case that is lightweight and super-durable, with inside supporting posts (to prevent crushing), interior tie-down straps, and foam padding (to prevent gear from rubbing together). Your case should be waterproof, with strong locks and latches, a comfortable handle, and maybe even rollers for pulling it through international airports. If you travel frequently, buy a case with a valve that equalizes air pressure so the gasket doesn't burst when altitude changes. A good case should offer a separate compartment for arrows, which need to be cushioned and individually mounted to protect the fletching. You want a separate storage compartment for broadheads, sharpeners, knife, tab or glove, and all of the hundred-and-one extra things you take on a trip.

Should you purchase a double-bow case? Do you have two bows? Cases for two take-down bows are available. Imagine that you have booked a hunt to northern

The Well-Stocked Case. *A well-stocked bow case opened for inspection the first day of a safari in Tanzania. The archer, Michigan's Bob Eastman, has hunted in Africa many times and understands the value of taking back-up gear in a sturdy case.*

Canada for woodland caribou and expect to spend $4,000 on travel, booking the guide, and mounting the expected racks. You will certainly take an extra shot-in string, but should you take an extra bow, as insurance against disaster? In a lifetime of experience, some disaster strikes every hunter at least once. How much do you worry, too much or not enough? Are an extra bow and perhaps a separately shipped bow case worth it? Most traditional archers end up with multiple bows, and it becomes an individual choice that you should carefully consider, weighing the costs and benefits over the lifetime of a quality case.

Padded, soft-sided cases with separate arrow compartments are excellent for short trips or for keeping your bow in storage—though for storage, a hard case is preferable to prevent an accident caused by curious children or meddling visitors. Some states require that bows be cased on the way to a hunting area; for this a zippered cloth case is adequate. Check your local regulations.

ARROW RESTS AND CUSHION PLUNGERS

Rests are not controversial, or not exactly. . . . Longbows usually require little other than a smooth leather strike plate because shooters often cant the bow—hold it not at the vertical but at an angle so that the arrow rests easily in the notch above the grip.

Several options are available for recurves, though. At the Olympic level, specialized equipment of every sort is required, but if you are a bowhunter or recreational shooter, you may discover that a simple rest and perhaps a cushion plunger will help smooth out arrow flight.

Recurves can be shot off the shelf if your arrow is spined properly and fletched with forgiving feathers and if you develop a smooth release. The old standard was the Bear Hair rest, a simple strip of carpet for the shelf plus a separate leather side plate. The Bear Hair's synthetic carpeting comes with an adhesive backing so that once you mount it, all you have to do is trim it with scissors to the shape of the shelf. It's quiet and effective, especially on bows with crowned rest shelves.

Your shooting style and gear set-up may require something more elaborate than a piece of carpet, though, and a number of rests attach to the recurve with adhesive. The simplest of these stick-on or "shoot-around" rests is a piece of hard rubber molded with an arm to support the arrow. In a step up from the simple rubber arms, look for a stick-on with a Teflon-covered arm, Teflon being extraordinarily slick (though not oily) as well as very quiet, in which case you might also want a cushion plunger.

Simple Rests. Longbow shooters rely on little more than a cushioned pad on the arrow shelf. The essential choice is the Bear Hair, a thin carpet (really just to quiet the noise of the arrow being drawn over the arrow shelf) with a separate leather strike plate against which the feathers can brush as they speed past. One step up for a recurve is a shoot-around rest, a simple soft plastic rest that can be used with a cushion plunger to cradle the arrow and help diminish natural oscillation as the arrow passes around the riser.

The cushion plunger was invented to help the arrow flow around the riser and stabilize faster. It screws through the designated hole in the riser. When you lay your arrow on the rest arm, the arrow balances against the tip of the plunger, the tip being a hard, self-lubricating, and, hence, silent plastic. Inside the brass or aluminum plunger body is a steel spring that you can adjust for side pressure, which is dependent on arrow spine.

Upon your shot, the arrow leaves the string and begins to flex in what is called *archer's paradox*. Unlike release shooters whose arrows flex in the vertical plane, finger shooters release arrows that bend side to side as the moving string curves around the fingertips, which, no matter how quick you are, can't release and get out of the way fast enough. The spring-mounted tip of the cushion plunger moderates or "cushions" the side pressure from the arrow. This helps prevent the arrow from banging against the riser, helps diminish the natural side-to-side fishtailing, and stabilizes the arrow faster.

Two cautions with a cushion plunger. First, you must make sure it is tight in the plunger hole in the riser. It screws in and out fairly easily and you must be careful not to over-tighten and strip the threads, though this was a more common problem with older magnesium risers, which were made of a softer metal than are aluminum risers. The second caution is to be sure the plunger and your bow-mounted quiver are compatible. Because plungers come in various lengths, a long plunger might interfere with the proper mounting of your quiver.

Armguard. *An armguard protects your forearm from string slap. If you think a bruise from the bowstring striking your unprotected inner forearm is of small consequence, just wait until it happens to you—and it is the second time that will make you cringe in pain. Hamskea's slip-on armguard is constructed from 3mm Neoprene on each side with Spandex gussets in between. An armguard can also hold loose or bulky sleeves out of the way of a shot. You may want several types of armguards—they're inexpensive—especially a leather or synthetic strap-on guard.*

THE STABILIZER

Today's bow stabilizer has come a long way from the simple weight-forward concept, the hunk of iron of yesteryear. At one time shooters who screwed the thirty-six-inch Easton stabilizer to the back of their bow used it primarily to lean on between shots at the competition stake, or at least that attitude was prevalent. Now stabilizers include a lot of innovations for dampening noise and vibration, but this will not significantly help traditional shooters.

High-level competition archers use all manner of stabilizers that screw into the accessory insert positioned on the back of the bow. Their idea is to give them a balanced bow platform, weight neither to the left nor the right, so that upon release, the bow rocks straight forward, in line with the flight of the arrow. Of course, they're wearing a sling so they never drop the bow. Plus, high-level competition recurves are routinely very light in draw weight, maybe up to forty-five pounds, and a competitive archer would never worry about the noise of a shot, which, in any case, is hardly more than a raindrop falling on a maple leaf.

Bow Sling. Every competition archer uses some type of sling on his or her bow hand. A sling allows them to shoot with a superbly relaxed grip, knowing that after a shot, when the bow jumps forward, it will not drop out of their hand. Adjustable in length, this sling attaches to the stabilizer hole. Relatively few hunters shoot with slings as it is something else to worry about, and they usually get only one shot (in competition one may shoot dozens or scores of times a day).

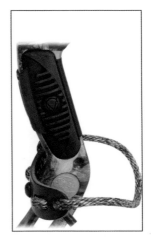

Stabilizers come in all sorts of lengths and weights. You will occasionally see a recurve with a stabilizer, but never a longbow. A short stabilizer is all that would ever be truly necessary, and if you have some interest in this item of equipment, buy one that has some rubberized vibration dampening built in, just to cover all the bases.

Stabilize-Me . . . or Not. Octane's Balance X adjustable stabilizer in black or a variety of camo patterns is customizable in length from seven to eleven inches and is weight adjustable from 0.4 to 6.4 ounces. The adjustability makes it a fine stabilizer for someone who shoots multiple bows.

TARGETS

Shooting traditional archery is a skill. To be any good you have to practice, and many find avenues for shooting year round, even in the snow and ice zones: in the garage, in the basement. But when the pro shop's shooting lanes are closed and you need a week of practice before the club tournament, the solution is a portable target.

You can of course set up a tree stand or climb onto the roof and shoot in the backyard, perhaps into stacked hay bales, but some cities have ordinances that prohibit shooting in the municipal limits. Not everyone has room for stacks of bales, either, and there is a financial cost as well as labor involved in building a compressed, stand-up hay bale target. Unless you live in the country, the better alternative is a portable foam or bag target.

Quite a variety of 3D foam archery targets are available. If you are a bowhunter, you can buy a target that looks like a deer or a bear. Rinehart, Delta McKenzie, and others make self-healing foam targets that realistically look like big and small game, even zombies, giant mosquitoes, and predatory dinosaurs. For a hunter to shoot at a target that resembles his quarry—raise a hand if you're waiting for the zombie apocalypse—is a type of mental conditioning. Perhaps it takes the edge off the jitters when the time comes for a shot at the real thing. Some of these targets have the vitals pressed into the target so you can learn at a distance where to place you arrow.

Look for a 3D target that is relatively easy to store and move; they often come apart in two or three sections. It should have stakes to support the legs—often a couple two-foot sections of rebar are adequate—and a replaceable "kill zone." If you shoot often enough, especially with broadheads, you will soon shoot-out the heart-lung zone of a target, and given the price tag for a realistic 3D target—roughly $300 and up, plus shipping—it's nice to save the majority of the target and just replace the central portion.

Your target will last much longer if you shelter it from the weather, but the other concern is broadheads versus field points. Why not practice like you hunt? If your season or a hunting trip hinges on making one great shot, and it often does, prepare for it. Shoot practice points a minimum of the time and your broadheads as much as possible.

Life-Size Targets. *Shooting at a life-size 3D target will sharpen your hunting skills because it adds an element of realism and helps you learn to judge distance. Look for a target with a replaceable core in the vital zone—these targets are relatively expensive—and a target that comes in several sections for compact storage. Both Rinehart and Delta McKenzie build self-healing foam targets such as this whitetail buck.*

179

Not all targets are designed for broadheads, though. Look for a self-healing target that your broadheads won't quickly destroy. If you also shoot recreationally, perhaps in a 3D league, check to see if the target has scoring zones that help you learn arrow placement for premium scores. Usually these zones correspond to the kill zone, but only roughly. A target's carton or the manufacturer's catalog or Internet site will tell you explicitly what kind of arrow point can be used and maybe even what bow draw weight the target is rated for. Some targets will not perform with a heavy arrow or with high-energy crossbow bolts.

It is not necessary to spend a small fortune on a 3D animal target however. Following some large national and regional shoots, used targets can be purchased on site at a discount. This prevents the local sponsoring organization from having to store the targets, which en masse are quite bulky, and allows them to recoup some of the up-front costs of running a tournament. It can also be a great way for you to acquire a good target at a reasonable price.

Target. The self-healing Cube Hybrid archery target from American Whitetail has four shootable sides covered with a waterproof wrap imprinted with high-definition graphics. It will stop arrows to 420 fps and comes in two sizes: 22x22x20 and 18x18x20. The Cube Hybrid is constructed with a foam shell and inner compression core that rotates by hand for even wear. The wrap will not fade or tear. Optional broadhead cores are sold separately.

Several companies have introduced six-sided block or cube targets that are great for any kind of shooting. These can simply be tossed into the yard and shot from lots of angles and positions. When you've finished shooting for the day, simply pick this target up by its handle and put it into storage. And these targets are much less expensive than, say a painted, standing, 3D whitetail buck.

You could just shoot at targets on the ground—clumps of grass with your Judo points or old stumps with your field points—like they did when "roving" in the old days. This is more and more impractical as the United States becomes more urbanized, though. Besides, a good target offers a uniform material and will save your arrows and heads from bends and breaks. In the long run, a good target is well worth the cost.

CHAPTER SEVEN

BIG GAME—THE TRADITIONAL CHALLENGE

Now This Is a Goat! *Loosely distributed from Colorado through North America and Alaska, the mountain goat is a terrific big-game challenge for hunters with traditional equipment. Terrain can be forbidding. The goat is wary of a growing population of mountain lions. Licenses are difficult—sometimes one in a lifetime. Guides are expensive and the shooting angles can be steep. Don't wait another year to collect your money and apply!*

You can hunt almost everywhere in the world. In the Arctic, an archer can stalk musk ox; when threatened on the vast tundra the odorous bovine circle and face outward. In Australia, a hunt for water buffalo or feral hogs or even, for the adventurous, the wild and cross-bred dingo can be arranged, and in neighboring New Zealand, only a thousand-plus miles away, almost anything goes—typically day or night, with no seasons or limits or licenses—for the myriad introduced deer and goats and elk and tahr that once threatened to eat the islands down to their volcanic bedrock. Sub-Saharan Africa, of course, has a tradition of bwana safari that goes back almost 200 years; its herds of wildebeest and antelope and its famous predators continue to attract hunters from around the world. Though hunting archers are uncommon, Europe has red deer and bear, ibex and chamois. Asia has sustainable populations of moose and sheep. South America is similar to Australia and New Zealand in that virtually all huntable big game was introduced from elsewhere, red and fallow deer and wapiti, for instance, the native tapir being classified as "endangered or vulnerable."

Rangefinder. Bushnell's Scout DX 1000 ARC Laser Rangefinder provides distance readings from five to 1,000 yards with ± ½-yard precision and six-power magnification. Within 125 yards, the processor provides ¹⁄₁₀-yard precision. Distance measuring with Angle Range Compensation gives true horizontal distance and holdover. If you are taking a traditional safari to Mozambique or Montana, hunting unfamiliar game in unfamiliar territory, take a rangefinder!

Every place you travel your experience can be dramatically different. English is the national language of Australia and New Zealand, but they still drive on the "wrong" side of the road! In other nations and time zones, you will hear exotic languages and experience moments of uncertainty when you can't understand a single word. You will be exposed to unusual foods and spices. When you fly, switching air carriers and bush flights, and perhaps ride horses, mules, or camels, you will re-learn all of the frustrations of traveling.

Baggage may be lost, flights delayed. You will learn about saddle sores and petty officials who hold out their hand, quietly demanding an unexpected bribe (a "gratuity," from their point of view, *la mordida*) to move your party expeditiously through customs. Wherever you travel with your archery gear, however, you will be an object of friendly curiosity and you will be escorted by a guide.

The International Experience. Traveling to hunt can be frustrating, disappointing . . . and magnificent! You will have unusual experiences and encounter people who have curious lifestyles, languages that sound incredible, and cultural norms that are unfamiliar. You will be introduced to food that you would not eat at home. Don't wait another minute. Go now! (East Africa bush plane crash photo courtesy of Michigan bowhunters Bob Eastman and Matt Dunaskiss)

YOUR GUIDE, SHOULD YOU CHOOSE TO ACCEPT . . .

You could try to hunt New Caledonia for rusa deer on your own, but you would first have to locate the island group on a map. On your own, you could easily arrange the travel, research the customs and the law, and maybe even find someone local to

183

help—in other words, find a guide. You could take your life in your hands and travel to Afghanistan for argali sheep or try to hunt Russia for great bears, although the odds of anything good happening to an unguided hunting party in that former (or perhaps future) Communist dictatorship are non-existent.

Most nations, in fact, require that you make arrangements, including hiring a local guide, through a licensed outfitter. In fact, most US states (and Canadian provinces, the Maple Leaf nation being, it may surprise you to learn, a foreign country) with populations of big game other than deer—sheep or brown bears or moose, for instance—normally require that non-residents work through licensed outfitters.

As you make reservations for the great hunt, the expensive hunt away from home, looking at the guide as "an expense" will only cause anguish. Your guide is your key to property access. He will know the habits and general whereabouts of game populations. Your outfitter will provide local guides, horses and wall tents, perhaps food and a cook and transportation, too. He will know local butchers if you are successful and the minutiae of the state's game regulations. (Generally, regulations increase in complexity with the increase in game species and habitats available. Gone are the days when a state fish and game department printed out its deer hunting regulations on a single sheet; now they are complex and voluminous and require an army of petty bureaucrats to micro-manage.)

The Freelance PH. *Peter Dafner is a freelance professional hunter. Originally from South Africa, he maintains a residence in Namibia and guides clients—mostly Europeans—throughout the countries of sub-Saharan Africa. As an experienced guide, Peter must work under the auspices of licensed outfitters; your consideration for his knowledge and hard work are vital to maintaining his way of life.*

If you get a good and experienced guide, one who fulfills your expectations, he will be worth whatever you contract to pay. And many guides offer several levels of service: options for spike camps or one-on-two guiding, a camp cook or a skinning and field-dressing service. (Ethically speaking, if you shoot an animal, it then becomes your responsibility. You need to understand this point and verify it in your contract.)

A good guide knows the "lay of the land," and whether you travel to Wyoming to hunt pronghorns or to Alaska to hunt caribou, this professional knowledge is always worth more than you will pay. Plus, in parts of the world where dangerous game might appear at any time—predatory bears on Kodiak Island or a tiger in India or a jaguar in Mexico—your guide will carry a rifle. (Your archery gear will kill just as surely as a rifle. As a "stopper," though, delivering a huge, knock-down "smack" of kinetic energy, the rifle offers a measure of security that even a deeply penetrating arrow cannot match.)

The one thing a guide cannot (or should not) guarantee is a kill; perhaps he shouldn't even guarantee a good shot. Remember that you are paying for a hunt, not for a kill. You are paying for the best chance, not for a certain opportunity. Indeed, you are paying for uncertainty, paying for the right to introduce your particular brand of uncertainty into an otherwise calm environment. Guides will advertise client success rate, and the rate may designate either a good shot (making the perfect shot is your responsibility) or a kill, but if he guarantees a kill, take care to understand the situation.

A guaranteed kill is the hallmark of a game farm. Highly controversial, it is the rare bowhunter who has not tried this brand of hunting at least once. Such farms or ranches (many are located in Texas) breed captive herds of exotic animals or purchase old zoo animals from auctions—hypocritically, most zoos only want the young, energetic animals for their displays, a colt or cub earning more "oohs" and "ahs" from the viewers than older animals, and once an animal reaches a certain age, they sell them at auction; animals unsold at the auction are "humanely put down,"—or even accept animals from collectors who decide, for whatever reason, that they cannot keep the growing tiger or giraffe any longer. In a sense, they provide a service and give people an opportunity. After all, where else would you ever see a Père David's deer from China? The "down side" of high-fence hunting ranches is that the experience is "canned," the animals being habituated to certain feeding times, for example. So, if you only have an hour or two, the guide can take you right to the animal, which has become semi-tame.

A high success rate may well mean the guides are highly skilled and understand the area and local game patterns, and this increases your chance of success. So a high success rate, either for taking game animals or a shot opportunity, is well worth consideration and checking references. Ask all of the usual questions when interviewing references, including those which seem intrusive or too personal—especially those. What would you have changed about the experience? Were you fairly charged? Did you see game? Was anyone in your party unhappy with the guide or the outfitter, and why? The usual questions. If you are going to pay a lot of money, you have a right to ask a lot of questions . . . and get a lot of answers.

Of course, an outfitter or guide will steer you toward his best and most memorable clients as references, and those clients will talk at length about their successful stalk. That's human nature. So the best approach is to get everything in writing and review all of the possibilities that you and your hunting friends can think of: If the moose runs into the water and dies, what equipment do you have to get it onto the bank, and does your guide roll up his sleeves to help you retrieve and field dress it . . . or does that cost extra? Then, pay any extra charges on time. Guides are part of a small and elite community of outdoorsmen, even if they are usually broke and dressed in rough working clothes, and they are always underpaid. If you don't hold up your end financially or are undisciplined, word will spread, and you may not find the most sincere welcome in other camps.

THE 15 PERCENT: ABOUT TIPPING

The question of tipping a guide always comes up when planning for a hunt. When and how much do you tip? Unless you have worked as a service professional, a waiter, hair stylist, valet parking attendant, or a hunting guide, you have no clue how important this is. The general rule is that if you are buying an expensive experience such as an African big-game hunt or a Canadian bear hunt and don't think you can pay for the hunt and the taxidermy and the travel and still give your guide a good tip, don't go.

Tipping percentages vary by industry. If you pay $20,000 for a hunt, expect that a generous tip to a competent guide and perhaps the camp cook is in order. If your purchase—and a guided hunt is a purchase—is $2,000, you would naturally pay less because the experience and service rendered is less in economic value and probably in emotional return as well. In a restaurant where the server and the bus boy and the dish washer are paid (by 2013 standards) about $4.50 per hour (ask if you could live on that), your 15 percent tip means the difference between standing on their own or asking for government assistance, because even if their service is necessary to society, no one can afford to live on such a low wage. Abroad, especially in the far outback where game is plentiful and wages are abysmal, a generous tip may mean the difference between poverty and a reasonable standard of living for a driver or skinner or camp cook and his family.

A general guideline of 10 to 20 percent is reasonable. If your guide worked hard for you and was helpful and in generally good spirits despite bad weather or bad luck—very important in a hunting camp—the minimum tip is about 15 percent.

Your contract with the outfitter (or perhaps directly with the guide) may already include a gratuity so double check it or ask if it is unclear before handing over cash. And when you give a tip, the most effective and appreciated manner is to hand it directly to the guide and/or the cook with your word of thanks. (Although US dollars are an international standard and accepted practically everywhere, especially in the cities, local currencies are far easier to use "in the bush.")

If the guide service was terrible or flawed in some manner (perhaps inexperienced or simply incompetent) or the guide was in a terrible mood, some minimal tip is still very important. If you have worked through an outfitter and the guide is simply an employee, some of the choices he has made were decisions by his boss—and we all know how that feels! Other bowhunters will follow you, so imagine that you are in a sense "paying it forward," buying his best work for the next hunter. Be sure to discuss this with the booking agent or outfitter as well.

For a traditional bowhunter the good-faith tipping obligation is especially important to get right. Because of the limited effective range of your arrow, your guide will need to work that much harder to get you in position. It's one thing to point out the moose in the Yukon valley and have a rifleman take it at 200 yards. It's quite another to sneak to within seventy-five to 100 yards and then belly crawl to twenty yards.

Most booking services and guide businesses are reputable and experienced, and they are interested in providing a high-quality hunt. Most will deliver what you pay for plus more. A flight to Tanzania to hunt elephants, for instance, may deposit you in the exotic, if ramshackle, Julius Nyere airport outside Dar es Salaam for hours, or you will have a chance to shop with the outfitter for food in a village market where few native people have ever interacted with an American. If you are open to the experience, open to interacting with strangers, you will see clothing and hear languages and mingle with crowds of people who are not like the people "back home." This in itself will almost be worth the price of the safari. It isn't strange or foreign; it's new and exciting.

BUT WHAT IF . . . ?

At some time in your hunting career, it's bound to happen that you will hire a guide who just can't or won't get it done to your satisfaction. You'll be ready to hunt before the cook, who has been drinking, gets out of bed . . . or your guide becomes frustrated glassing the valley or irritated because you insist on sneaking closer . . . or your

Moose Guide. *Professional guide Wayne Zaft owns the bow-hunting-only Wayne Zaft Hunting Adventures camp, a spacious but motley group of trailers 100 miles north of Edmonton, Alberta, and east of the town of Athabasca. On Google Maps–Satellite View, it is easy to see the manner in which the landscape was scoured during Earth's last glacial epoch. Temperatures can be extreme. The wilderness is vast and unforgiving.*

outfitter arrives at the airport hours late while your party waits in the rain, or doesn't show up at all, taking your deposit and leaving you stranded.

There is little recourse if you are in a foreign country, certainly if you do not speak the language—although English has replaced French as an "international language." (At a time like this, you will also discover what little help or even empathy the US embassy will offer. Embassy employees will treat you as an annoyance and may even become suspicious and legalistic, while giving the "red carpet treatment" to locals with questions or complaints.) You will have to work very hard for even a partial refund or an apology from a negligent outfitter. Unless the service is sanctioned by an organization like Safari Club International or licensed by a state or province, you may have to suck it up with the best good humor you can muster and learn from the experience. In that case, find ways through existing magazines and Internet sites, bowhunting organizations, and booking agencies to warn other hunters. Denying clients to a bad service will be some satisfaction, however minor.

You will feel enormously relieved—worrying about connections prior to the hunt, whether the guide speaks your language, then nervousness about receiving a well-cared-for trophy, and myriad other concerns—if you book a hunt through a reputable service. Several are available that cater exclusively to bowhunters, but look for one that is well-versed in archery and has a track record of satisfied clients, such as Bowhunting Safari Consultants. Booking through a reputable middle-man, one that comes with superior references, may cost a little extra, but it is like taking out an insurance policy for your adventure.

Blood Trailing. *Rarely will a big-game animal simply drop when hit with an arrow (or a bullet, by the way), and one of the great experiences for a bowhunter is following a blood trail. After all, an arrow kills by causing an animal to hemorrhage. Blood trailing, which often takes place in the dark because most big game is killed in the last hour of daylight, is an art, and teamwork is a huge benefit to quick recovery.*

Hunting with the bow and arrow is so much different from rifle hunting that an experienced service with a thorough understanding of archery will pay bountiful dividends. Guides who have a wonderful understanding of game habits and rifle ballistics are often puzzled by, and even unhappy with, the way a bow works, by the effective shot distance a traditional archer requires, and by the concept of "blood trailing." In Africa, traditionally, professional hunters resisted all things related to the bow and arrow, their excuse—sometimes very valid and sometimes just plain stubbornness—being that dangerous animals lurked in the bush.

Expectations are very different between those hunting with rifles and those with bows. Riflemen experience a greater percentage of kills on a hunt because they can shoot effectively at a much greater range, and there is a general sense that they pay to shoot something. Archers have an entirely different expectation, which is to have a high-quality hunting experience with the understanding that, at best, their success rate—when measured by "kills"—is half that of riflemen.

Cape Buffalo. The difference between riflemen and bowhunters is a matter of the experience. Higher kill percentages are expected by riflemen, while bowhunters willingly acknowledge that they will have less kills while still having a high-quality hunting experience.

Two characteristics generally determine the quality of a hunt with a guide and both begin with you, the client. If you treat your guide as a professional who provides expert service based on specialized knowledge—just like a banker or doctor back home, regardless of the rough clothing and "uncivilized" working environment, for example—chances are much greater that your hunt will be a success.

Secondly, if you approach a hunt with a degree of respect and even humility, realizing that hunting is a privilege, you will almost certainly have a memorable trip, even if you return home empty-handed. You do not have control of the game or the weather, and you only have marginal control of the guides, but you have complete control of yourself, your preparation, and your attitudes and emotions, and you can have a successful experience even when things go wrong.

The traditional approach means accepting the inherent limitations of the gear and the ethic we have discussed in this book. It also means that many of the mod-

Longbows in the North. Denny Sturgis, Jr. with his TD Black Widow PLX longbow in Canada's Northwest Territories, July, 2010. His Dall sheep hunt was a success and a great thrill. Sturgis has carried longbows across Canada and Alaska and made numerous trips to five continents, including nine African safaris.

ern devices designed to make hunting easier and arrows lighter and faster will not be part of your gear. You have little use for modern laser bow sights or release aids, regardless of the quality of materials and craftsmanship and innovative design. You are taking a chance at hunting in the most elementary fashion, relying primarily on yourself, your own instincts, and your own discipline, and this gives you, if you are open to it, a personal relationship with your quarry. Taking the life of a deer or an antelope becomes a private action because you are in its living room, and on most days you will be alone when you draw back the string.

Aside from a few tiny populations of native hunters left in the wild, most of them in the vast though diminishing jungles of South America and Asia, the traditional bowhunter is the best hunter in the world, because he or she must be. You must be close, and being close means that any mistake is critical; you can't tip your arrows with poison; your arrows carry enormous energy (or momentum), but they are slow and heavy.

The founders of the archery-only Pope and Young Club, the US-based club that records big-game trophies taken with the bow and arrow, were all traditional bowhunters: Glen St. Charles, Fred Bear, and others. They modeled the archery-only club after the established firearms club, the Boone and Crockett Club. Of course, at the time of the archery club's founding, there were no compound bows or crossbows in the field. If you wanted to bowhunt, you needed a recurve or longbow. Even today—or especially today since the club now has far more members that are modern archers than members that practice traditional archery—it is typically controlled by older traditional archers who routinely take more than their share of superb big-game trophies, and all in a fair-chase manner.

The club serves a useful purpose as the center for a community of dedicated bowhunters. As an institution, however, it fails because it is fundamentally very conservative, occasionally becoming its own worst enemy.

THE BIGGEST AND BEST

Here, it is necessary to interject a note about one of man's inherent failings: measuring.

As archers, we are involved in a human competition complex in all of our games (indeed, perhaps in all life activities, from driving the biggest car to possessing the largest bank account). Our targets are not simply blobs of white or gold; they are graded, zoned, colored concentric circles with the gold, the "bull's eye" in the center. Whoever shoots arrows into the center of the bull's eye wins, and this often involves a rigorous system of measuring and evaluating no less exacting than the excessive, game-slowing, and ultimately boring reviews of plays in the US National Football League—60,000 people waiting for endless minutes for an official to decide whether

Pope and Young Measuring. *Trained and accredited volunteer measurers of the archery-only Pope and Young Club examine a whitetail mount. They will measure each beam, each point, each broken spike and arrive at a composite score to place it in the organization's record book.*

a receiver's toe was out of bounds or the nose of the football "broke the plane" of the goal line before the runner fumbled.

What would happen if, on a competition venue, the bull's eye were offset to the left side of the target? The international competition committee would dissolve in recrimination; our finest Olympic archers would melt down, unable to shoot; the world of archery would dissolve in chaos and despair. Agonizing to endure, it would be great fun to watch.

The world of hunting is practically the same, however, especially the pursuit of the largest animals. This is generally called *trophy hunting*, although the Pope and Young Club prefers to call it "quality hunting."

Trophy hunting is a way for older, experienced bowhunters to maintain their interest after the initial years of excitement have worn away. It is a way of entering into competition—measuring—the size of their accomplishments and comparing them to those of others. It is a way of establishing who is "Number 1" and a hierarchy or "pecking order." Pope and Young suggests that the information gathered

Recurve on the Ruaha. *Hunting only with a recurve bow, Michigan's Bob Eastman takes a warm-up shot on the banks of the Greater Ruaha River in Tanzania prior to heading to his leopard blind. Eastman has been fortunate to hunt in Africa more than thirty times, taking every legal big-game animal on the continent, including the incredibly difficult sitatunga and bongo. His world record elephant by bow, taken in Angola in 1975, scores an amazing 270. Africa is open for bowhunters, but given the continuing pressure on land and resources from a poverty-stricken and expanding population, such opportunities may not last much longer.*

when big animals are killed and hunters self-report the location and circumstances is used in scientific studies, although this claim by our brother bowhunters is patently preposterous.

The club mandates trophy standards for every species. These standards are established by measurement and designed to "honor the animal," though there is little enough honor given the animal and great attention given the bowhunter who killed it. Deer and caribou have antlers that are measured for length and girth. The antlers must meet minimum total scores to be accepted into the record book. Most North American animals are so scored; bears and cougars by skull dimensions; elk and moose in a manner similar to deer.

For a young or novice bowhunter and especially a traditional archer, the rule of thumb is to ignore the constant talk of record books. Concentrate on enjoying the outdoors and working hard to take pleasure in seeing game, and if a good shot on a buck or doe or any legal game presents itself, take it. Take the first good shot.

When you become an experienced hunter and shooter or when your ego demands entry into the stroking competition for larger and bigger, then consider the rack or the size of the animal. When you are beginning, ignore the antlers completely and concentrate on the mechanics of your shot, of placing the arrow into the heart of the vitals and then celebrating either the ache of missing or the elation of

The Biggest Deer of All. *Calling or grunting moose is not a science, but it is an art and one not quickly mastered. In the wilds of the pays du nord, the vast northern country of Canada, coaxing a bull moose to hunt you—especially with such a short range instrument as a traditional bow—will be an experience you will never forget. For this spine-tingling opportunity, tip your guide well whether you make the shot or not: You pay for the chance to hunt, not kill. Moose can be hunted in several states of the United States, but demand for those tags is very high, and your chance of being drawn in your lifetime is middling at best.*

Florida Gators. An alligator hunt in the American Southeast can be exciting and dangerous. Once on the endangered species list, alligators have made a stunning comeback, and locals say that if you leave water in the bathtub overnight, you'll have a gator inside by morning. Jim Morrow (right) killed two enormous alligators with a recurve bow.

making a good, clean shot that makes the deer or pronghorn circle once before falling, taking a final breath, and expiring quickly. This is the essence of bowhunting; this is the peak experience and it is what those who describe themselves as "trophy hunters," those who in videos on television slap their sides and howl with false elation and excited thumbs-up signs, have perhaps forgotten.

Now let's see what's out there to challenge and excite the traditional archer.

DEER

There are only two species of native North American deer: whitetails *(Odocoileus virginianus)* and mule deer *(Odocoileus hemionus)*. A third group, the Pacific coastal (or Columbia) blacktail, is a regional variation of the mule deer with enough individuality to be considered a legitimate subspecies. Whitetail offshoots include the isolated Sitka deer of Alaska, which is a close relative of the blacktail (and consequently of the mule deer), and two diminutive cousins to the whitetail: the Coues deer of the American Southwest and the tiny and endangered Florida Key deer. Interbreeding between whitetails and mule deer results in deer that you will informally hear referred to as "mule-tails."

Whitetails are found in forty-eight of the fifty US states in populations that sustain, indeed, encourage, hunting. In many areas of the east and the Midwest, deer are so numerous that they have become comfortable in suburban edge environments or even in large urban parks. Chances are high that public or private lands within fifteen minutes of your house will have sustainable deer populations and hunting opportunities as well.

Indeed, America's urban deer populations have become especially problematic but may offer bowhunting opportunities in unexpected places. Urban-zone deer are hunted in the same manner as deer in the deep forest—pattern and patience.

Finding places to hunt, whether it is on private land or through a club that leases land or in a wildlife management zone open to public hunting, and then studying the habitat to understand deer movement is called "scouting." Unless you are impatient, scouting for deer is almost as much fun as hunting. It can be a social event, getting you out of the house at any time of the year and teaching you about your neighbors, natural resources, and your wider community. Scouting is to deer hunting as sharpening a knife is to trimming a steak or priming a wall is to applying the final coat . . . though it is more fun than that!

Few people suddenly decide, on their own, to learn a foreign language or learn to drive a bulldozer or to take up traditional archery. Although a powerful experience in a book or at the movies might spark your curiosity—a significant bump of interest in archery, especially among young women, followed the 2012 movie *The Hunger Games*, which featured a young heroine; a similar bump among young men occurred following the 1982 movie *Rambo: First Blood*—you will typically be introduced to a subject, find admirable mentors, and become engaged in the topic through a friend or family member. Most likely they will also guide you in learning about hunting and again, most likely, your first quarry will be whitetail deer.

It is not that whitetails are easy game, for they are not, but they are the most numerous, most wide-spread, and arguably most durable of America's big game. We understand their needs for food and seclusion and where their populations are high—which is most areas in the United States despite zones with a now endemic disease called chronic wasting—and they are relatively easy to pattern. With a well-placed arrow, your traditional gear will be fully capable of taking any deer on the continent, from the smallest yearling doe to the grandest "book buck." For years, since bowhunters began demanding sensible hunting regulations that recognized the bow and arrow as legitimate, though limited, deer hunting gear has included a tree stand. Just thirty years ago, commercial tree stands were in their infancy and states were slow to accept their value. Minnesota, for example, forbade placement of stands higher than six feet off the ground, perhaps sharing the generally poor national experience of hunters nailing boards on trees and falling, with disastrous consequences, from do-it-yourself platforms.

Three types of tree stands are entirely compatible with traditional hunting and climbing up out of the deer's line of sight, perhaps twenty to twenty-five feet. At about twenty pounds with straps and accessories, climbers come in two pieces—a foot platform and a seat/arm platform—and allow you to climb many, though not all, trees in the deer woods. Fixed-position stands average twelve to fifteen pounds. They require attaching separate steps or a ladder to the side of a tree, climbing, and chaining the stand around the trunk. Positioning and use of either of these stands is an intricate operation, replete with the danger of falling. A ladder stand is less dangerous than a climber or fixed-position stand and thus offers fewer problems from fall injuries. Ladders are heavier and bulkier though, and more visible. They may require—depending on their length and weight—assistance transporting and erecting against a tree.

Whichever type of tree stand you hunt from, a fall-assist option securely attached to the tree is now used by every intelligent hunter. Hours on stand, sometimes in the cold and dark while waiting for a deer to cross your shooting lane, can be boring, and all hunters, at one time or another, find they have dozed off. In the "old days," hunters used little more than a rope around the waist and the tree, but eventually learned—after numerous well-publicized and certainly lonely and agonizing deaths—just how inadequate this was. Today's fall-assist harnesses allow you to hang from a stand in the vertical position, leaving your hands and feet free to save yourself or place a call to your hunting buddy. Some will even lower you safely to the ground.

When you buy a stand and harness, look for the TMA logo, the logo of the Treestand Manufacturer's Association. The TMA logo assures you that the manufacturer guarantees building to accepted industry standards and carries insurance to protect themselves and their customers in case of a manufacturing defect.

For those who are uncertain about climbing trees in the dark before legal shooting hours or of climbing down after dark, the past dozen years have witnessed an explosion in ground-blind development. Portable, camouflaged pop-up blinds are now a popular choice of many bowhunters who find that the interiors give them concealment and, if they are equipped with some odor control elements, give a minimal scent signature, too. In many situations, ground blinds are wonderful additions to a hunter's tool kit, the primary danger perhaps being that they encourage carelessness—noise, eating, reading, or even sleeping when one should be alert.

Deer can be hunted actively as well as passively, though no technique is foolproof or works 100 percent of the time. "Rattling deer" by banging antlers

Deer and Bowhunting. *Hunting and, derivatively, hunting and shooting companies in America have grown in the last half century as a result of the superb health of the whitetail population. While there are occasional incidents of blue tongue and chronic wasting, and the spread of "deer ticks" with Lyme disease, the size of the population allows—unlike in Europe or elsewhere in the world where the common man has a much more difficult time finding an opportunity—virtually everyone to go into the field with a significant possibility of being successful.*

together and thus imitating the clash of fighting bucks is well known for bringing in curious bucks. Using a fawn distress call will also sometimes cause deer of either sex to come running in search of a coyote or bobcat to thrash. The use of modern decoys, either 2D or 3D deer, is especially effective when coupled with a curiosity scent or some food flavoring like apples (if apples grow in your hunting area). All of these techniques are fun to experiment with and, if used judiciously, can turn the long hours of waiting and watching into an active and thoughtful pastime; in a sense, they encourage the deer to hunt you.

BLACK BEARS

Unlike whitetails, whose numbers may be larger on a continental basis than at any time in history or pre-history and are growing—and obviously estimates of numbers prior to the modern era are only scientific wild guesses based on further gross estimates of food resources and habitats—black bear populations are stable in a broad swath of territory from Maine to Alaska. Generally, the black bear (*Ursus americanus*) is half the size of a grizzly or brown or polar bear and is non-aggressive, although contrary examples aren't rare. Black bears eat grubs and berries, "anything that does not eat them first," and this makes them susceptible to close-range shooting with the bow and arrow.

Most bears are taken by hunting over bait. This means an outfitter (or an individual hunter if you can independently secure a license) puts out a pile of bait prior to the season in an area known to have bears and then checks periodically to see which baits are visited. Bait can be road kill or sweet bakery scraps. Because bears have a notorious "sweet tooth," honey is often used at the bait, sometimes melted or even burned so that its sweet odor carries for miles downwind. The outfitter then erects a tree stand within shooting range, and it is the client's responsibility to sit as silently and carefully as a fallen leaf until the bear appears at the bait. Baiting bears is hard work; it is time-consuming, but it isn't rocket science.

Formerly, bears were chased with dogs in the same manner as cougars, but numerous states have outlawed bear hunting with dogs.

Bears can also be called to a hunter with a "dying rabbit" squeal or distress call. It is not everyone's most popular dream, however, regardless of the black bear's timid nature, to sit nose to nose with an omnivore that can outrun, out-climb, and surely out-fight the meanest martial arts combatant.

Black bears make wonderful bowhunting quarry. Nothing in the northern forests quite compares to their stealth. One moment the woods are silent as a tomb, and the next a bear is pawing at the bait. You will swear that it could not have appeared so silently.

In addition, bear hunting is "laid back." Unlike deer hunting's agonizing refrain—"Sun's up in swamp!"—when everyone in camp rolls over in the sleeping bag and groans at 3:30 a.m., you need not go to your bear stand before mid-afternoon. Days are long in the north, longer the farther north one hunts, although hunting bears can still be done in the extreme south as well. Sleep late. Go fishing. Eat a leisurely lunch and bed down for a nap. Take a few practice shots . . . and then head out to the stand. Sooner or later you'll be right on time.

The question of a bear's edibility has to be posed here. Deer are designed by the ultimate creator to be eaten, either by wolves or cougars or bears or man, but bears have a strong and generally disagreeable flavor that most people find inedible. With a meatloaf that cooks the ground bear meat in its own fat, you will probably want to throw it away the minute you smell it. On the grill, however, when the meat is mixed with other ground meats and plenty of spices and where the fat drips off . . . it is, like carp taken from fresh water, worthy of consideration.

As far as equipment is concerned, your traditional gear, the same shooting gear you use for deer, will harvest any black bear. The trick with black bear is shot placement. The heart is low in the chest, the shoulder is thick and forward, and the bear is covered with thick black hair, which can make proper shot placement difficult to estimate. It is important to pick your spot and not become so interested in the animal's movements around the bait. A spot a third to halfway up the chest with the near-side leg forward is about right. The bear's hair will soak up plenty of blood, so a complete pass-through is to be preferred.

When shooting from an elevated stand for bear, the shoulder blade will cover some of the vital area. Unlike deer, whose ribs will split with any well-placed arrow carrying sufficient energy—or momentum, if that is your preferred measure—the best shot from a tree stand will be slightly from the bear's rear. Also unlike deer, there is no reason to hunt from a stand so high that you need oxygen. If you are still, without moving or sneezing, the bear will know you are present; it just won't care. And usually, an experienced guide will position the bait in a 55-gallon drum or between heavy logs so that the bear must move in a manner that gives you a good shot opportunity. This makes choosing your shot easier and may even give you time to relax and enjoy the sight of one of nature's most adaptable creatures so close.

PRONGHORN

America's antelope isn't a true antelope, but that is an argument we care less about than the fact that, except for outlying states in its range such as Texas and Arizona, the pronghorn (*Antilocapra americana*) is thriving in the West. (The Sonoran branch of the pronghorn family in Mexico is listed as endangered.) Because its Western high plains habitat is open rangeland, it is one of the few species you can enjoy watching for hours, sometimes for days, without being able to take a shot.

By speaking of open-range habitat, it is useful to note that little of such territory with viable pronghorn populations actually remains. Isolated government-owned acreage like the 115,890-acre Fort Pierre National Grassland in central South Dakota remain open to the public, but most of the West is divided and sub-divided by barbed wire for cattle. The overall population of pronghorns is stable-to-expanding, but the animal has a peculiar behavior around fences; it will not or can not jump over them, even a fence that a child could clear stops an entire herd of pronghorns. Wildlife managers encourage ranchers to omit the bottom rung of fencing or even to raise it slightly because the speedy mammal will scoot beneath fencing if it is able.

Unlike deer and caribou and elk, which possess bony antlers, the pronghorn—affectionately called a prairie goat—has horns composed of a slender blade of bone. The visible exterior, a black sheath of a waxy "hair-like substance" grows around the bone and is shed each year. Even the females have horns, though much smaller.

Although the pronghorn's head gear is distinctive and beautiful, the animals possess other qualities that make them desirable, especially for traditional bowhunters. First, they are lightning fast, racing at speeds in excess of sixty miles per hour; and because of their large heart-lung system, they can sustain this speed over the prairies for longer than you can keep their image in the spotting scope. Secondly, an antelope has large, luminous eyes that protrude from the sides of its head and provide wide-angle vision believed to be about the same as that of a man looking through eight-power binoculars. Third, unlike bear meat, antelope are unusually fine-tasting, often naturally flavored with sage; better than venison if the animal is properly cared for in the field—careful not to contaminate the meat with fluids from internal organs—and cooked with skill.

Again, your traditional gear will be perfect for hunting pronghorns, but the manner of hunting is different. Typically you will hunt pronghorns from the ground; this means that everything you do must be done meticulously, from building a blind to moving into shot position, because pronghorns are ultra-wary, skittish, and very fast. For a rifleman, this is not a special problem because the effective shot distance of a .243 or $.25/_{06}$ Remington is so much greater; but for a traditional archer whose arrow makes a distinctive arc and delivers a great punch, though relatively slowly, this means scoring on the prairie ghost is a meticulous process of getting everything right. And a frustrating quality of pronghorns is that they often "hang up" just out of bow range, standing broadside and watching the waterhole or the water trough where you are hunting, and while they are watching, you had best not be moving or they will see you and the speed of their departure will astonish you.

Pronghorn are usually hunted from a pit blind near a source of water, because water is the animal's weakness on the dry and dusty prairie. If you are lucky, your blind will be sheltered from the constant wind; if you are not lucky, you will need a hat, a bandana to cover your eyes and nose, and a pair of eyeglasses or sun glasses to keep your vision clear of blowing grime. And a pronghorn may run into a waterhole at any time of day, so hunting them can be a tedious process.

An option for bowhunters who may not like a pit blind—watch for prairie rattlesnakes and scorpions before you jump in and sit down—is sitting on a windmill platform. Attached to a well and pump, the windmill turns when the wind blows to pump water into a stock tank, which the pronghorn visit when no natural pond is nearby. The benefit of a windmill seat is that you can see for miles across the prairie, and the blades of the windmill turn frequently as the wind blows, habituating the pronghorns to movement. The down side is that you are exposed to the elements; the elevated position can be dangerous if you are the least bit careless; pronghorns can see you, so outrageous movement won't be tolerated; and the noise of the windmill turning and moving, a continuous clanking and scraping, can drive you mad.

Another option is to position yourself among the round hay bales prevalent in farm and ranch country, perhaps even erecting a portable blind among them if they are not stacked too tightly together. If you are cautious this gives you great freedom of movement and, accustomed to the stacks of bales and to ranch machinery, the goats will be as relaxed as goats ever get.

At times, prairie goats can be attracted to decoys. The old standard was to hang a white handkerchief on a fence and find a spot to crouch down within shot distance. While few of the curious prairie goats were probably taken in this manner by bow-hunters, the fluttering kerchief would always stop them and they would stare for hours, or so it would seem to a nervous hunter, but usually at a distance beyond bow range.

Today's 2D and 3D decoys are much more effective decoying pronghorns. Because a big goat weighs less than 100 pounds, a lifelike decoy is easily portable.

ELK

Arguably the most magnificent of North America's commonly hunted animals, the elk in all of its niches and high mountain valleys is the "trophy of trophies." Even smaller elk are twice the size of a big deer. The autumn vocalizations of rutting bulls (called bugling) are inspired, multi-octave, and spine-tingling. The antlers are astonishing in their elegance, and the animal's adaptation to mountains and prairies well deserves our admiration.

Elk have even been reintroduced to states that long ago crowded and, yes, hunted them to extinction in the pre-management era: Michigan, Tennessee, and others. The species is so adaptable that when they were introduced to New Zealand and Argentina, they out-competed other species, and their numbers grew to the point that they are now considered pests, invasive species.

Unless you are spectacularly lucky and draw one of the few Eastern tags—don't hold your breath—an elk hunt means a trip "Out West." Depending on the environment and the outfitter, an elk hunt could involve a long horseback ride into the foothills of the Rocky Mountains of Colorado, or perhaps bugling and stalking in Idaho or a Canadian province, or even sitting on a tree stand in the rain-drenched forests of western Oregon.

Your hometown deer-hunting gear could probably use an upgrade for elk. Compared to whitetails, the animal is enormous. While its vitals area is notably larger than a deer, its ribs are sturdy and shot distances might be greater. In addition, if your hunt involves calling and stalking, the uphill-downhill terrain that many elk herds inhabit is going to require practice before the trip. Unlike pronghorns or perhaps even big horn sheep or mountain goats, the elk will not stand still for long while deciding whether you are a threat. You must be ready to shoot from unexpected positions and angles. For such a large animal, it is capable of moving through evergreen forests, impossibly thick with blow-downs, either like a truck or a ghost. You will have to be alert all the time.

One of the aspects of bowhunting for elk that is understood but not actually accounted for is that elk are indeed very large critters. This means that you must mentally adjust from shooting deer at twenty or thirty yards, or you will either miss entirely or perhaps hit the elk with a wounding and non-critical shot.

Wapiti. It is customary to hunt elk in the Western United States and Canada, but significant efforts have been made, successfully, to restock this spectacular big-game animal in eastern states. With a well-placed arrow, a traditional bow is fully capable of taking a 1,200-pound bull elk.

The best way to work around this problem—and it may be totally unconscious, but that does not make it less real—is to practice with a life-size elk target. You can purchase a 3D target—wonderful, but very expensive—or cut one from cardboard, but having a sense of the dimensions will help you create effective distance-judging habits and consequently proper shot placement.

This is as good a time as any to talk about wounding a big-game animal and not recovering it. You know that the moment you nock an arrow on the string, you are responsible for that arrow. If you miss, you need to find it, because leaving an arrow with a sharp broadhead for someone to stumble on or to leave one embedded in a tree where some unlucky logger may hit it with his chainsaw is not acceptable. When you shoot an arrow, you need to find it. It will happen in the lifetime of every archer, however, that you will loose a shot and, despite looking for hours, you won't be able to locate the arrow. It happens. Do the very best you can and realize that not one of us is perfect.

And speaking of perfection . . . If you are long into bowhunting, you are going to wound an animal that, try as you might, you cannot recover. No archer wants this, but it happens. (It also happens to gun hunters, but they don't obsess about it like archers do.) A deer, and certainly an elk, is a good-sized target with relatively modest vitals: heart, lungs, liver. These animals move to their own rhythms, often unexpectedly; the wind blows a branch; you over- or underestimate the distance; the adrenaline flooding into your bloodstream causes you to execute a poor release; the deer "jumps the string," its muscles tensing for a leap from the unknown noise and your arrow flying high . . .

At some time you will hit a deer or a feral hog and you will not be able to find it. You follow the drops or sprays of blood, mark the trail, and are careful not to trample the evidence of the shot. You may even find a bloody arrow that has passed completely through, in which case the animal will bleed from both sides as it runs away, or a bed thickly matted with blood. And then suddenly, the blood trail ends—a drop, a speck, a turned leaf, and finally nothing. You search for an hour, two, three hours. You come back the next day with friends, ask other hunters, even watch for buzzards or crows that might gather around a carcass, and still nothing. The animal has vanished.

If you are on a guided hunt, depending on the regulations (or the depth of your wallet), your hunt may be over. Even though you did not recover the animal, you still have to pay the trophy fee. It's a bitter pill to swallow, but you knew this could happen before you signed the contract (or you should have).

There are several consolations. First, fretting and remorse and agonizing and unwillingness to give up a search are acceptable. Every hunter understands this; not one likes it. It should cause you to think hard about the situation and analyze what went wrong. Use it as a learning experience and get over it. You have fallen off the bicycle. Figure out why, and climb back on.

Secondly, there is substantial evidence in the bowhunting literature—much of it anecdotal but some based on real attempts to verify shot results—that big game that is not quickly and cleanly killed from a shot in the vitals often recovers. The animal might pull out, with its teeth, an errant arrow that hits a major joint if it has not penetrated too deeply. The animal may bleed a bit, and your shot will certainly cause pain, pain being a natural part of every animal's existence, including man's, but the animal will most likely—though not always—recover. There are plenty of bowhunting anecdotes about killing a deer and, upon field dressing or butchering, finding an old broadhead encapsulated in a cyst inside the body cavity.

Shooting an animal is not the end of a hunt. In some ways it is only the beginning. Your next job is to relax and wait for a half hour before making any significant noise or climbing out of your stand or blind. Unless you can see it from your position—and sometimes, though rarely, a deer dies quickly and within sight of the archer—give the animal time to lie down, bleed out, and die. If you can relax at this critical moment, finding it will be easier. Whatever you do, do not holler in excitement or shout into a cell phone. Let those actions wait until you have found the animal and are posing for pictures. The two jobs immediately following a successful shot are finding your quarry quickly and then field dressing it for processing. A lot of books have been written on these subjects alone: dissecting—pardon the pun—the shot angle or the point of impact, the hair or quality of blood on an arrow (frothy blood from an arrow through the lungs, for instance), following blood spattered on leaves and bushes, and keeping the animal clean once you remove the entrails.

The Inventive Bowhunter. *The author's bowhunting mentor Don Friberg, a retired official of the US Fish & Wildlife Service, finds an ingenious way to pack out a bow-killed trophy elk in Oregon. It is often said that once the game animal is on the ground, the fun is over and the work begins, but that ignores the reality of family cook-outs and the pleasure of having taken such a fine big-game animal with a traditional bow.*

CARIBOU

Caribou populations in North America are stable, and hunting pressure is light. The greatest threat to caribou comes from habitat destruction from oil drilling with its subsequent road building, flooding for hydroelectric power stations, and the rise of ocean levels from global warming.

For caribou, called reindeer in the Old World, a trip to northern Canada will put you in a wall tent with a cook who speaks French or perhaps an Inuit dialect. Bowhunting success rates are high, but getting your antlers home through the airlines needs to be studied and negotiated in advance or at least understood to avoid disappointment. If you are interested in registering your trophy with a record-keeping group like Pope and Young, you don't want the skull-cap split, and you do want to protect the tips of the antlers when you and your guide pack them. If that is immaterial to you, then splitting the antlers and taping them together will save space, will make carrying easier, and will probably be less expensive.

You want cold days and nights, because when the weather warms, billions of mosquitoes and black flies come out of hibernation, and on the tundra biting insects can drive you mad. When that happens, no oily bug sprays or lotions—in any case these are harmful to your traditional gear—will provide sufficient protection, and a head net only restricts your vision. An old-fashioned full body suit from Bug Tamer or Cabela's is the very best solution. These suits are lightweight, effective, and easy to pack (and also very useful for turkey hunting in the spring or early-season deer hunting in the fall).

Boo! If you are going to spend $3,000 to $4,000 for a caribou hunt, buy a target that will give you a sense of proportion. Whatever the subspecies, caribou are easily twice the size of deer, and the size of their antlers can dwarf the antlers of the average deer.

The caribou experience varies from terrain heavily covered by conifer forests to open tundra. In any case, supplement your gear with a good set of binoculars as they will come in handy for judging movement and antlers at a distance. When elk hunting, a cow elk will occasionally be your trophy—no antlers but a hundred-plus pounds of meat with fine edible qualities. For caribou, use your binoculars to shop for huge headgear; if you are accustomed to deer, caribou antlers (and body size—smaller than elk but much larger than a deer) will surprise you. Practice accordingly. You are not interested in paying $4,000 to fly to northern Canada or Alaska, hire an outfitter, and return home dragging a box of half-frozen cow caribou steaks through customs, even if the cows do have small antlers.

In this case you want a great experience and a life-long trophy for the wall. If you are lucky, you will see wolves, watch in fascination as the Northern Lights dance overhead, catch lake trout for dinner, and, later in the week when you are beginning to reek of body odor, jump madly in and out of a half-frozen lake or stream. All, unforgettable experiences.

OTHER HUNTING CHALLENGES

Wild Turkey. Michigan's Tim Hooey has hunted across North America with every imaginable legal weapon, from longbows to high-power rifles. The most difficult big game—some will argue with the adjective "big" when applied to this bird, in which case they should stop hunting small ones—he says might be high-mountain sheep and wild turkeys. "The wild turkey is extraordinarily sensitive," Hooey says, "and without benefit of decoys and ground blinds, few archers would ever score on a tom."

Exploring the bowhunting world of North America may not be boundless, but it is wide. We have touched on several opportunities that you can explore with traditional gear at a reasonable price, recognizing that dollars may not be the best measure of an experience, but that they are the unit of exchange.

An off-season hunt at a game ranch may not be your cup of tea, but for some species, primarily the imported exotics—blackbuck antelope or Axis deer or scimitar horned oryx, for example—it will be your only chance in a lifetime to hunt or perhaps even view these animals in the outdoors. Some species, such as the Père David's deer, which are extinct in the wild, are kept alive in a few wildlife sanctuaries in China and England and in America as curiosities. As long as they have an economic value, they will remain a viable species.

Puma. *Racing for hours up and down mountainsides, following the baying of hounds, is exhausting and, if and when the cougar (mountain lion or puma) is treed or cornered, terribly exciting. Bowhunting cougar is a test of stamina, willpower, and shooting ability.*

Hunting magazines are full of advertisements to hunt red stag in New Zealand and trophy dimensions on the ranches there are staggering. An occasional story will mention bear hunting in Russia or feral hogs in Poland, but the gem, the gold standard for the traveling hunter, has always been a hunt in Africa. Art Young and Saxton Pope went to Africa and bowhunted lions; Howard Hill took an elephant, as did Fred Bear; Bob Eastman and a few other American and Canadian bowhunters have taken all of the big game available except the threatened and endangered species, and Eastman accomplished the trick with a recurve. So when you pick up your bow for the first time and consider loosing your first arrow, put the idea of an eventual African safari in a corner of your conscious mind, begin saving, and start studying books and stories online and in magazines. An African hunt has all of the ingredients for being *the trip of a lifetime* . . . and the continent is changing so rapidly that your opportunities will not last forever, probably not through the end of the twenty-first century.

AFRICA

PLB. *In remote areas of the world and the United States, carrying a cell phone is no certainty that you can be located in an emergency. A Personal Locator Beacon can save lives—perhaps yours.*

Africa is a troubled continent. With virtually limited resources and many unstable governments, it has given, since the time of first European contact, far more than it has received. Today's aggressive economic power invading the lands south of the Sahara is China. Creeping southward also is the scourge of militant Islam, bent on destroying and enslaving. In a century, Africa has traded one set of overlords for another, European for Asian. Despite the tides of history, the continent's resources in big game are still astonishing.

Africa is worth as many visits as you can muster the finances and time to pay for. In New Zealand or Australia, you'll find customs somewhat similar to ours; plus, the people speak English, though at times you will be hard pressed to understand the local patter. In Europe, the languages will be difficult on the ears, but the customs and the clothing and the food will be vaguely familiar, vaguely similar to home, whether you are in France or

Romania. Even the game in these places is similar to the deer, elk, bear, and hogs that you hunted at home. Africa though, will almost certainly be shocking for a North American bowhunter.

In Africa, you will immediately be recognizable as a foreigner, and, in rural districts where you will find the big game, villagers stare. To your eyes, they are the exotic specimens, but you are on their soil, and you may feel like the proverbial fish in a glass bowl, even—or perhaps especially—in the field as a traditional bowhunter. This is your chance to feel exotic. In all, North Americans are 5 percent of the world's population, so this is your chance to be a patient and wise diplomat for your country and to demonstrate how truly effective the bow and arrow can be. No pressure, though . . .

The old days, the historic and romantic days of hunting Africa, are gone, except for the super wealthy. The days that Ernest Hemingway, Karen Blixen, Robert Ruark, and Peter Capstick wrote about are gone. And the great, commercial elephant hunting safaris of Bell, Sutherland, and Neumann are long over. Those were fantastic days of billowing tents and cocktails by starlight, of lines of chanting porters carrying canvas-wrapped bundles of food and tools on their heads. Those were the days of month-long or even six-month safaris. Those were the days of double rifles, double martinis, and close danger.

Today, the bow and arrow are widely accepted as efficient tools for taking all but the biggest game, such as elephant and hippopotamus. About the effectiveness of the bow for killing Africa's cats and antelope and pigs there is no doubt. Discuss the thick-skinned species of elephant and hippo and Cape buffalo (or white rhino, if that is at all possible, the poaching of rhino for their horns to provide fabulous Oriental medicinal ingredients having all but destroyed the species) and you will likely find yourself lost in the argumentative bush of bow weight, energy delivery and arrow momentum, shot placement and angle, and a hundred and one other questions.

You can hunt Africa with your whitetail gear if you intend only to hunt the thin-skinned creatures, the antelope or a warthog. But if you are stepping up to a member of the Big Five or hippo, you want to shoot the most powerful bow and the heaviest combination of arrow and broadhead that you can effectively handle. Unless you choose to hunt from a blind positioned near a waterhole, in which case you can silently check distances with a laser rangefinder because your movement will be disguised by the sides of the dark blind, you will want to extend your practice to sixty yards if possible. On foot, in Africa, many eyes and ears will be watching, and a chance to shoot at a trophy animal from only twenty or so yards will be rare. To paraphrase Robert Ruark, "Bring enough bow."

The demonstrated effectiveness of the bow and arrow democratized African hunting. Today it is not only the Captains of Industry or Heralded Heart Surgeons or Bank PooBahs who can hope to hang wildebeest or leopard trophies on the wall. Today teachers and union members, accountants and small business owners have a chance to book their African experience at a reasonable price, and much of this is due to archery and the archer's ethic that intention must precede action and the hunt is at least as important as the kill.

In the twenty-first century, your African hunt can be of one or two different types, both lasting a far shorter time than the classic safaris. For either, you will fly into an African airport where your outfitter or one of his assistants will meet you and help you and your gear move through customs. He will also help you with exiting and will work with you to see that any trophies you collect are properly tagged, prepared, and shipped. The last point is critical since you will depart once your hunt is over, but unlike hunting elk in Oregon or caribou in Newfoundland or bears in Maine, your trophy horns and skins must be processed locally for international shipment and carefully tagged for inspection by wildlife authorities.

The least expensive African hunt is a week at a game farm in South Africa or perhaps Namibia, where you will hunt from an elevated blind (a "hide" or perhaps a "machan") over a waterhole. This can be an extraordinarily productive way to hunt—or not, depending on the availability of water on the prairies—and these African ranches are not a canned experience because the abundant game is, unlike the customary ranch experience in Texas, native and totally wild; there may be fences, but you can walk for days without encountering one, and the animals feed naturally, rather than eating delivered goodies shoveled out of the back of a pick-up truck at periodic intervals.

The most expensive hunt is a true safari, or what passes for one in today's political and market atmosphere. For this hunt, you will take a bush plane from the international airport to your destination, invariably a grass and sand landing strip far out on the veldt. You will spend nights in tents, probably a semi-permanent base camp, because competition for space is so intense that outfitters vie for concessions from their government, and such concessions are not cheap, especially if they are known to hold populations of in-demand species. On a modern safari, you will ride beside the professional hunter in the high seat of a Range Rover or Toyota while you scout the concession for game. When something is spotted, a buffalo or impala or zebra, you will glass it to judge its trophy quality—or whether it is even approachable, such game often being surrounded by others of its species—and if you decide to attempt a stalk, the first person out of the vehicle will be your professional hunter with his .375 H&H or whatever rifle he prefers, followed by a tracker, a government "game scout," and then you.

On safari, you will not go into the bush without a back-up, a hunter with a gun. The land is home to lions and leopards, wild dogs and hyenas, and even a well-placed arrow will not protect you if you are rushed; only a heavy bullet with a ton of wallop—the .375 may deliver 4,000 ft/lb of energy depending on the range—at close range can do that. All of these animals can out-run and out-fight you. Lions and leopards can out-climb you. And all of them are hungry, all the time.

Whatever you choose to hunt, you must study the game available before you go and then perhaps make a list of what your financial capability will be. To be crassly commercial, every animal carries a price tag. Every species is valued separately, from a heavy, spiral horn eland to the grunting warthog, and on most ranches, animals are also priced by size of their horns, every inch of trophy adding several hundred dollars of value. So before you place an arrow on the string, be certain that you understand what you are shooting.

And this final thought on the commercial aspects of hunting Africa. Every hunter misses now and then; it happens. Every hunter, despite his or her most ardent practice and best effort, occasionally wounds an animal that is not recovered, despite all efforts to find it, despite the trackers and dogs. This also happens in Africa, but in Africa the outfitter is responsible to his government for the sustainability of the nation's wildlife resources, and if you hit a sitatunga, for instance, and it jumps into a black lake where it is eaten by crocodiles, you still must pay the trophy fees for that animal. Draw blood and the cash register rings. Shoot with the end in mind.

THE PH

The PH, professional hunter, has been the subject of romantic novels for a hundred years. He has been portrayed as a brave and ruggedly handsome white man, a hard drinker who understood the game and the dangers of the bush. He was a crack rifle shot, of course, and spoke several native languages, inspiring courage and loyalty among his men.

Like all romantic myths, there are elements of truth in the picture, but it is heavily glossed by Hollywood and popular novelists. This much is true however: Whatever he was, he knew little or nothing about archery and would laugh at the idea of using a stick and string to take a giant kudu, much less a lion or Cape buffalo.

Today's PH is by and large a different soul. He is a student who has learned primarily from books rather than in the rough and tumble of bush camps. He has worked his way up through classes and certificates, rather than by repairing a broken-down vehicle with chewing gum and bailing wire. Today's PH will certainly know the IUCN status of every huntable species in his concession, but he may struggle to evaluate the trophy quality of a sable. He has book-sense and, if you are very lucky, he has common sense as well.

The PH. *Paulo Shanalingigua is a professional hunter and owns Pori Trackers in Tanzania. Supporting a part-time crew of a dozen local men—game trackers, skinners, cooks, and various other specialties—Shanalingigua has learned about the limitations of the bow and arrow from his American clients. He was the first black PH in his country, a thrilling and harrowing story he tells in the recent book The African Diary of Bob Eastman. Shanalingigua is a professional who provides a specialized service, and the tip you leave should be discussed long before you touch down in Dar es Salaam's Julius Nyere International Airport. Would he advise his sons to follow in his footsteps? "Probably not," he says.*

One thing today's PH shares with the guides of old is a love for the land and a well-founded knowledge of its animals. This is not a profession for a man who expects to get rich quickly, because guiding is hard work. Your guide will rise before you and have his men prepare your hot water for a quick bath and breakfast; he will fall onto his camp cot after you are snoring, having made arrangements for the following day. He will organize the cooks and skinners and trackers and all of the support that is required to put a foreign bowhunter successfully into the field, bring him (or her) back safely and happily, and send him home.

Being a professional hunter means that at some time in your career you will be bitten by a venomous snake, attacked by a lion or buffalo; you will be cold, thirsty, frightened, in pain or discomfort, and still must deal with cranky clients. Being a PH is still not a job for the weak or the inattentive. It remains a difficult job and a great, if vanishing, profession.

Where PHs Go to Die. Once a famous African PH working for Safarilandia Mozambique, Rui Barbosa Quadros had been bitten by poisonous snakes and lions, gored by Cape buffalo, and chased by Communist guerillas. When he died alone and penniless in 2010, he had lived a life of high adventure and paid for it ultimately in blood, sweat, and tears.

The Père David Deer. *Now extinct in the wilds of China, which was its natural habitat, this species of deer can be found on select hunting ranches in America. China has reintroduced the deer into a zoological garden from a stock smuggled to England a century ago, but in the most curious twist of fate, the only way the Père David can be kept from going completely extinct is for sportsmen of the world to pay to hunt one on a stocking ranch. This will guarantee that ranchers allow the species to breed and will maintain the necessary genetic diversity for a viable species.*

CHAPTER EIGHT

SO, NOW WHAT? COMPETITION . . .

Many Games, Many Nations. In Hungary, riders still practice the sport of shooting the bow and arrow from horseback. The Eurasian steppe produced most of the well-known mounted archers, including the Scythians, Parthians, Huns, Avars, Bulgars, Magyars, Turks, Mongols, and Cossacks. As the most common troop type among the classical Mongol hordes, warriors were born to the saddle. Equipped with a powerful recurve composite bow and hand weapons, mounted warriors were lightly armored and highly mobile. Their effectiveness and maneuverability on the battlefield nearly allowed them to conquer the known world. (Photo courtesy of Csanády)

You have a bow and arrows and you have taken a few shots at the local range or at a friend's backyard target. Now what?

Most of us grow up into hobbies like stamp collecting, banjo playing, or small engine repair. We learn from parents or even school chums and so almost naturally fall into similar tracks. We also follow our mentors into hunting or competition, but there is a wide world of opportunity awaiting; a world of travel and friendships . . . and a deepening understanding of and appreciation for archery.

Hunting to Eat. *The native Rikbaktsa peoples are hunters, gatherers, and agriculturalists who live in the Amazon rain forest of northwest Mato Grosso Province, Brazil. Traditionally male children receive their first bow between the ages of three and five years old. In this photo, a Rikbaktsa archer competes in Brazil's 2007 Indigenous Games. (Photo courtesy of Valter Campanato/ABr.)*

Other than pleasure or pure recreational shooting, such as old-fashioned roving, shooting a bow can roughly be divided into two areas: competition and hunting. Hunting is extremely popular among traditional shooters, but many of these men and women also shoot in competitive events that simulate a type of social hunting. After all, recreational competition sharpens their skills and engages them in a community, a communication network of mutual interest. So let's take a look at the three most popular competitive avenues for longbow and recurve shooters.

Uniting the Nations. *Perhaps there are always two strains in human affairs—that which would unite and that which would divide; the black and white; the yin and yang. As much as the bow and arrow have been used in warfare, they have been a part of friendly competition that brings the people of the world together. (Photo courtesy of Easton Archery)*

ARCHERY SHOOTERS ASSOCIATION (ASA; WWW.ASAARCHERY.COM)

The ASA was founded in Georgia in 1993 by a group that wanted to televise archery competition. They believed they could make archery as interesting and as exciting for the viewer as it was for participants by using multiple cameras, personality interviews, and sharp editing. The same inspired programming had developed a huge following for golf and, fifteen years later, would do the same for poker—and there is no more static activity than playing cards! The group was not perfect, but it was ahead of its time.

The idea developed a thread long held in archery circles that promotion and growth of the sport depended on the electronic media, which at that time meant the flourishing cable television market. Even old-timers realized that with diminishing rural populations, archery needed a continual influx of young shooters, and this depended on the small screen of the TV (or today, the even smaller screens of handheld mobile devices like smart phones). Watching an international FITA—now called World Archery—tournament where men and women stood in a line and silently, unemotionally, shot at distant round targets was as much fun, all agreed, as watching grass grow. This was exemplified by television coverage of the Summer Olympics, which focused exclusively on active, energetic sports where strength, agility, and movement were key to winning—boxing and basketball and even rowing—and totally ignored archery.

While the "exciting television" angle eventually fell by the wayside, the competitive shooting environment that developed has flourished, following the organizational lead of the older but more regionally limited International Bowhunting Organization (IBO). Headquartered now in Kennesaw, Georgia, the ASA typically holds its major competitions in the Southeast, in the zone from Texas to the East Coast, and north to the Ohio River. The six McKenzie ASA Pro/Am Tour Schedule competitions are three-day events. They typically attract several thousand archers from all over the United States and require hundreds of staff and volunteers. These outdoor get-togethers are terrific for fine shooting and a congenial atmosphere.

On day one, archers travel, check into a motel (or set up a tent), look over the venue, and unlimber their gear. Most will also take a few shots at a practice range. Shooting for score takes place the second and third days and consists of two rounds of twenty individual 3D targets set at unknown distances (there are some known distance events but the original impetus for ASA was to simulate the bowhunting experience) from the shooting stake. Each life-size 3D foam target—bear, deer, turkey, or other—has scoring zones faintly imprinted on the side that roughly equate to the vital areas of a big-game animal. With the naked eye, it is almost impossible to see these zones from the shooting position, so a shooter should be familiar with them before the shoot in order to ensure they shoot their best. Serious shooters carry a reference card to remind themselves of scoring sectors and then double check the shooting lane with binoculars before loosing an arrow

What makes the shooting difficult, other than the unknown distance and the pressure of shooting in front of a crowd or in unpredictable weather, is unfamiliar terrain. While there is a huge emphasis on safe shooting, the shooting lanes—from the stakes to the targets—may be irregular with overhanging branches, leaning stumps, or brush partially obscuring the targets (though not the scoring zones). At some events, competitors may be required to climb a stair and shoot from an elevated platform, to fling an arrow across a ditch, or to shoot up- or downhill, all of which make distance estimation tricky, especially in an unknown environment.

Shooters walk through a venue in groups of three to five after the shotgun start. The trick is to judge the distance to a target—no distance estimation aids such as laser rangefinders are allowed—and then to shoot an arrow into the highest eight-, ten-, or twelve-ring scoring zone. Targets are set generally perpendicular to the shot; angled shots, such as the classic quartering away bowhunting shot, are discouraged because the foam skin of the target can cause deflections, arrows hitting at angles in the scoring zones and glancing dangerously off to the side. Archers shoot in a rotation and then go forward together to score arrows. If an arrow even touches the next higher scoring zone, it counts as the higher score.

Although it is competition and a winner can pay for their trip and pocket a little money as well, shooting is friendly, and when rain falls or the afternoon sun makes it difficult to see the target because of glare off sights or eyeglasses, a member of the group will usually step up to hold an umbrella over the shooter. Shooters have fun, but they are inevitably courteous and serious about shooting.

ASA has developed several interesting rules, among them a "dress code" (you thought you left this behind in elementary school): "All competitive shooters are required to wear collared shirts, or may compete in an ASA sponsor's factory-issued competition clothing, which may include Henley collars or mock turtle necks (no T-shirts.) Professionals and amateurs will be allowed to compete while wearing shorts (men's shorts must have a minimum inseam of six [6] inches.) All competitive shooting classes are prohibited from competing in T-shirts, tank tops, cut-off jeans, or short-shorts."

In ASA shooting, archers are divided (and sub-divided) into classes by type of equipment, by professional or amateur status, and by sex and age. Men and women shooting modern compound bows, for example, compete separately, and both the youngest and oldest competitors have specific categories, as do archers who have extreme differences in experience. Rules for these categories specify individual maximum arrow speeds based on a minimum arrow weight of five grains per pound of draw (the top ASA arrow speed allowed is 280 fps), target distances (from twenty-five to fifty yards), and equipment selection. Taken as a whole, the rules are complicated, and to fully understand each nuance, you must check the online rule book, as rules change over time and can be exceptionally picky. This, according to ASA's shooting rules, governs arrows:

> Arrows of any type may be used provided they subscribe to the accepted principle and meaning of the word arrow as used in target archery, have not been altered from the manufacturer's original specifications (except cut to size), and that these arrows do not cause undue damage to the 3-D targets. An arrow consists of a shaft with a field or glue-in point, nock, fletching (which may only consist of individual vanes used to stabilize the arrow and which may

not be connected to each other by any means above the shaft) and, if desired, cresting. The maximum diameter of arrow shafts will not exceed .422″; the field or glue-in point for these arrows may have a maximum diameter of .425″

In the traditional class, ASA regulations specify that the bow must be either a recurve or longbow "without wheels or cams." The maximum shot is twenty-five yards and maximum speed allowed is 280 fps! "No release aid, no sights, a single stabilizer up to 12″ in length measured from the point of attachment, no overdraws, no draw checks, must have one finger touching the arrow nock, and must use one consistent anchor point. No marks on the sight window, string, or bow to use as an aiming or judging reference. All arrows must be identical in size, weight, and construction." However, most competitors use binoculars so they can review the target prior to their shot and then check arrow placement afterwards.

A few years ago ASA used a high and low twelve-ring, and sometimes a fourteen-ring that was outside the eight-ring. It may seem odd that such a high-scoring ring was in a zone where a hunter would not want to shoot at an animal, however it related to an individual shooter's evaluation of risk versus reward; if you thought you could make it or needed the extra points to advance in the standings, you might give the fourteen-ring a shot. Like the twelve-ring, the fourteen-ring was fairly small and a miss often resulted in a low eight or five score. So you had to be pretty sure of the range and of your ability to hit such a small circle before committing to shooting at the fourteen-ring. This element has been changed recently to the requirement to clearly "call" if your intention is to shoot the high twelve-ring. (Note that ASA says, "When the upper 12 is called that will take the lower 12 out of play on that target for that shooter. The group must acknowledge the shooter's request to score the upper 12.")

Despite the overabundance of rules—but anytime money is involved and is awarded as a prize, there will be plenty of rules—ASA shooting is tremendous fun, and major shoots attract a thousand archers. ASA has worked hard to vary the formats within an acceptable structure of competition and to include, for example, occasional celebrity and team shoots to maintain interest and entice manufacturers into sponsoring opportunities. The rules, though complex and at times irritatingly picky, are designed to ensure that all competitors have a chance to win within their selected class and division; thus, the rules "level the playing field."

In addition to the national shoots, ASA has developed a local structure called the ASA Federation that holds local shooting events. Dozens of clubs across the South and as far away as California, Wisconsin, and Vermont participate in Federation shoots. Local events put archers in touch with one another and provide a measure for potential national success, and affiliation locally will always make you a better shooter.

INTERNATIONAL BOWHUNTING ORGANIZATION (IBO; WWW.IBO.NET)

IBO Fun. The object of archery is to have fun. If you can mix in a little hunting and competition like these IBO shooters, who are scoring and pulling arrows from a 3D mountain goat, then your purpose has been accomplished. If you can introduce a youngster to the thrill of traditional shooting, you are doubly blessed. The IBO dress strictures are much more relaxed than those of its southern cousin, the ASA. (Photo courtesy of Ameristep)

The IBO is actually the older of the two national 3D shooting circuits, and it uses Rinehart targets exclusively. With headquarters located in Vermillion, Ohio, IBO was originally conceived by a group of bowhunters in 1984. Their aim was to unify the world's hunting archers into a cohesive force that could influence legislation, increase standards of education and shooting abilities, and have fun in a competitive environment: "Promote, encourage and foster the sport of bowhunting." Of course bowhunters, like any active and thoughtful group—snowmobilers or marathon runners—are as easy to corral as a yard full of house cats. Nevertheless, the IBO has thrived in the three decades since its inception.

A more varied set of shooting formats—indoor as well as outdoor—is sponsored by the IBO than by the ASA. Of course, some of that has to do with location, because the founding states for the IBO were Indiana and Illinois. (The broad swath of states from New York through Missouri, containing more than half of America's licensed archery hunters, is traditionally the heart of bowhunting in the United States.) Still, the IBO occasionally holds well-attended national shoots as far south as Georgia and Alabama. The organization's events begin in January and run up against the opening of archery deer (and elk) seasons in September, with individual and team events. And the IBO pays special attention to longbow and recurve shooting with a mid-summer Traditional World Championship.

One of the ideas incorporated into the by-laws is a financial incentive. A percentage of the entry fees and monies collected from sponsors is paid back to top winners (the ASA is similar). This means an average archer can take home a little cash if he or she has a hot shooting weekend, or perhaps one of the dozens of door prizes given away at each shoot. It also has resulted in a class of opportunistic archers who have turned professional—typically the class with the largest cash payouts—superbly honing their skills and gear, developing their market value through sponsorships with equipment manufacturers or outfitting businesses, and all the while keeping their "day job." Invariably the men and women who are consistently at the top of the official standings, which are highlighted in print and online, are those who are diligent in practice and pay very careful attention to targets and their gear set-up. This is as true for the traditional class as for the open pro divisions. Payouts for traditional classes are smaller because there are fewer participants, the majority of America's bowhunters having been lured into more expensive (and less fun) compound shooting by its relative ease with high let-off and the highly publicized speed craze.

The IBO has its own target and scoring system for local and national events, because targets are either 2D silhouettes—less expensive and easier to store but not as realistic—or 3D targets. The host club determines both target selection and pay-outs per class and division. (The host club for the 2013 Traditional World Championship, for instance, was Cloverdale Conservation Club in Cloverdale, Indiana.) In recognition of its bowhunting orientation, the IBO allows a wider angle for targets in relation to the shooting stake, at least in theory: "Care shall be taken when setting targets not to over rotate or excessively lean the targets to ensure that the entire vital area can be safely shot." Official IBO targets have eleven-, ten-, and eight-ring scoring zones; an arrow anywhere else on the body scores five points, and if you place an arrow into the horns or antlers, you get a big fat zero. Maximum arrow speeds are a little higher in IBO shooting—290 fps—and stake placement for unmarked distance shots extend from fifty yards (blue) to about twenty-five yards (white). When shooting, the archer must touch the appropriate stake with some part of his or her body. At times, stakes are set to challenge the archer with various shooting positions, and unlike informal golf matches, there are no "mulligans"— each archer gets a single shot at the target.

The IBO takes a more varied approach to traditional shooting. A recurve or longbow could compete in the other classes (except crossbow), but unless you are a magnificent shooter, your odds of winning against a bow that shoots 100 percent faster and whose arrows are launched with a mechanical release would be nil.

Local color. Women now compete in the archery and horse-racing events of Mongolia's Naadam festivals, traditionally "the three games of men." The games are Mongolian wrestling, horse racing, and archery. (Photo courtesy of Zohar Bar-Yehuda)

- The "Recurve Un-Aided" class bars sights but allows a rest, a plunger, and a draw check or clicker. Unlike other classes, Recurve Un-Aided class permits string- and face-walking.

- The "Longbow" class requires wood arrows. Interestingly, this class specifies: 1. The bowstring, when the bow is strung, may only contact the nocks of the bow; and 2. No stabilizers, counterbalances, or weights of any kind may be attached or built into the bow, except a bow quiver "clearly designed to hold arrows."

- The "Traditional" class allows recurves or longbows and allows aluminum, carbon, or wood arrows with at least three feathers or vanes no less than four inches long.

225

- Archers in the "Female Traditional" class must use the same equipment as the Traditional Class with the exception that any arrow and fletching combination may be used as long as all arrows are matching in size and weight. Also, any rest may be used.

And since you asked, the IBO does not have a formal dress code.

NATIONAL FIELD ARCHERY ASSOCIATION (NFAA; WWW.NFAA-ARCHERY.ORG)

According to John Yount, who compiled a history of the NFAA, now headquartered in Yankton, North Dakota, the archery club in Redlands, California, began writing rules for competitive instinctive field shooting in the 1930s. An organization gradually coalesced to promote it because members wanted to be free of the more rigid constraints of target archery as dictated by the National Archery Association (NAA), which recently rechristened itself "USA Archery" (www.teamusa.org/USA-Archery.aspx) as part of a worldwide branding effort to maintain interest in the Olympics. Members of the club wanted to improvise games that would interest and attract new archers.

Modern Olympic Games. At the 2012 Olympic Games in London, Ki Bo-bae of Korea and Aida Roman of Mexico thrilled the crowd with a first-ever shoot-off for the women's gold-medal title. Ki won the shoot-off and the gold medal with a final arrow that measured only millimeters closer to the center of the gold. Roman's teammate, Mariana Avitia, took the bronze earlier in the day, giving Mexico its first-ever Olympic archery medals. If you look closely, you can see the separator of the finger tab protruding between the fingers of her right hand, the sling on the finger and thumb of her left hand, and the clicker on the bow riser. In the second photo, her arrow launched and in flight, Ki Bo-bae shows excellent posture and follow-through. (Photos courtesy of Easton Archery)

Yount writes that the initial twenty-target course in California was laid out in rugged country, which few of today's archers would appreciate. "Many a target had a fifty- or sixty-yard climb up a forty-five-degree trail, and one shot was 160 yards across a very deep ravine that is still full of arrows. There were no straw butts on this or any of the other early courses. The target was simply pinned to a pile of dirt." In those days, all archers were "traditional" and shot heavy wood arrows, but things have changed since the NFAA's official founding in 1939.

What is field archery today? It begins with the "field round," and it is similar in format to the NFAA's "hunter round" and "animal round." Imagine walking along a path through the woods. You are among a group of shooters, four being the preferred number. The path may wind uphill or down. It is both similar to and different from the typical 3D course laid out by the IBO or ASA. When you come to a stake, the distance is clearly marked. You know, for example, that it is twenty-nine yards to the target, and this is the core difference. The NFAA gained popularity among people who thought of themselves as archers first and hunters second.

NFAA separates field shooters by style, division, and class or flight, as well as sex. Men and women may shoot in the same groups, but will compete separately for high score.

- Style refers to the type of shooting equipment used, and until you choose your own style, it can seem confusing: freestyle, freestyle limited, barebow, competitive bowhunter, bowhunter freestyle, bowhunter freestyle limited, freestyle limited recurve/longbow . . . and traditional.

- Division refers to the separation of competitive archers by category: professional, master senior, senior, adult, young adult, youth, and cub. The NFAA says all divisions are available for both male and female archers.

- Class and/or flight refers to the separation of competitive archers according to skill level.

The typical field round is twenty-eight targets, and each competitor is allowed four arrows per target. The NFAA's Range Guidelines say, "Field ranges are often laid out in fourteen-target 'loops,' where all of the shots are outward, away from the center of the loop." This means that on the field round, you will shoot 112 arrows, whereas on a day of IBO shooting, you might only shoot twenty arrows in addition to a few practice shots.

According to the NFAA: "Some of the shooting positions let you shoot all four arrows from one marked stake; some shooting positions have stakes at four different positions where you walk toward the target on each shot, or in a fan position. The distances vary according to the round you are shooting."

Shot distance at the round NFAA targets varies from about seven yards to eighty yards, and the NFAA uses four different size targets; larger for longer shots, smaller for closer shots. There is a possible twenty points per target, and a perfect round is 560. The NFAA recognizes a peak shooting weight of eighty pounds and a top arrow speed of 300 fps. It also takes two pages of its voluminous official rules to help archers establish golf-like handicaps: "Handicapping is the great equalizer among sportsmen of differing abilities."

Bow mounted sights are not allowed in NFAA traditional shooting, or as the rule book says, "There shall be no device, mechanical or otherwise, in the sight window except the arrow rest, arrow plate or plunger button." No clickers, stabilizers, or levels are allowed, and only a single nocking point is permitted. Bowing to the inherent handicaps accepted by today's traditional shooters, the rules specify, though it is indeed a mixed compliment: "For all tournaments below the Sectional level, all traditional archers may shoot at Youth distances." In freestyle limited recurve/longbow shooting, sights (or scopes without a magnifying lens) and kisser buttons are allowed.

The NFAA is quite particular—and this is stylistically instructive, though in the mass of registered field shooters, the percentage is small—about the longbow, defining it in print as: "A one piece straight ended bow of any material, which when strung displays one continued unidirectional curve which is measured as follows: When the strung bow is placed with the bowstring in a vertical position, the angle as measured between the tangent of any point on the limb and an imaginary horizontal line must always decrease as this point is moved further away from the bow grip. Tip reinforcing not exceeding ½″ in height, as measured from the surface of the bow limb and not exceeding 1½″ in length as measured from the limb tip." Wood arrows are specified.

And yet this is only one of the NFAA-sponsored archery rounds . . . Aside from the regulated field, animal, and hunter rounds previously mentioned, NFAA has established patterns for an international round, a "Flint Bowman Indoor" round, a "Lake of the Woods" round, and various target rounds. The NFAA promotes a much wider variety of shooting venues than other national organizations. It hosts static indoor events, such as the historic Las Vegas Archery Festival where competitors stand at a line and shoot at round targets eighteen meters away. It either lends its name to a sponsor or hosts a variety of other events such as outdoor 2D competitions, where animal images printed on paper are pasted on cardboard, or 3D hunter events using foam animal targets. And remember that, in almost all NFAA shooting, distances are marked to give everyone an equal chance.

The NFAA approach is to have fun within a structure of competition that is the same all over the United States. The rule book, though complex and, at times, entertaining, is flexible, having been amended often. Thus, everywhere you shoot, you can compare scores within your division—whether you prefer release, fingers, bowhunting equipment, or are strictly a formal target competitor—knowing that the formats are comparable, the "playing field" is level.

And since you asked, the NFAA—perhaps betraying the senior bias of its directorate—does have a dress code, preferring "clean, neat attire, acceptable to public view."

Not acceptable? "Jeans or Denim of any color are not allowed during competition. Professional archers shall wear khaki, tan, black, white, or navy slacks, shorts, or skirts. Shorts and skirts can be no shorter than two inches above the knee. The waist of the attire must not fall below the waistline. Shirts/tops shall be of a collared design. Archers may also wear uniforms provided by sponsors. Shirts must have a standard collar, Henley collar, or mock collar. T-shirts, swimming suits, cut-offs, and obscene or vulgar slogans or pictures on clothing are prohibited."

The NFAA even regulates footwear, noting that "Open toed shoes/flip flops/sandals are unacceptable while competing." And anyone—an official, another competitor, or your ex spouse—can rat you out, the violations resulting in reprimand, probation, or even suspension from the NFAA.

And perhaps betraying the general baby boomer age and conservative orientation, the official rules not only specify the playing of the national anthem before competition begins, but also outlaw littering: "Anyone reported littering . . . will be dealt with." So be careful with that candy wrapper.

Lest you think that a hide-bound organization such as the NFAA has no sense of humor, however, the official rules do allow an Order of the Bone award for a member who "pull(s) a conspicuous 'boner' pertaining to archery hunting." So screw-ups of the world hold on. There is hope!

A NOTE ABOUT THE IFAA

The NFAA is part of a world-wide organization of field archers called, not surprisingly, the International Field Archery Association. The IFAA was founded in 1970 when a group of field archers from the United States, Sweden, England, Scotland, Wales, and Canada agreed on a set of basic rules by which field archery tournaments would be run. "We now represent over 50,000 field archers in over 40 member countries from all continents [forgetting, it would seem, Antarctica]."

International Fun. Shooting at international competitions is not just for the elite sponsored athletes who devote their lives to intense training. Participation in International Field Archery events introduces everyone who wishes to participate to the thrill of shooting in Europe or Asia or Australia and meeting people from those continents on their own terms—as well as testing your archery skills on a world stage. (Photo courtesy of Ameristep)

The IFAA is a little different in its regulations of shooting than the NFAA, but the beauty of the organization is that an archer can meet like-minded people from all over the world and learn about their equipment, their shooting styles, and their cultural perspective. In addition, IFAA tournaments are held both indoors and outdoors in dozens of foreign countries—Sweden, Argentina, New Zealand, South Africa, and many more—giving you an opportunity to travel to exotic environments with a purpose other than sightseeing. And the IFAA is hospitable to traditional shooting.

Perhaps because it encompasses so many languages and cultures, and crosses all international boundaries, the IFAA tournament system is flexible in its broad outlines and within the 300 fps arrow speed: "The International Field Archery Association (IFAA) sanctions a number of different Regional and World tournaments that are hosted in accordance with its rules. These tournaments all have their own specific rules and guidelines."

One of the IFAA's outstanding characteristics is its recognition that historical bows are a great pleasure (and a great challenge) to shoot. From its 2011 Archer's Handbook: "The recognition of the classic bow (also called historical or primitive bow) shall be based on the accepted design and usage during the period preceding the year 1900." Shooting historical bow designs in IFAA competition requires polyester strings (no historic string materials like flax or sinew or spun cotton) and wood arrows fletched with feathers. One of the cool, internationally flavored elements of the IFAA is that its website (www.ifaa-archery.org) illustrates—rather than just discusses—the types of bows and equipment allowed in various shooting categories. Check it out!

Relax. Have Fun. *In the end, after all the discussion of stance, arguments about aiming, and rulemaking about equipment, it all comes down to having fun. If you can't have fun shooting the bow and arrow, learning a traditional life skill, consider yourself officially "fun-challenged." (Photo courtesy of Ameristep)*

GLOSSARY

As you become more deeply involved in archery you will occasionally hear a term that you don't understand. You can either ask or you can look it up—or both!

In the definitions below you occasionally see the acronym "AMO." This stands for Archery Manufacturer's Organization, under which some of these terms were formalized, at least for the United States. This helps manufacturers and we individual archers with interchangeability of gear. Accepted definitions give us a way of evaluating preferences and performance across diverse platforms. The AMO has been dissolved and reincorporated as ATA, Archery Trade Association, yet the AMO acronym is still customary in defining some terms.

A

Adjustment range (compound bow): a) Draw weight: the minimum to the maximum bow weights over which the manufacturer recommends the bow be used. b) Draw length: the longest to shortest draw-length capabilities for which the bow was designed.

Anchor point: spot on side of an archer's face, often at the corner of the mouth (called a high anchor) or under the jaw (a low anchor), to which the hand pulling the bowstring is positioned on every draw; any spot used as a consistent location to anchor the archer's shooting hand.

Arm guard: a stiff material worn on the inside of the bow arm to protect it from the slap of the bowstring upon release.

Arrow: projectile shot from a bow, having a point on the forward end and stabilizing fletches on the rearward end (sometimes called a "bolt" when shot from a crossbow).

Arrow length: the length of the shaft from the deepest point of the nock notch to the end of the shaft, not including the point.

Arrowhead: the replaceable tip or point of an arrow designed to give the arrow proper balance, to protect the front end of the shaft from splintering on impact, and to aid in penetration.

Arrow plate: area on the side of a recurve bow's arrow shelf that comes in contact with the passing arrow; also called "strike plate."

Arrow rest: where the arrow rests during draw; the means used to support the arrow on the bow while it is attached to the bowstring and through the initial period of launch. Depending upon the bow and your style of shooting, the arrow rest may actually be your knuckles (longbow) or the arrow shelf (recurve).

Arrow shelf: bottom ledge or horizontal off-set of the sight window in a bow handle.

Arrow weight: weight of an arrow in grains at 437.5 grains per ounce.

Atlatl: a handheld spear- or dart-throwing device that preceded the invention of the bow.

B

Back of the bow: the side of the handle riser or limbs facing away from the archer when the bow is held in the shooting position.

Backing: a layer of material permanently attached to the back of the bow.

Barebow: a style of shooting without sights or other aiming aids (also called "instinctive").

Bare-shaft testing: the use of non-fletched arrows at close range to aid in adjusting nocking-point height—and, if used, plunger stiffness and arrow-rest position—or to determine arrow stiffness. The purpose is to tune the bow and arrow system for good arrow flight.

Barreled arrow: an arrow whose shaft is slightly tapered from the middle toward each end and has its greatest cross-sectional diameter near the center of the shaft.

Belly: the belly of the bow is the side seen by the archer when the bow is held in shooting position (also "face").

Billet: a) a piece of wood used in making self bows. Billets are commonly split from a side-by-side position in the same log to obtain similar limb performance characteristics and then spliced into the handle section of a one-piece recurve bow. b) A length of "raw" aluminum from which a handle riser is machined.

Blunt: an arrow tip that is not pointed. Fitting on the end of the arrow shaft, it is used for practice or to hunt small game.

Bow arm: the arm that holds the bow riser while shooting.

Bow draw weight: the bow weight marked on a recurve or longbow. It is predi-cated on the force required to pull the string to a standardized length of twenty-eight inches.

Bow face: the side of the handle and limbs that faces the archer when the bow is held in shooting position (also "belly").

Bow sight: a device attached to the handle (riser) to give one or more points of refer-ence. It typically fastens on the opposite side as the arrow shelf but is shaped in an "L" fashion, so that the sight pins can be seen on the arrow side.

Bow square: usually a T-shaped device used to measure string brace height and proper nocking height or location.

Bow string: the cord that attaches to both limb tips and transforms potential or stored energy from the limbs into kinetic energy in the arrow. Usually multiple strands of a suitable material used to connect the limbs and launch the arrow.

Bow weight: the actual physical or mass weight of the bow itself with no accessories mounted.

Bowyer: a bow maker or bow designer.

Brace: to string a bow.

Brace height: the distance from the grip pivot point to the inside edge of the bow-string measured at ninety degrees with the bow in the un-drawn position. The traditional term was "fistmele," which refers to the equivalent length of a closed fist with the thumb extended, indicating the proper traditional distance used between the deepest part of the grip and the string.

Broadhead: arrow tip with blades having cutting edges suitable for hunting.

C

Cant: to hold the bow at an angle while drawing and shooting.

Cast: a general reference to the distance a bow can shoot an arrow.

Center serving: a protective wrap around the central section of a string to prevent wear.

Centershot: the left-right horizontal placement of the arrow rest in the sight window of the riser. Can also refer to the amount the sight window is offset to achieve smooth arrow passage.

Clicker: usually a metallic, spring-activated device mounted inside the sight window of the bow and forward of the arrow rest. It gives a precise indication of when full draw is attained by snapping off of the point of the arrow and making an audible "click."

Cock feather: the odd-colored feather on the arrow in a three-fletch configuration. It is used to index the arrow for proper placement on an arrow rest or shelf.

Composite bow: a bow made of laminations of more than one material.

Compound bow: a bow featuring a system of eccentrics and cables used to increase bow weight rapidly to a maximum and then decrease it (let-off) rapidly as the archer approaches full draw.

Creep: a) the failure to hold solidly at full draw or at anchor point prior to release; b) relaxation of the internal molecular adhesion in synthetic strings, usually from heat or continued stress, which results in string stretch.

Cresting: decorative painted bands on the arrow shaft.

Crossbow: a horizontal bow mounted on a stock and using a trigger mechanism for holding the arrow at full draw and releasing it when the trigger is pulled.

Cushion plunger: a spring-loaded device mounted through the bow handle and against which the side of the arrow rests (for finger shooters). Usually adjustable for spring tension and degree of centershot.

D

Dead release: a finger release in which the drawing hand remains at the anchor point as part of shot follow-through.

Deflex: a bow design where the ends of the handle or the limbs at their attachment positions are angled toward the archer. The central portion of the riser bends away from the shooter. Or having the limbs curved or curled at the base so as to turn toward the archer when unstrung, reducing the strain on the limbs and also the energy stored by the weapon.

Dominant eye: the eye that exercises primary control of judging distance and hand-eye coordination.

Draw: to pull the bow string toward your anchor position.

Draw length: the distance at full draw from the nocking point to the farthest point of the grip is the "true draw length." The distance at full draw from the nocking point to a point 1¾ inches beyond the pivot point of the grip is the standard "AMO draw length."

Draw weight: the maximum level of force required to bring the string to full draw.

Dry fire: shooting a bow (releasing the string from full draw) without an arrow in position on the string—a dangerous practice that can destroy the bow and cause serious injury to the archer.

E

Efficiency: the relationship between a bow's draw weight and its arrow speed. The greater the speed for a given draw weight, the more efficient the bow is.

End: a group of arrows shot at one time and prior to scoring.

Eye: the end loop in a recurve or longbow string.

F

Face: a) the scoring area on a target; b) the side of the bow nearest the string (the belly).

Ferrule: the conical or cylindrically shaped portion of an arrow point that screws into an insert glued in the forward end of an arrow; that part of a screw-in broadhead that holds the cutting blades.

Field archery: an outside archery round in which the archer shoots from a variety of known distances.

Field point: an arrow point designed for practice shooting or competition.

Finger release: when one's fingers are placed directly on the bowstring (or into a protective tab or glove) for the purpose of drawing and releasing the arrow. (Most compound or modern shooters use a mechanical, handheld release aid.)

Fistmele: the distance from the base of the clenched hand to the tip of the extended thumb. Used as a measure of proper distance from the riser to the string when a longbow is braced or strung.

Fletch: a feather or plastic vane used in multiples and attached to the rear of the arrow to stabilize the arrow in flight.

Flight bow: a bow designed for maximum distance shooting (flight shooting). Often drawn by hand while lying on one's back and braced with the feet.

Flu-flu: an arrow used in wing shooting. It is generally fletched with complete spirals or multiple offset, full-height, untrimmed feathers. The size of the fletching is large enough that the flight distance is short and arrow speed diminishes rapidly.

Follow-through: the consistency of the position of various body parts such as head, bow arm, and drawing hand after the release of the string.

Footed shaft: a shaft with hardwood spliced into its forward section.

Force-draw curve: a graph created by plotting draw force (on the vertical axis) against draw length (on the horizontal axis) for a bow, as it is drawn from brace height through full draw. Also called "draw-force curve."

Forgiving: jargon for a bow style that appears to be more tolerant of a shooter's inconsistencies.

Freeze: an inability to move the bow to the aiming position while at full draw or the inability to release the bowstring smoothly. A symptom of target panic. "Snap shooting," releasing the string early, is a form of freezing or target panic.

Fulcrum: the point on a limb beyond which it is free to flex. The location of the pivot on an adjustable limb butt or the first meeting place of limb and riser if a non-adjustable butt.

Full draw: a) the condition of the bow when the bowstring has been drawn and the draw hand is at the anchor point; b) the position of a bow when drawn to its prescribed maximum draw length.

G

Gap: the relationship an archer sees between the tip of his arrow and the target. Used in barebow or instinctive shooting. Also the space between the pins of a bow sight.

Glass: often used as a shorthand to describe fiberglass composite materials.

Grain (abbreviated gr.): the smallest unit of weight in the English system. One pound = 7,000 gr.; one ounce = 437.5 gr.

Grip: the part of the bow riser held by the bow hand.

Gunbarrel: a method of aiming used in barebow shooting in which the nock end of the arrow on the string is placed close to the archer's eye, and one sights along the arrow shaft.

H

Handle: the section of a bow between the limbs or fads containing the grip, also called the "riser."

Handle length: the distance on a take-down recurve between the upper-and lower-limb fulcrum pivot points.

Helical fletching: fletching applied to an arrow in a helical pattern. The vanes or feathers form a slight helix around the shaft.

Hen feathers: on a three-fletched arrow, the two feathers opposed to the differently colored "cock" feather.

Hold: the pause at full draw while aiming before releasing the arrow.

I

Insert: a lightweight internal adapter that permits attachment of a point or nock to an arrow shaft (opposed to "outsert").

Instinctive shooting: a method of shooting in which no formal aiming method is used. The archer looks at the target and releases the string relying on natural coordination or calculation between his eyes and bow arm to direct the arrow to the point of concentration.

J

Jig: name given to devices or fixtures used for fletching arrows and making strings.

K

Kisser button: a marker placed on the bowstring so that it touches the archer's lip at full draw.

L

Let down: to slowly release the bow's stored energy from full draw without losing control or shooting an arrow; slowly return the string to brace height.

Let-off: the difference between the peak draw weight and the actual holding weight of a compound bow divided by the peak weight; expressed as a percentage.

Limb: the upper and lower flexing portions of the bow attached above and below the center handle section. The limbs flex as the bow string is drawn and are the means of storing the energy needed to propel the arrow.

Limb bolt: screw-in bolt that attaches a limb to the riser. The limb bolt is also used to adjust bow draw weight and limb tiller.

Longbow: a straight, one-piece (or take-down) bow, used to differentiate from compound and recurve bows.

M

Mounting holes: one of the holes in a bow riser with (generally) 5/16-24 threading for the attachment of various standardized accessories.

N

Nock(s): a) Traditional bow: The grooves at the tips of the limbs of a bow into which the bowstring is fitted. b) Arrow: The slot at the fletched end of the arrow into which the string is placed for a shot.

Nock-point locator: an attachment to the center serving of a bowstring used to consistently position the rear end of the arrow.

Nock throat: the notched part of an arrow nock that holds the arrow on the bow string.

Nocking point: the place on the bowstring where the nock (end) of an arrow is fitted.

O

Offset fletch: fletching applied at an angle to the arrow shaft with a straight clamp.

Open stance: the position of the feet on the shooting line where the left foot of a right-handed archer is behind an imaginary line extending between the archer's right foot and the center of the target.

Outsert: an external adapter to permit attachment of points or nocks to an arrow shaft.

Over-bowed: used to describe an archer with a bow that is too great in draw weight to pull and shoot comfortably.

Overdraw: a) the act of drawing a bow so that the arrow point is pulled past the arrow rest toward the archer; b) a condition resulting from the arrow rest being located closer to the archer than the grip's pivot point in order to permit the use of shorter, and thus lighter, faster arrows.

P

Paper test (tune): use of paper mounted on a frame for the purpose of recording the position of the point end and nock end of an arrow as it passes through the plane of the paper. The size and direction of the subsequent tear gives information about what part of the bow to adjust and in what direction.

Paradox (archer's): the flexing (and gradual stabilization) of the arrow as it passes around and then past the bow handle.

Peak weight: maximum draw weight during the draw cycle or the maximum draw weight recommended by the manufacturer that should not be exceeded.

Peek: to move the head or bow arm to watch the arrow either in flight or to see where it hits the target. Such movement introduces torque and interferes with arrow launch and flight.

Peep sight: any see-through aperture used for the purpose of aligning the bowstring with a front sight while at full draw, thus providing a three-point sighting system—anchor point, peep, and pin.

Pivot point (point of grip): deepest point and usually the smallest area of the grip; the point about which the handle tends to rotate if inadvertent torque is applied. The arrow-rest hole is located directly above the pivot point.

Pluck: to pull the string out and away horizontally from the anchor position as the string is released.

Point of aim: a means of sighting a bow and arrow in which the tip of the arrow is aligned with a specific object just prior to release.

Point-blank: aiming directly at the target.

Q

Quiver: device for holding arrows that can be attached to the bow or worn on the back or belt.

R

Recoil: a) the tendency of a bow to move forward when shot; b) vibration in the riser immediately following a shot.

Recurve limb: limb design in which the un-braced limb tips bend toward the back of the bow and away from the shooter.

Reflex: a bow design where the ends of the handle or the limbs at the fadeouts angle toward the back of the bow and away from the archer; having the limbs made such that, until strung, the ends of the bow project forward rather than backward.

Release: to shoot or loose an arrow.

Riser: the rigid center section or handle portion of a bow to which the limbs are attached and that holds the grip.

Round: a specified number of shots on a given shooting venue.

Roving: shooting over fields and woodlands at random natural targets.

S

Scope: an optical sight, usually magnifying.

Self bow: a bow made from a single piece of material.

Serving: a) wrapping the bow string with an appropriate material to prevent wear, such as at the center section or loop ends of the bowstring; b) wrapping the bow string to hold a peep or silencers in place (to serve).

Shaft: the body or main section of the arrow.

Shelf: part of the riser on a bow that forms a platform for the arrow or the arrow rest.

Sight: a device for aligning the bow with the target.

Sling: a strap or cord that allows the archer to shoot his bow with a relaxed bow-hand grip. Attached to wrist or fingers, the sling prevents the bow from dropping from the bow hand following a shot.

Snap shooting: shooting without pausing to aim carefully.

Spine: the amount of bend (deflection) in an arrow shaft that is caused by a specific weight being placed at the center of the shaft while the shaft is supported at a designated span; the "stiffness" of a shaft. Can be static (at rest) or dynamic (in flight).

Square stance: the position of the feet in which an imaginary straight line would touch the toes of both feet and extend to the center of the target.

Stabilizer: any device added to the bow for the specific purposes of reducing handle torque, maintaining bow-handle position during the shot and follow-through, and minimizing vibration and noise following release. Stabilizers add inertia to the system, thereby increasing stability.

Stack: a characteristic of longbow or recurve performance that shows an increasing rate of change in bow weight for each increment of draw length.

Static recurve: a recurve with sharply bent limb tips that do not flex when the bow is drawn.

Stave: a full-length, un-spliced piece of wood used for making a self-wood bow. Mated half-lengths are billet staves.

Stringer: a cord used to string the bow, drawing both limbs equally and without torquing them.

Stored energy: the amount of energy required to bring the bow limbs to full draw, measured in foot-pounds (ft-lbs).

Stroke (power): the distance over which force is applied to the arrow during launch, i.e., from full draw to the instant the arrow separates from the bow string.

Swage: the tapered shaping of an arrow fore-shaft to directly accept an arrow point, commonly five degrees. The rear shaft tapers 11½ degrees to accept an arrow nock.

T

Tab (or glove): a protection for the digits that draw the string. Also provides better release performance. Usually leather, with rubber and synthetic inserts.

Take-down bow: any bow designed to come apart in the handle area in two or three parts, usually consisting of a riser and the upper and lower limbs.

Target panic: the inability to release an arrow from full draw or a continuing compulsion to let the arrow fly too soon.

Tiller: the difference between the limb-to-string distances measured where the limbs are attached to the riser. Usually the upper distance is slightly more than the bottom one, resulting in a "positive tiller." Tiller reflects the power-balance between both limbs.

Tiller (reverse): when the lower limb-to-string dimension is greater than the top limb-to-string dimension.

Tillering: the adjustment of tiller on traditional bows by shortening or lengthening the distance from the riser to the string. Most bows are tillered to approximately ¼-inch positive measurement on the upper limb to equalize the loading on both limbs because of the non-symmetric bow-hand placement on the grip and the draw hand location.

Torque (bow): the unintentional twisting of the bow around the vertical axis by the bow hand during shooting.

Toxophilite (antique): an archer.

Tuning: to adjust the elements of your shooting set-up (bow-string nock, draw weight, arrow-rest height, etc.) to achieve best arrow flight.

V

Vane: the web or flat, expanded part of a feather. Also, the synthetic fletching used instead of feathers on many modern arrows.

INDEX